'THE MOST HAUNTED HOUSE IN ENGLAND'

Frontispiece   *Above :*   The twelfth-century Borley Church, opposite Borley Rectory.

Below :   The Rectory nestling amongst the trees, photographed from the tower of Borley Church.

'THE MOST HAUNTED HOUSE IN ENGLAND'

TEN YEARS' INVESTIGATION
OF BORLEY RECTORY

By

HARRY PRICE

With Illustrations

LONGMANS, GREEN AND CO.
LONDON ⬦ NEW YORK ⬦ TORONTO

LONGMANS, GREEN AND CO. LTD.
39 PATERNOSTER ROW, LONDON, E.C.4.
17 CHITTARANJAN AVENUE, CALCUTTA
NICOL ROAD, BOMBAY
36A MOUNT ROAD, MADRAS

LONGMANS, GREEN AND CO.
55 FIFTH AVENUE, NEW YORK
221 EAST 20TH STREET, CHICAGO
88 TREMONT STREET, BOSTON

LONGMANS, GREEN AND CO.
215 VICTORIA STREET, TORONTO

First published 1940

PRINTED IN GREAT BRITAIN
BY WESTERN PRINTING SERVICES LTD., BRISTOL

PREFACE

I HAVE done little more than edit the remarkable records[1] that constitute the major portion of this monograph. The evidence for the haunting of Borley Rectory is mostly in documentary form and, where possible, I have reproduced verbatim the oral and written testimony which, in nearly every case, is first-hand. As I am merely the narrator of the story, I cannot, of course, assume responsibility for the validity of those incidents that did not come within my own personal experience.

Without the kindly co-operation of a great number of people, this book could never have been written. I desire to put on record my sincere thanks to all those who helped me in compiling it. Especially, I am grateful to the following persons: The Misses Bull, Mr. Walter Bull, and the Bull family generally, for permission to print their experiences and for their hospitality in many ways; the Rev. G. Eric Smith, the Rev. L. A. Foyster, the Rev. A. C. Henning (successively Rectors of Borley), and their wives, for much help and hospitality during my ten years' investigation. To Mr. Foyster I am specially indebted for permission to reproduce extracts from his Diary. To Lady Whitehouse and her nephew, Dom Richard Whitehouse, O.S.B., I am grateful for contributing two of the most interesting and convincing chapters in this work. By courtesy of the editors of *The Times*, *The Month*, and the *Daily Mirror*, I have been able to reproduce extracts from their journals; and Dr. C. E. M. Joad has kindly permitted me to quote his experiences as originally related by him in *Harper's Magazine*. I am also

[1] Now deposited in the Harry Price Library of Magical Literature in the University of London.

indebted to the many correspondents of *The Times* for permission to include their respective letters on the bricking-up of nuns.

Among those of my official observers to whom my thanks are specially due are Mr. Sidney H. Glanville, Mr. Mark Kerr-Pearse, and Lieut.-Colonel F. C. Westland. These gentlemen took infinite pains in making plans of the Rectory, taking photographs of the wall-writings, etc., and in rendering help in a hundred ways. That they were strangers to me before my investigation began only adds to my indebtedness to them. Finally, I must thank all my official observers for the expenditure of time, trouble, and money in visiting Borley in the interests of science, and for the care and skill in preparing their various reports and protocols. The fact that a few of these records were negative, does not lessen my indebtedness to them.

In conclusion, I must put on record my obligation to Captain W. H. Gregson for permitting me to chronicle his strange experiences, and for his assistance rendered both before and after the fire that consumed the Rectory—an event that so dramatically brought down the curtain on the most extraordinary and best-documented case of haunting in the annals of psychical research.

H. P.

CONTENTS

LIST OF ILLUSTRATIONS

* *By courtesy of the 'Daily Mirror'*

ILLUSTRATIONS IN THE TEXT

CHAPTER I

LUNCHEON INTERLUDE

O N Tuesday, June 11, 1929, I was having lunch at a friend's house in South Kensington when his telephone bell rang. We had reached the coffee stage and I remember we were discussing why *Poltergeister*, in spite of their mischievous and annoying tricks, never appear to harm anyone—they are merely playful and troublesome. Before we had solved the problem a maid entered the room and said I was wanted on the telephone.

Excusing myself, I walked into the hall to answer the call. It was from the Editor of one of the London dailies, and the matter was somewhat urgent. It appeared that he had rung up my office, had spoken to my secretary, who had given him my friend's telephone number.

The Editor was rather excited. One of his staff, Mr. V. C. Wall, was at that moment investigating the remarkable incidents that were occurring at a rectory about sixty miles from London. The rectory in question was that of Borley, two and a half miles from Long Melford, Suffolk (and the same distance from Sudbury), but just within the Essex border. The most extraordinary things were happening at Borley Rectory, and the Editor asked me whether I would care to visit the scene of these occurrences and take charge of the case. I thanked him very much, and said I would make immediate arrangements to join his representative. I was told that the incumbent of Borley was the Rev. G. E. Smith. As I replaced the receiver, I little dreamt that there was ten years' work ahead of me probing the mystery of what was to become the best-authenticated case of haunting in the annals of psychical research.

CHAPTER II

THE ADVENTURES OF A JOURNALIST

WHEN I returned to my office after lunch, I saw that the midday post had arrived and amongst my usual delivery of Press cuttings, I found the clippings from the Monday morning's papers, giving an account of the Borley happenings up to the previous Sunday night, which Mr. Wall had telephoned to his paper.

Here is Mr. Wall's report:[1]

'Ghostly figures of headless coachmen and a nun, an old-time coach, drawn by two bay horses, which appears and vanishes mysteriously, and dragging footsteps in empty rooms. All these ingredients of a first-class ghost story are awaiting investigation by psychic experts near Long Melford, Suffolk.

'The scene of the ghostly visitations is the Rectory at Borley, a few miles from Long Melford. It is a building erected on the part of the site of a great monastery which, in the Middle Ages, was the scene of a gruesome tragedy. The present rector, the Rev. G. E. Smith, and his wife, made the Rectory their residence in the face of warnings by previous occupiers. Since their arrival they have been puzzled and startled by a series of peculiar happenings which cannot be explained, and which confirm the rumours they heard before moving in.

'The first untoward happening was the sound of slow, dragging footsteps across the floor of an unoccupied room. Then one night Mr. Smith, armed with a hockey stick, sat in the room and waited for the noise. Once again it came—the sound of feet in some kind of slippers treading on the bare boards. Mr. Smith lashed out with his stick at the spot where the footsteps seemed to be, but the stick whistled through the empty air, and the steps continued across the room.

'Then a servant girl brought from London, suddenly gave notice after two days' work, declaring emphatically that she had

[1] *Daily Mirror*, June 10, 1929.

2

seen a nun walking in the wood at the back of the house. Finally comes the remarkable story of an old-fashioned coach, seen twice on the lawn by a servant, which remained in sight long enough for the girl to distinguish the brown colour of the horses.

'This same servant also declares that she has seen a nun leaning over a gate near the house. The villagers dread the neighbourhood of the Rectory after dark, and will not pass it. Peculiarly enough, all these "visitations" coincide with the details of a tragedy which, according to legend, occurred at the monastery which once stood on this spot.

'A groom at the monastery fell in love with a nun at a near-by convent, runs the legend, and they used to hold clandestine meetings in the wood on to which the Rectory now backs. Then one day they arranged to elope, and another groom had a coach waiting in the road outside the wood, so that they could escape. From this point the legend varies. Some say that the nun and her lover quarrelled, and that he strangled her in the wood, and was caught and beheaded, with the other groom, for his villainy. The other version is that all three were caught in the act by the monks, and that the two grooms were beheaded, and the nun buried alive in the walls of the monastery.

'The previous Rector of Borley, now dead, often spoke of the remarkable experience he had one night, when, walking along the road outside the Rectory, he heard the clatter of hoofs. Looking around, he saw to his horror an old-fashioned coach lumbering along the road, driven by two *headless men*.'

Mr. Wall stayed at the Rectory over the week-end and sent a further report[1] of his adventures to London:

'*Long Melford, Monday.*

'With a photographer, I have just completed a vigil of several hours in the "haunted" wood at the back of Borley Rectory, a few miles from Long Melford.

'This wood, and the whole neighbourhood of the Rectory, is supposed to be haunted by the ghosts of a groom and a nun who attempted to elope one night several hundred years ago but were apparently caught in the act.

'Although we saw only one of the manifestations which have, according to residents, occurred frequently in recent years, this by itself was peculiar enough.

'It was the appearance of a mysterious light in a disused wing of the building—an appearance which simply cannot be ex-

[1] Ibid., June 11, 1929.

plained, because on investigation of the deserted wing it was ascertained that there was no light inside—although the watchers outside could still see it shining through a window!

'When we saw the mysterious light shining through the trees we suggested that somebody should go into the empty wing and place a light in another window, for the sake of comparison . . . the Rev. G. E. Smith, the Rector, who does not believe in ghosts, volunteered to do it.

'Sure enough, the second light appeared and was visible next to the other, although on approaching close to the building, this disappeared, while the Rector's lamp still burned. Then we were left alone to probe the mysteries of the haunted wood.'

After reading Mr. Wall's accounts of his adventures at the Rectory, I sent a telegram to the Rev. G. E. Smith, asking whether it would be convenient for my secretary and me to visit the Rectory on the following day. In an hour or so I received the necessary permission, with the added invitation to arrive in time for lunch.

CHAPTER III

THE RECTOR'S STORY

O N the following morning, Wednesday, June 12, 1929, my secretary, Miss Lucie Kaye and I prepared for our trip. In case the reader may wish to know what a psychic investigator takes with him when engaged on an important case, I will enumerate some of the items included in a ghost-hunter's kit.

Into a large suitcase are packed the following articles: A pair of soft felt overshoes used for creeping, unheard, about the house in order that neither human beings nor paranormal 'entities' shall be disturbed when producing 'phenomena'; steel measuring tape for measuring rooms, passages, testing the thickness of walls in looking for secret chambers or hidey-holes; steel screw-eyes, lead post-office seals, sealing tool, strong cord or tape, and adhesive surgical tape, for sealing doors, windows or cupboards; a set of tools, with wire, nails, etc.; hank of electric flex, small electric bells, dry batteries and switches (for secret electrical contacts); 9 cm. by 12 cm. reflex camera, film-packs and flash-bulbs for indoor or outdoor photography; a small portable telephone for communicating with assistant in another part of building or garden; note book, red, blue and black pencils; sketching block and case of drawing instruments for making plans; bandages, iodine and a flask of brandy in case member of investigating staff or resident is injured or faints; ball of string, stick of chalk, matches, electric torch and candle; bowl of mercury for detecting tremors in room or passage or for making silent electrical mercury switches; cinematograph camera with remote electrical control, and films; a sensitive transmitting thermograph, with charts, to measure the slightest variation in temperature in supposed haunted rooms; a packet of graphite and soft brush for developing finger-prints. For a long stay in house with supply of electricity, I would take with me infra-red filters, lamps, and ciné films sensitive to infra-red rays, so that I could take photographs in almost complete darkness.[1] For special cases, as in my broadcast[2] from the 'haunted manor' at Meopham, Kent, I use an electric signalling instrument which automatically reveals to the investigator (who has no need to leave his base-room) a movement of any object in any part of the house, or a change in temperature in the 'controlled' rooms.[3]

Speeding northwards I turned over in my mind the best way to tackle the Borley problem, and by the time we reached Chelmsford, I had formulated a plan of campaign. We got to Sudbury at midday and found we could no longer continue our route unaided. We stopped and asked the way. A dozen willing guides immediately put us on the right road and even offered to accompany us. The 'Borley ghost' was almost the sole topic of conversation for miles around and the good people of Sudbury were consumed with curiosity as to what we intended to do—and how we intended to do it!

A mile or so out of Sudbury, on the Long Melford Road, we saw a sign-post to Borley and in a few minutes our car entered one of the drive gates leading to the Rectory. I was astonished at the great size of the house.

We were welcomed by the Rev. G. E. Smith and his wife, very charming and hospitable, and I should like to take this opportunity of thanking them publicly for their interest in my investigation and for the assistance they rendered during my prolonged inquiries.

During lunch I heard the whole story of their adventures.

---

[1] This kit is illustrated in my article 'Psychical Research,' *Encyclopædia Britannica Year Book*, 1939.

[2] March 10, 1936.

[3] This set-up is illustrated in *Fifty Years of Psychical Research*, London, 1939, Plate opposite p. 268.

It tallied with what Mr. Wall had printed in his paper. But the following is a more detailed account, as it is the epitome of a number of interviews with Mr. Smith, by one of my helpers, Mr. S. H. Glanville, and myself.

The living of Borley had been offered to, and refused by twelve clergy before Mr. Smith accepted the living. He went into residence at the latter part of 1928. He was not informed that the Rectory was alleged to be haunted. The house was found to be excessively cold[1] and difficult to heat. The water supply was quite inadequate for their needs, there being no pipe supply inside the house.[2] All water had to be obtained from a well. The house was so large that some of the upstairs rooms were not needed and were permanently closed. The place was depressing and Mrs. Smith became ill.

Soon after Mr. Smith and his wife moved into the Rectory, certain minor demonstrations of a supposed psychic nature occurred. For example, one summer afternoon, when Mr. Smith was alone in the house, he left his bedroom and upon passing under the archway leading to the landing, heard distinct sibilant whisperings over his head. He was at a loss to account for this, and walked slowly across the landing, followed by the sounds. As he passed under the archway leading to the chapel (see Plan, page 22) the sounds instantly ceased, as though a wireless set had been switched off, though there was no radio instrument in the neighbourhood. He returned across the landing, but nothing further was heard. These sounds were heard several times afterwards, though no words were distinguishable.

Upon another occasion, at dusk, when he was crossing the landing, he was startled at hearing a woman's voice again coming apparently from the centre of the arch leading to the chapel. The voice started with a moaning sound, gradually rising into a *crescendo* and ending with the words: 'Don't, Carlos, don't!' dying away in a sort of muttering.

---

[1] A fact confirmed by every one of my observers. See *post*.
[2] Later installed.

The volume of sound, at its highest pitch, was slightly louder than would be used in ordinary conversation. 'Carlos,' by the way, was supposed to be the nickname by which the builder of the Rectory was known, though this is denied by surviving members of the family.

Other phenomena experienced at the Rectory included mysterious bell-ringing, the slow and deliberate footsteps that patrolled the passages and upper rooms, and the apparitions seen by the two maid-servants successively employed by Mr. Smith.

When Mrs. Smith was returning from church one night, after dark, and was entering the house by the back—or scullery—door, she noticed that the window of the school room (No. 11 on Plan, page 22) was lighted up, and presumed that the maid was there with a lamp. Upon entering the house, she found the maid in the kitchen. The girl told her mistress that she had not been upstairs at all. They therefore went up together, and found the room in darkness. The same thing happened on a later occasion, when the choir had just finished their evening practice. Mrs. Smith took all the members of the choir and showed them the lighted window. Then they all went up to the room, but it was again in darkness.

Mrs. Smith also told us that when she has been in the dairy in the evening, she often saw a figure leaning over one of the drive gates. The figure was always dark and shadowy. She several times went out to investigate, but never found anyone there. This particular figure leaning over this particular gate has been seen by various people, who all speak of its strange and sudden disappearance.

One of the maids employed by the Smiths was quite definite that she saw the traditional 'coach.' One afternoon she ran to Mrs. Smith with the news that she had seen 'such a funny old coach' on the lawn. A Press photographer took a picture[1] of her pointing out the exact spot where it disappeared and the girl herself told me the same story.

[1] *Daily Mirror*, June 10, 1929.

Another maid, the one they brought from London, saw a figure dressed in black leaning over the gate. It so frightened her that she stayed only two days.

Very curiously, Mr. Smith heard many more strange noises in the winter than in the summer. As to *Poltergeist* phenomena, the most peculiar was the 'shooting' from the locks of their keys—found usually two or three feet away. This happened periodically and I, too, witnessed this phenomenon.

On another occasion, a vase that normally stood on the mantelpiece of their bedroom was found smashed to pieces at the foot of the main stairs. No one was in the house at the time, the Smiths being in the garden. Curious sounds in various parts of the house were heard from time to time, but except for the figure leaning over the gate, nothing was seen that could not be accounted for.

During the first few weeks of their tenancy, before they had actually moved in, Mrs. Smith was turning out the various rooms when, in a cupboard in the library she found a parcel neatly wrapped and tied with string. Upon removing the wrappings, she was astonished to find the skull of, apparently, a young woman. It was in perfect condition, and the teeth were also perfect. Failing to find any reason why the skull should be preserved in the library, Mr. Smith and the sexton reverently buried it in the church-yard in the presence of the churchwarden and the widow of the previous Rector.

By the time we had finished lunch I had heard the whole story of the manifestations, the history of the Rectory, the various legends connected with the place and other informa-tion which will be dealt with fully in subsequent chapters.

I found the Smiths very intelligent, delightful, and much-travelled people who were, like myself, utterly sceptical as regards 'spirits.' They knew nothing about psychical research, and the subject did not particularly interest them. Though puzzled by what they had seen and heard they, being God-fearing people, were not afraid that anything would harm them. What finally drove them from the Rectory was the lack of amenities there and *not* the 'ghosts.' But I am anticipating.[1]

---

[1] Inspired by the traditions of Borley, and some incidents alleged to have occurred at the Rectory, Mrs. Smith has written an entertaining novel, *Murder at the Parsonage*, which she hopes to publish some day.

PLATE I

Right :
Borley Rectory from
the lawn.

Below :
The large summer-
house facing the
Nun's Walk.

Above :
The stream in the
garden.

Left :
The Nun's Walk,
facing large
summer-house.

CHAPTER IV

THE STORY OF THE RECTORY

IN order that the reader shall possess a proper orientation of Borley Rectory, its history, lay-out, and grounds, I now propose to give in some detail an account of the building and its appurtenances. If he pleases, the reader can skip this chapter and the next. If he is wise, he will not do so, as it is important for him to visualize the background of the story; and for him to have an exact conception of the building and its surroundings is, I think, necessary. Plans of the house (pages 16 and 22) have been carefully prepared by Mr. Sidney H. Glanville, and these should be consulted when reading the text.

The name Borley, in Essex, is the modern spelling of the Anglo-Saxon *Barlea* (meaning 'boar's clearing' or 'boar's pasture') as written in Domesday Book, the record of the great survey of England prepared (1086) for William the Conqueror. The small village—or hamlet—lies on the right (west) bank of the River Stour, which here divides the counties of Essex and Suffolk. Borley is fifteen miles from Bury St. Edmunds, two and a half miles from Long Melford, and about the same distance from Sudbury, Suffolk, to the north-west of which it lies. Sudbury and Long Melford, on the Great Eastern Railway, are the nearest stations. Sudbury is 58½ miles by rail from Liverpool Street.

The population of Borley is 121, most of the villagers being engaged in agricultural pursuits. The village is scattered, picturesque, extremely quiet, and strangers are seldom seen. The tower of the twelfth-century church (dedication unknown), which faces the Rectory on the other side of the road, is a landmark seen for many miles.

Borley Rectory, in the Diocese of Chelmsford, was built in 1863 on the foundations of at least two—and probably more—earlier dwellings. There is a persistent tradition that a fourteenth-century monastery formerly occupied the site. A number of persons interested in Borley have sought for information concerning the early history of the place, with little result. But Dom Richard Whitehouse, O.S.B.,[1] was fortunate in finding references to Borley in Sir William Dugdale's[2] *Monasticon Anglicanum*,[3] where it is stated: 'Edward III[4] in the 36th year [*i.e.*, 1362] of his reign gave to the Prior and Community of Christ Church, Canterbury, the Manor of Borley in the county of Essex in exchange for the customs and revenues together with all the rights which the said Prior and Community could in any way have in the town and port of Sandwich. . . .' A later entry in the time of Henry VIII gives a certificate of valuation of Borley Manor amounting to £32 14s. 4d. As Richard Whitehouse observes, there is thus definite evidence that Borley Manor, by Sudbury, wherever it was situated, became the property of Benedictine monks in the fourteenth century.

Thirteen years after Edward III gave Borley to the Benedictines, Simon of Sudbury was appointed Archbishop of Canterbury—a further link between Borley and the Benedictines. In July 1377, he crowned Richard II. In 1380 Simon became Chancellor of England. Falling foul of the peasants, who were in revolt, the Kentish insurgents dragged Simon from the Tower of London and beheaded him on Tower Hill on June 14, 1381. A suggestion has been made that Simon still haunts Borley and the neighbourhood. Simon was a great benefactor to his native town and rebuilt part of the church of St. Gregory at Sudbury, and founded a college there.

I think there is little doubt that the Manor House occupied the site of the present Rectory, the previous Rectory being what is now Borley Place, a building nearly opposite. But

---

[1] See Chapter XV.   [2] 1605–86.
[3] Published during 1655, 1664 and 1673.   [4] 1312–77.

according to some authorities, there was also another Rectory on the site of the present building, belonging to the Herringham family. Memorials in the church opposite appear to confirm this view.

What is quite certain is that the Waldegrave family played a major part in Borley during some three hundred years, according to Mr. J. M. Bull.[1] The family held the manor and were patrons of the church. A descendant of Sir Richard Waldegrave,[2] who was speaker in the House of Commons in 1402, was Sir Edward Waldegrave,[3] the first member of this family connected with Borley. He was imprisoned during the reign of Edward VI for his loyalty to the princess, afterwards Queen Mary. By Mary he was knighted, and he received from her the manor of Chewton in Somerset. Chewton Priory, Bath, is now the seat of the Waldegrave family.

Sir Edward Waldegrave was Member of Parliament for Essex and Chancellor of the Duchy of Lancaster. After Mary's decease he suffered a reverse of fortune, and he was a prisoner in the Tower of London when he died on September 1, 1561. His tomb is at the east end of the nave of Borley Church. He is buried with his wife, Frances, who survived him for thirty-eight years. 'Their effigies lie side by side, the man in armour and the wife in a tight-fitting bodice and skirt with flat cap on head and large ruffle round neck.'[4] Their six children are represented on the sides of the tomb. There is a tablet on the north wall of the chancel to the memory of a daughter, Magdala, who died in 1598.

It is not quite clear where the Waldegraves' residence was situated, but probably they lived at the Manor House on the site of the present Borley Rectory. A legendary account of a castle near by is current. The story is that Sir Edward and his family lived in the castle, the Manor House being occupied by his chaplain. The castle itself is

---

[1] *A Short History of Borley and Liston Churches*, 1937.
[2] Died 1402.   [3] *c.* 1517–61.   [4] J. M. Bull, *op, cit.*

said to have been destroyed by Cromwell's troops. Nothing appears to be known of any existing ruins of the castle.

For our purpose, it will be sufficient if I name the Rectors of Borley since the present Rectory was built in 1863 by the Rev. Henry Dawson Ellis Bull. He was born in 1833, and died on May 2, 1892, aged fifty-nine years. He was Rector of Borley from 1862 to 1892, a period of thirty years. He will be referred to in this monograph as the Rev. Henry Bull. He is buried in Borley churchyard.

He was succeeded by his son, the Rev. Henry (Harry) Foyster Bull, who was born in 1862 and died on June 9, 1927, aged sixty-five. He was Rector of Borley from 1892 till 1927, a period of thirty-five years. He will be referred to as the Rev. Harry Bull, as everyone called him. It will be noted that the Rev. Henry Bull and his son were incumbents at Borley continuously for sixty-five years. Harry Bull is also buried in the churchyard.

After the death of the Rev. Harry Bull in 1927, there was difficulty in finding a successor, and the Rectory remained empty for some time. However, as we have seen, in 1928 the living (the patrons of which were the Bull family) was offered to the Rev. Guy Eric Smith who was inducted to the living, October 2, 1928, remaining until Easter, 1930. The living is worth £298 per year, with house.

When the Rev. G. E. Smith found it was not possible to live in the place, the Bull family offered the benefice to a relative, a cousin, the Rev. Lionel Algernon Foyster, who resided at the Rectory from 1930 to 1935. It was then decided by Queen Anne's Bounty, or the Bishop, or both, that, on account of the strange happenings in the house, and the reputation it had acquired; and on account of the unsuitability of the place as a residence for a small family, no more Rectors should live there.

So in 1936 the livings of Borley and Liston, a neighbouring village, were merged into one, the Rev. A. C. Henning being appointed minister of both parishes. Mr. Henning lives at the charming and comfortable Liston Rectory, a mile or so from Borley. And that is the present position. Borley Rectory was placed in the hands of house agents and towards the end of 1938 was sold to Captain W. H. Gregson. Though the edifice cost some thousands of pounds to build, it was offered to me for £500. Soon after Captain Gregson purchased it, the place was burnt down under curious circumstances, which the Captain will himself relate later in this story.

As we have seen, the present Borley Rectory, which stands on a rise, sombre and gloomy in a large neglected garden, and entirely surrounded by a belt of high trees, was built in 1863 by the Rev. Henry Bull. Before, and during building he lived at Borley Place, an old and picturesque house on the opposite side of the road. With the exception of Borley Place and two cottages a few hundred yards away, the Rectory is completely isolated. When the Rectory was completed, Henry Bull moved in. The original building was, roughly, L-shaped, as can be seen from the Ground Plan (page 16). As Mr. Bull's family grew, he found he needed more room, so he added (1875-6) a wing, indicated on Ground Plan, making the building almost rectangular, and almost completely enclosing an uncovered bricked courtyard. This wing gave him a number of excellent store houses, etc. on the ground level and three extra bedrooms on the first floor. These are numbered 9, 10, 11, on the First Floor Plan (page 22). That this extra accommodation was welcome is evident when I mention that the Rev. Henry Bull had fourteen children, twelve of whom survived. In addition, he had a large domestic staff.

Borley Rectory[1] is a solid, unpicturesque, red-brick building of two stories, ground floor and first floor, with two bay windows on the side of the house overlooking the lawn. These windows are spanned, at the top, by a glass-roofed veranda, under which, in the centre, are French windows opening out of the library or study (later our Base Room)

[1] From notes taken before the fire which almost destroyed the place early in 1939.

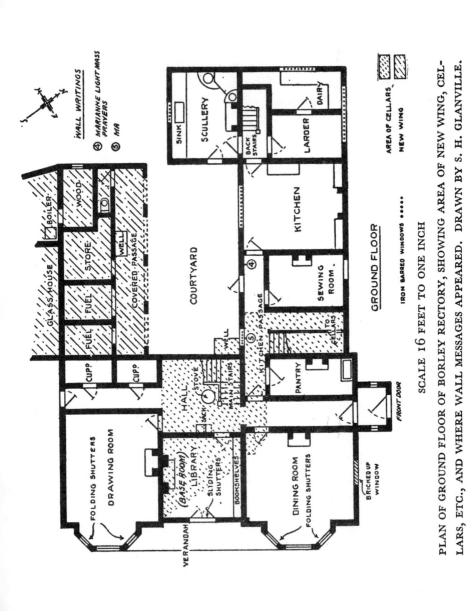

PLAN OF GROUND FLOOR OF BORLEY RECTORY, SHOWING AREA OF NEW WING, CELLARS, ETC., AND WHERE WALL MESSAGES APPEARED. DRAWN BY S. H. GLANVILLE.

to the lawn. Although situated at the side, as one enters the house, this is really the front of the Rectory. The side of the house in which are the front door and entrance porch is separated from the road by a broad drive with gates at either end. The porch, too, has a door, so that two doors, both of which can be locked, have to be negotiated before the house can be entered from the drive. Other 'orthodox' entrances to the house include the French windows already mentioned; a back entrance leading from courtyard into scullery; another door leading from kitchen passage into courtyard; and a small door giving access from the garden to the main hall. All these entrances are marked on the Ground Plan. The 'unorthodox' entrances to the house are, of course, by the windows, all with good shutters or fastenings, and the trap-door in the courtyard, by means of which one can get into the cellar. It will be noticed that the windows of the domestic quarters are heavily barred (indicated on Plan). This was *not* done to keep burglars out, but was intended to keep the maids from surreptitiously slipping out of a night when they ought to have been in bed. The iron grids also had the effect of preventing 'followers' visiting the girls, unknown to their mistress.

Speaking of windows, the first thing that a visitor notices when he enters the carriage drive from the road is a large bricked-up window to the left of the entrance porch (see Ground Floor Plan and Plate II). The disfigurement quite spoils the appearance of this side of the house and one immediately wonders why it should have been done. When first I saw it, I at once suspected that the Window Tax was the cause. But I recollected that this imposition was repealed in 1851—twelve years before the place was built. The window in question was let into the wall of the dining-room, and was intended to illuminate that apartment. Then why block it up?

I began to make inquiries and from three different sources learned that the window was bricked up because the spectral 'nun,' of whom more anon, *habitually peered into the room*

c

from the drive, thus annoying the Rev. Henry Bull, who had the window removed and the aperture bricked in.

Pursuing my inquiries, I then heard that the window was not blocked up because of the too inquisitive 'nun,' but because people passing along the road could see the Bull family having their meals. Candidly, I do not believe that this was the reason at all, because (*a*) very few people use the road past the Rectory, and fewer must have used it at the time when the window was removed; (*b*) the carriage drive is so wide (as can be seen from the photograph), that it must have been a sheer impossibility to see through the window from the road, as I have proved for myself by trying to peer through other windows on this side of the house; (*c*) the hedge and belt of trees separating the drive from the road form an impenetrable screen that would discourage anyone trying to peer in at the window, even if the drive were not so wide. In any case, a light curtain or blind would have prevented any person from seeing what was going on in the room. That is, any normal person. But it might have been thought that such a screen would *not* prevent an entity such as the 'nun' from peering into the room. Whatever the reason, a drastic remedy was decided upon, and the window of the principal living-room was strongly and permanently bricked up, as it remains to-day, completely spoiling this side of the house. The illumination of the room by day is obtained only from the bay window overlooking the lawn.

Borley Rectory is rather like a rabbit-warren, but a rabbit-warren that can be effectively sealed if one does it systematically. It contains ten rooms on the ground floor, in addition to many cupboards, store-houses and cellars. Some of these are not directly connected with the living-rooms (see Plan). The principal rooms are the dining-room, drawing-room, library, and Sewing-Room, together with a large hall. Judging by the number and size of the 'usual domestic offices' in the shape of kitchen, larder, dairy, pantry, etc., both food and labour must have been cheap and plentiful—and the domestic staff exceptionally sweet-tempered. To try to 'run' such a house to-day would break a woman's heart, so badly designed and awkward is the lay-out of the whole place. Neither gas, electric light, nor mains water are available and there is no central heating. It is impossible to warm the place properly. I know, because I have tried.

The main ground-floor rooms are large, and the whole place is strongly and well built. The windows of the drawing-room, dining-room, and library can be barred by very strong folding burglar-proof shutters. Another question I asked myself: 'Why such heavy shutters in a remote country hamlet, well off the beaten track, where even a wandering tramp must be something of a novelty?' I have not yet found the solution, but the shutters came in very useful when sealing the house during our investigations.

The rooms themselves on the ground floor call for little comment. As I have stated, they are large and lofty. A word must be said about the mantelpieces in the dining-room and drawing-room. Both (Plate IV) are of marble, rather ornate, and came originally from Italy. They were exhibited, I believe, at the Great Exhibition in London in 1851. The mantelpiece in the dining-room is adorned with quaint marble busts of two monks, well carved, and symbolic of the traditions connected with the Rectory.

The cellars are most curious and of an extraordinary shape. As can be seen from the Plan, the entrance to them is by a staircase from the kitchen passage. They extend under this passage, under the main hall, under three-parts of the library, and under a corner of the dining-room. A partition wall divides them. The area is indicated by the hatching on the Ground Floor Plan. They are very solidly built, with provision for storing a large quantity of wine, etc., though during the whole of my connection with the Rectory they contained—to paraphrase a remark re Romeo's apothecary—nothing more exciting than 'a beggarly account of empty bottles.' A shallow well, properly in the courtyard, extends into the portion of the cellar under the kitchen passage. It was covered in with some boards, rotten and antique, and was 'discovered' by one of our observers literally putting his foot in it, and nearly falling in. The cellars are damp and the walls are slimy.

On November 1, 1937, Mr. Sidney H. Glanville and Mr. M. Kerr-Pearse, thoroughly examined the cellars and the foundations of the house generally, and made some curious discoveries. The strange shape of the cellars is due, apparently, to their partly conforming to the foundation walls or footings of an ancient building that was previously on the site. My friends noticed, as I had, that a part of the cellar floor had subsided. So they dug up this portion and found what appeared to be the foundations of a much older house, the bricks being the old-fashioned two-inch bricks. The cellar wall, indicated on Plan, that runs diagonally under the library is composed of these bricks. Portions of other walls in the cellar were found to be composed partly of two-inch bricks, and partly of the modern type. The foundations of the ancient building were traced more or less satisfactorily, and this old site would face, roughly, south. It is interesting to note that *exactly* over the subsidence, and where the old bricks were discovered, but outside the Blue Room on the first-floor landing, is the spot (marked + in First Floor Plan) where several observers 'felt cold' and shivered, and other phenomena occurred. This became known as the 'cold spot' and will be discussed later.

Little need be said about the courtyard, the general conformation of which can be seen from the Plan. Under the covered passage (indicated) is the large and heavy hand-wheel, the rotation of which pumps water into a large cistern under the eaves of the house, whence it is now led by pipes through the building. The system, if archaic, is efficient, and there is a good supply of water which, I understand, is decreasing in volume.

A word must here be said about the well itself. It is of brick, and Mr. Glanville, by means of a flare and sinker, ascertained that, from the ground surface to the water level, the depth was 71 feet. The total depth of the well is 80 feet. At a depth of 61.9 feet Mr. Glanville's flare and sinker were sucked or blown into a cavity on the house side of the well. This suggests that there must be a passage or hole of some sort leading out of the well side, nearly 62 feet below ground level, but for what purpose is unknown. Perhaps it leads into one of the subterranean passages. The well is covered with a heavy iron plate.

Not structurally connected with the Rectory in any way are some stables and garage, over which are rooms occupied successively by groom-gardener, caretaker, etc. This detached unit is known as the 'cottage' and plays little part in the story of the Borley hauntings—with one outstanding exception, which will emerge in due course.

Three staircases lead from the ground level of the house to the first floor. The main staircase leads from the hall to the landing outside Room No. 6 (the 'Blue Room'). A second staircase leads from the kitchen passage to the side of the bathroom; and the 'back stairs' indicated on Ground Plan lead from the kitchen quarters to near Room No. 2. Most of these staircases have doors, which can be fastened and sealed.

There are fourteen rooms on the first floor, including the large lavatory, the larger bathroom (formerly, I think, a bedroom), and the Chapel, which has altar rails (indicated). As can be seen from the Plans, the Chapel is a structural continuation of the porch, and is surmounted by a steeple-shaped erection. The 'Blue Room' and Room No. 7 are the principal bedrooms, and in the former apartment both Henry Bull and Harry Bull breathed their last. It has always been associated with strange happenings and uncanny events. The windows of all the rooms are normal and call for no comment.

Between the lavatory and the bathroom are some stairs leading to what, by compliment, have been called attics. These stairs lead merely to the joists and rafters under the

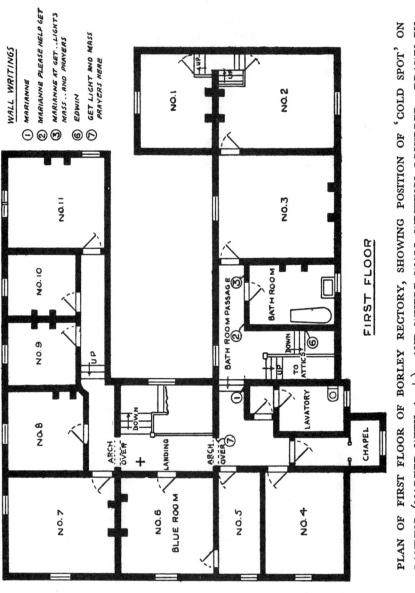

WALL WRITINGS

① MARIANNE
② 'MARIANNE PLEASE HELP GET'
③ 'MARIANNE AT GET ...LIGHTS MASS ... AND PRAYERS'
⑥ EDWIN
⑦ 'GET LIGHT AND MASS PRAYERS HERE'

NO. 1
NO. 2
NO. 3
NO. 11
NO. 10
NO. 9
UP
NO. 8
ARCH OVER
LANDING
DOWN
ARCH OVER
BATH ROOM PASSAGE
BATH ROOM
③
②
①
⑦
UP
DOWN
TO ATTICS
LAVATORY
CHAPEL
NO. 7
NO. 6
BLUE ROOM
NO. 5
NO. 4

FIRST FLOOR

PLAN OF FIRST FLOOR OF BORLEY RECTORY, SHOWING POSITION OF 'COLD SPOT' ON LANDING (MARKED WITH A +), AND WHERE WALL WRITINGS OCCURRED. DRAWN BY S. H. GLANVILLE. SCALE 16 FEET TO ONE INCH.

roof. They give access to the water cistern, and from these same rafters are anchored the wires that control the old-fashioned system of bell-levers and bells that are hung in the kitchen passage.

There is little more I need say here about the first floor, except that there are two arches over the landing passage on either side of the Blue Room; and that the Chapel has imitation stained-glass windows.

CHAPTER V

THE NUN'S WALK AND THE GARDEN

THE grounds of Borley Rectory were at one time of considerable extent. Some nine acres formed the area of the original gardens, etc., but most of this has now been let off for farming purposes. The present garden comprises about two acres, including the large lawn in front of the main living-rooms.

The 'Nun's Walk' (Plate I) is the name, acquired during the life of the Rev. Henry Bull, of a long path that skirts the lawn on the side farthest from the large summer-house. It is completely visible from this summer-house, and partly visible from the windows of the principal living-rooms and bedrooms.

The path acquired its name because, it is alleged, on many occasions a sombre figure of a nun has been frequently seen to walk or glide along this path, usually at dusk, or a little later, and always on July 28th of each year. Collating a number of reports and traditions, I have discovered two main versions of the route that the nun is alleged to take. One, is that she is seen to leave the path by the side of the Rectory nearest the drawing-room, where the 'walk' begins. Keeping an almost perfectly straight line the figure walks along the path for the full length of the lawn, and disappears amongst the trees that overhang a small stream that traverses the garden.

A second version of how and where the nun walks is that she is said to step over the low boundary wall that runs parallel with the 'walk,' on the far side of the lawn, and near the house. Having traversed the 'walk' for half of its length, she turns left, crosses the lawn at right angles to the 'walk,' enters the clump of old trees near the large summer-house, passes through the hedge into the road—and disappears.

The large octagonal summer-house (Plate I) situated opposite the Nun's Walk, was built by the Rev. Henry Bull for the special purpose, I was told, of being able to watch, in comfort, for any appearance of the nun. Whether this is true or not, it is a fact, as can be seen by the photograph, that two sides of the octagon are entirely open and free from obstruction, and a third side is open for more than half its height. This arrangement is ideal for observational purposes as any person or persons within the structure can obtain a very wide angle of view. The summer-house is well and strongly built, and is still in good repair. The interior seating is round the periphery of the house, and to the centre pole is attached a table. Both Henry Bull and his son Harry spent much time in the summer-house.

There is a smaller summer-house (Plate II) in the copse at the end of the garden, almost hidden by the trees and brambles that have been allowed to grow there. This, too, was built by the Rev. Henry Bull, and was erected at about the same time. This retreat was also much used by Henry Bull, who would often resort there in the early hours of the morning in order to 'commune with the spirits.' It plays little part in our narrative.

Through the end of the garden runs a small stream (Plate I) bordered by trees and bushes which are now much overgrown. It is into this stream, according to one story, that the figure of the nun disappears. It is crossed by a small bridge. The stream empties itself into a pond, in which, it is said, someone once drowned himself.

Much overgrown with brambles, and in danger of being altogether missed by a stranger exploring the garden, is a collection of wooden headboards bearing the names of pet cats that have been buried there from time to time. This cats' cemetery is at the end of the Nun's Walk, near the stream. Three headboards still remain and on them are painted respectively the names 'Gem,' 'Rollo,' and 'Sandy.'

A very curious incident occurred in the cats' cemetery, which will be related later.

A portion of the garden of Borley Rectory is the site of the burial place of some of the victims of the Great Plague which ravaged England in 1654–5. Occasionally, a skull is turned up by the spade and other remains have been found. These gruesome relics are invariably reverently reinterred in the churchyard opposite.

The remains of a portion of an underground tunnel can be seen in the farmyard of Borley Rectory. Apparently it had caved in at some period in the remote past. It is impossible to trace it very far, and no one appears to know for what distance it is blocked. Future investigators might well make it their business to explore this tunnel. But portions of the tunnel—or *a* tunnel—have been discovered in various places in a direct line between Borley and Bures, a township seven miles from Borley, on the River Stour, and partly in Essex and partly in Suffolk. Bures is six miles south-east of Sudbury and the remains of a nunnery or similar religious foundation have been found there. The story is that a secret passage or subterranean tunnel led from Borley Monastery or castle to the nunnery at Bures. Whether this tunnel—of small, ancient bricks—was used as a means of escape from some possible danger, or for some military purpose; or whether it was constructed as a purely domestic arrangement between the monastery and nunnery, is a matter of conjecture.

I have been told that the entrance to a second tunnel, or perhaps the entrance to a branch of the Borley-Bures tunnel, is still extant in the farmyard of Borley Place, the ancient house opposite the Rectory. A tunnel from Clare is supposed to meet the one from Bures somewhere in the Rectory grounds.

I have now related all that need be told here about the Rectory and grounds. Other details will emerge during the account of the strange happenings that have occurred there. I will now detail the various legends, stories, traditions, and phantasms connected with the Rectory.

Above left :   Front entrance to Rectory from drive, showing   PLATE II
bricked-up window on left of porch.
Above right :   One of the drive gates, by the side of which Fred Cartwright
saw the " nun " four times.
Below left :   The bricked courtyard of the Rectory.
Below right :   The summer-house in the copse.

CHAPTER VI

THE BRICKED-UP NUN AND OTHER LEGENDS

O F the many stories and traditions connected with
Borley Rectory, the one about the nun is the most
persistent and picturesque.

The 'nun' legend has several variants, but the principal
one is that a beautiful young novice at the nunnery at Bures
fell in love with one of the lay brothers at Borley Monastery.
Or perhaps the lay brother fell in love with the novice.
There is no precise information on this question. The lovers
arranged to elope and the novice met her sweetheart, by
appointment, in the woods that surrounded the Monastery.
Perhaps she traversed the seven miles from Bures to Borley
via the tunnel which I mentioned in the last chapter. The
lovers took into their confidence another lay brother, and
—according to the story—the three escaped from Borley
in an 'old-fashioned coach' drawn by a pair of bay horses.
They chose—rather foolishly—a bright moonlight night for
their escapade, were missed from their respective foundations, and chased. History does not reveal by whom they
were chased, or in what they were chased. Probably on
horseback. But, as is usual in similar stories, they were
caught and taken back to their respective superiors—repentant, I hope.

After, I imagine, a full and contrite confession, the novice
was adjudged guilty of having broken her vows—if she had
made any—and she was condemned to be bricked up alive,
in a convenient niche built in the convent wall—rather
hurriedly, I expect. So she was walled up accordingly,
with nothing but the traditional loaf of bread and a pitcher
of water—and her own sad thoughts. A big price to pay for

such a venial sin! The lay brother, I mean the lover, was just hanged. I do not know what happened to the driver accomplice. Perhaps he turned king's evidence—or its equivalent—and got off scot free. But the nun, the coach, the bay horses, and the spectral driver have been careering about the scene of the tragedy ever since, again according to the story. It is a fact, however, that many people claim to have seen the nun, the coach, *and* the coachmen. Sometimes these are headless.

Obviously, there are several snags in the above charming story of frustrated love. The first is, was a nun *ever* bricked up alive, anywhere, at any time?

On April 18, 1939, I gave a lantern talk[1] to the London Ghost Club, my subject being Borley Rectory, and of course mentioned the walled-up nun. My lecture was duly reported in *The Times*,[2] and the account started a long and interesting correspondence in the columns of this journal as to whether nuns ever were bricked up alive. Dr. Letitia Fairfield, Senior Medical Officer of the London County Council, opened the discussion in an amusing letter[3] in which she says:

'Mr. Price claims that the manifestations are caused by the spirits of a nun and a lay brother who eloped together in a black coach and pair, the nun being subsequently "bricked up" and the lay brother hanged. I fear that these unscrupulous phantoms have been pulling Mr. Price's leg. . . . Remember that these deplorable events must have happened—if at all—before the Reformation. Where at this date could the guilty pair have obtained a coach, as coaches were unknown in England till after 1550? Legal historians would, I think, be even more interested to learn how the lay brother managed to get himself hanged.

'If he was in fact hanged, it must have been for the apportation of the horses and not of the lady. Nor is it clear how the novice could be "bricked up," as this punishment has been shown over and over again to be mythical. Can Mr. Price produce any evidence for his legend or, indeed, any example of a capital sentence being imposed in England on a monk or nun for a breach of vows? Men have been hanged, drawn, and quartered often enough for keeping their vows, but not for breaking them.

[1] *Ten Years' Investigation of Borley Rectory.*   [2] April 20, 1939.
[3] *The Times*, April 22, 1939.

(The famous deacon who was burned for marrying a Jewess is perhaps an exception.) One might add that, judging by their subsequent spiteful conduct to well-meaning investigators, these two young persons seem to have been singularly ill fitted for the religious life.'

I answered[1] Dr. Fairfield's good-natured criticisms by gently suggesting that she had been jumping to conclusions, or had misread *The Times* report of my lecture. I pointed out that it was *not* 'my legend,' but one that had been current for fifty years. Also, I said that as a matter of fact, I did *not* believe in the legend, and did *not* believe in 'spirits.' Dr. Fairfield is probably right about the bricking-up of nuns, and undoubtedly right about there being no 'black coaches' at the time when Borley Monastery flourished.

Another correspondent, Mr. H. J. Tarry, Verulam, St. Thomas Drive, Hatch End, Middlesex, called attention to Sir Walter Scott's account of a bricked-up nun. He said:[2]

'Readers interested in this subject will find the story "on those the wall was to enclose alive, within the tomb" vividly described in Sir Walter Scott's *Marmion*, Canto Second—"The Convent." In the appendix by the author appears: "It is well known that the religious, who broke their vows of chastity, were subject to the same penalty as the Roman Vestals. A small niche was made in the massive wall of the convent, and a slender pittance of food and water placed therein, and the awful words *Vade in Pace* were the signal to immure. The remains of a female skeleton some years ago in such a niche were discovered among the ruins of the Abbey of Coldingham, Berwickshire. It is hardly likely, however, that in latter times this punishment was often resorted to."'

The Rev. Walter Crick, of Eastbourne, called attention in *The Times*[3] to the fact that in classical times women were bricked up as a punishment. He says:

'There can be little doubt that the barbarous punishment referred to by Sir Walter Scott was derived directly from ancient Rome. Classical authors make frequent allusion to the grim ritual which was followed when the punishment was inflicted and the victim: *Sanguine adhuc vivo terram subitura sacerdos* was

[1] *The Times*, April 29, 1939.   [2] Ibid., May 3, 1939.
[3] May 6, 1939.

taken out to the *Campus Sceleratus* near one of the city gates,[1] to be buried alive; and Pliny has a story of a vestal named Tuccia, who was falsely accused of broken vows, and appealed to the goddess to vindicate her, with the happy result that she was able to carry a sieve full of water from the Tiber to the temple. Only a few years ago the grave of another vestal, as to whose name and long term of honourable service there can be no doubt, was discovered near Tivoli. The inscription says that her name was Cossinnia, that she served as a vestal for 66 years, and was honoured by a public funeral, "*manu populi delata*"; and on the breast of the skeleton was found "a doll (?) about a foot high, ornamented with necklace, bracelet, and anklets of gold." '

The late Dr. J. H. Middleton, in an article[2] on the goddess Vesta says that the vestals or virgin priestesses were not unfrequently falsely accused of unchastity: 'Cases of un-chastity and its punishment were rare; and, as the evidence against the vestal was usually that of slaves, given under torture, it is probable that in many instances an innocent vestal suffered this cruel death' of being buried alive.

The Times correspondence was concluded by Paymaster Captain C. Tyers, R.N., of The Plains, Ampton, Suffolk, who pointed out[3] that in Egypt, too, burial alive was the punish-ment meted out to 'vestals' of Isis who broke their vows. He said: 'I saw in Cairo Museum in 1913 the "mummified" body of a woman so punished who had obviously died of suffocation while trying to move the lid of the sarcophagus with hands and knees. The body was as well preserved as any of the other mummies. When I inquired about it during a visit a year or two later, I was told that it had been removed to the museum cellars as too gruesome for exhi-bition.'

The reader has now before him the evidence, or some of it, *pro* and *con*, for the bricking-up or burying alive of females who had broken their religious vows. Apparently, this practice was common in classical times, but it is extremely doubtful if any woman was so immured in this country,

[1] The Porta Collina. H.P.
[2] *Encyclopædia Britannica*, Eleventh Edn., 1910, Vol. 27, p. 1055.
[3] May 9, 1939.

and the reader is now able to assess the value of the 'bricking-up' portion of the Borley legend.

The late Father Herbert Thurston, S.J., carefully analysed the 'evidence' for the walling-up of nuns and others and concluded that such a thing never happened. In a most interesting summary of alleged cases, including that of Coldingham Abbey, which he published in *The Month*[1] for June 1892, he concludes: 'Perhaps such charges are to be found, but I can only say that I have not yet heard of a case, nor met any controversialist who pretended to quote one.' In *The Month*[2] for January 1894, he returns to the subject and attacks Rider Haggard for printing in his novel, *Montezuma's Daughter*, a sensational scene where the nun, Isabella de Siguenza, is immured alive in a coffin-shaped niche in a convent wall.

As regards the 'black coach' of the legend, it is also doubtful whether any such vehicle that could be called a coach was in common use in this country, at Borley or elsewhere, in the thirteenth or fourteenth century. The word 'coach' comes from the Magyar *kocsi*, derived from the place-name Kocs in Hungary, where a four-wheeled covered carriage was in use in the fifteenth century.

According to Mr. J. A. M'Naught,[3] an authority on carriages, coaches existed at the beginning of the fifteenth century, but their use was confined to ladies of the first rank. It was undignified for a man to ride in a coach. When Richard II, at the end of the fourteenth century, was fleeing before his rebellious subjects, he went on horseback, while his mother used a coach. The first real coach in England was made in 1555 for the Earl of Rutland, and no trace of proper doors or glass windows appeared before 1650. Springs on vehicles were not employed before 1804. In 1550 there were only three carriages in Paris, and in

---

[1] 'Walled-up Alive,' in *The Month*, June 1892, pp. 172–94.
[2] 'Mr. Rider Haggard and the Immuring of Nuns,' in *The Month*, London, January 1894, pp. 14–29.
[3] See his article 'Carriage,' in the *Encyclopædia Britannica*, Eleventh Edn., 1910, Vol. 5, pp. 401–6.

1635 London could boast of only fifty public conveyances, and their number was restricted because it was thought they would 'break up the roads'!

So I think that we can rule out any possibility of the Borley lovers having used a coach for their elopement. If a phantasmal coach has been seen, and there is evidence for this, its original must have existed at a date much later than that of the monastic foundation.

Another version of the nun-and-coach story tells how the lovers fled in the coach, the lay brother himself driving. A short distance from Borley the young people quarrelled, and the lay brother, in a most unbrotherly fashion, strangled the girl. A third variant says that the young monk rescued his sweetheart by night from the nunnery at Bures, and that during their escape by coach from the precincts, they were seen, chased, captured, and at once put to death.

If we have disposed of the coach,[1] so far as the lay brother and monastery are concerned; and have laid the legend of the 'bricking-up,' we certainly have not laid the ghost of the nun, as readers will realize before they have finished this story. The nun has been seen many times by many people, and the evidence is incontrovertible. She has been seen walking, standing under a tree, gliding along the Nun's Walk, and leaning over a gate. She has been seen as a typical Sister of Mercy, a sombre figure, a shadow, and as a substantial young woman attired in typical nun's clothing. She has been seen by individuals singly, by two persons together, and once by four persons simultaneously (the daughters of the Rev. Henry Bull), proving that the figure was objective. She has been seen to vanish spontaneously and she has been watched out of sight. Not once, I think, has she *appeared* suddenly to any observer. The evidence will be submitted in due course. She has been seen in daylight, by moonlight, and at dawn—four times by one man, on different occasions.

---

[1] For an interesting account of many other spectral vehicles, see 'The Lore of the Phantom Coach', by G. M. Mayhew, in the *Occult Review* for June, 1922.

Another story connected with Borley is that of the screaming girl. The legend has it that a few years after the Rectory was built a young woman was seen clinging to the window-sill of the Blue Room (Room No. 6 on Plan). She was screaming at the top of her voice. Finally, unable to continue her hold, she had perforce to let go, and she crashed through the veranda roof and was killed. Her spirit is alleged to haunt the place, but no evidence is forthcoming to support this story. It is said that she was attacked in the Blue Room by someone unnamed, and, *via* the window, made her escape to her death. This legend was told to me by a man I met during my many inquiries at Sudbury, and there is not the slightest confirmation for any part of it—except that the figure of a young woman dressed in white or blue was seen leaning out of the Blue Room window—or rather the aperture where the window once was—by two persons simultaneously a week or so after the fire had reduced the upper part of the house to ruins. The story of the clinging girl is comparable with a similar legend associated with the haunted house in Berkeley Square,[1] London.

Other spectral actors in the Borley drama include the apparition of the Rev. Harry Bull, and the figures seen wandering at the scene of the fire by villagers and a local policeman. Also, a few black 'shapes' were noted by various persons.

In addition to the phantasms seen by various people, the following phenomena have been recorded by visitors, residents, servants, and official observers: *Poltergeist* manifestations; the spontaneous displacement of objects (telekinesis); the appearance and disappearance of objects within the house; voices, footsteps, banging of doors and similar noises; the spontaneous combustion of portions of the house; mysterious wall-writings; paranormal bell-ringing; inexplicable and sudden thermal variations; 'touchings' felt by observers; singing, as if by a choir; music, strange lights; rumbling sounds outside the building, as if made by

[1] See *Haunted Mayfair*, by Harry Price, a brochure issued by Maggs Bros., Ltd.

D

a heavy coach; the galloping of horses when no horses were near; the odour of scent and less pleasant smells; fright caused to animals for no ascertainable reason; a column of smoke seen in the garden; strange footsteps in the snow;[1] raps, intelligently directed in response to questions; fulfilled prediction through the Planchette, etc. Though most of the above phenomena have been recorded during recent years, manifestations have been known to occur at the Rectory for at least half a century.

[1] Compare similar phenomena in the snow in the case known as 'The Devil's Hoof-marks,' recorded by Rupert T. Gould in *Oddities*, London, 1928. See also *The Times*, February 16, 1855, for original accounts of the phenomenon.

CHAPTER VII

AN EXCITING DAY

IF the reader has properly assimilated the information
contained in the last three chapters, he will be able to
visualize the background to the Borley mystery, with
its traditions of nuns and monks, stories of phantom coaches,
and the other ingredients of which good ghost stories are
composed. He will also have a clear mental picture of the
Rectory itself, its successive inhabitants, the lay-out of its
many apartments, and the conformation of its grounds.

After lunch on June 12, 1929, my secretary and I began
a minute examination of the Rectory from rafters to cellars.
With yard-stick and steel tape we measured every room,
passage and piece of furniture, and made a working plan of
them. We sounded the walls for possible cavities or hidey-
holes, examined all cupboards, explored under stairways,
and, with powerful electric torches, crawled on our hands
and knees along the joists and rafters under the eaves. On
one of the rafters, to which the bell levers were anchored,
we discovered the following inscription in rough black
painted characters: 'Bells hung by S. Cracknell and Mercur,
1863.' This positively fixes the exact age of the house.
Dusty and slightly bruised, we scrambled back from the
'attics,' and resumed our search. We sealed the door
behind us. As we came to a window, we sealed that, too.
We examined the chimneys and fireplaces, took more
measurements, and satisfied ourselves that at least the upper
portion of the house could not be invaded without our
knowing it.

Returning to the ground floor, we re-examined every
room and the domestic quarters, looked in ovens and

35

copper, tried to move the fixed pieces of furniture, such as dressers and shelves, and found everything normal. We particularly examined the numerous bells in the passage, traced each wire from its respective bell right through the house up to the rafters. We tested each bell as we traced its course through the house. Some of the wires were broken, or had been cut, in order to stop the incessant ringing.

Torches in hand, we then descended to the cellars. We found these dark and damp, floors and walls slimy, and young frogs, toads and newts were hopping about on the cellar floor. It was difficult to avoid treading on them. On the walls I saw a number of lizards, of a dark green hue, similar to the species known as *Lacerta agilis*. These reptiles were very much alive and quickly slid off at our approach. Scores of old—and empty—wine bottles were stacked in the niches, and a lot of old rubbish was lying about. We examined the place for secret entrances and found none. Everything was normal. What we did *not* discover on this, my first visit, was the old and rotten well cover which was later found by one of our observers. This cover was flush with the cellar floor, from which it was indistinguishable. As we came up the cellar stairs into the kitchen passage we sealed the door behind us.

After a good wash, I interviewed the gardener who had helped to bury the skull found in the house, and cross-examined Miss Mary Pearson, the Rectory maid, as to what she said she saw and heard.

Of the two maids employed by the Rev. G. E. Smith, the first, brought from London, stayed for two days only. She was frightened by a nun, wearing a hood, that she had seen at the gate at the bottom of the garden. The second maid, Mary Pearson, a very intelligent girl, not only saw the nun, but saw the coach, too, *and* a headless man. I interviewed Mary and could not shake her testimony. The following information is taken from my original notes (June 12, 1929):

'Mary has seen a coach on the lawn, with two bay horses.

The first time she saw it, it was going down the garden; the second time, up the garden. When she stopped to look, the coach disappeared. First time she saw the coach was at 12.30 p.m., three weeks ago. The second time, two days later, from the road. Coach went through the trees. It was "like a big cab." On both occasions it was the same coach, with two brown horses. She saw no coachman. She also saw a man, headless, behind a tree. She chased it into the garden, where it disappeared. She had also heard scratchings at the drawing-room window, which could not be accounted for.' There seems little doubt that Mary thought she saw the objects she described to us. Young persons (especially young girls) and adolescents are admittedly good 'percipients.'

It will be remembered that on the night previous to my arrival, Mr. V. C. Wall had, with others, seen a strange light in one of the upstairs rooms of the Rectory. This was Room No. 7 on Plan, a room that was unfurnished and unused. Immediate investigation proved that no light was there, although it was still seen from the garden while the investigators were actually in the room, satisfying themselves that there was *no* light in the room. A number of the Bull family died in this room.

After tea on the first day of my visit, and after *another* search of the house and grounds, Mr. Wall and I arranged that, when it was dusk, we would take up our vigil in the garden for a long observational period. So, soon after sunset he and I made our way to the large summer-house to take up our posts. It was decided that I was to keep my eyes on the window of Room No. 7, while my companion kept watch on the Nun's Walk at the point exactly opposite the summer-house, at the door of which we were standing, smoking our pipes. Previous to the commencement of our vigil, we had sealed up every door and window in the Rectory with the exception of the French windows of the study, in which the Rev. G. E. Smith, his wife, and my secretary were on guard. The maid servant had gone home.

We had been smoking in silence for more than an hour when suddenly Wall gripped my arm and said 'There she is!' With that exclamation he dashed across the lawn to the Nun's Walk. Taken by surprise, as I was intently watching the window of the Rectory, it was a second or so before I could direct my gaze to the spot indicated by Wall. It was nearly dark, but against the darker background of the trees I fancied I could discern a shadowy figure, blacker than the background, gliding towards the end of the garden and the little stream. But I was not certain. From experience I know what tricks one's eyes can play one when seeing a 'ghost,' and a subconscious elaboration of details, plus imagination, is liable to deceive. The night was still, and there was no stir amongst the trees to mislead me into thinking that I saw something move. So I am not certain that I saw the nun: I merely record the fact that I thought I saw something blacker than the trees move along the path.

When Mr. Wall returned to me, breathless and excited, he told me his story. As he was gazing steadily at the Nun's Walk, he saw a portion of the dark background begin to move. It was a shadowy figure moving towards the stream. Here is his own story[1] in a few words:

'The first remarkable happening was the dark figure I saw in the garden. We were standing in the summer-house at dusk watching the lawn, when I saw the "apparition" which so many claim to have seen, but owing to the deep shadows it was impossible for one to discern any definite shape or attire. But something certainly moved along the path on the other side of the lawn, and although I immediately ran across to investigate, it had vanished when I reached the spot.'[2]

Having discussed the figure, we decided we would remain in the garden no longer as it was now quite dark. We crossed the lawn towards the house with the intention of entering the study *via* the French windows. We had just set foot on the path under the veranda and were about to enter the room, when a terrific crash was heard and one of

[1] *Daily Mirror*, June 14, 1929.
[2] Compare Mrs. Lloyd Williams's account of seeing the 'nun,' page 219.

the thick glass panes from the roof fell in pieces at our feet and splashed us with splinters. The hole can be seen to this day. Very startled, we sought for a possible missile and found a piece of brick or tile on the floor of the veranda. It was *not* an ordinary tile, but looked more like a common half-brick.

We entered the study and found that nothing untoward had happened during our vigil. Of course, our friends had heard the smash and were just as puzzled as ourselves. Thinking that, in spite of our search, someone *might* have been in one of the upper rooms and had played a trick on us, we hurried upstairs and again made a search of the rooms and windows, especially those of the Blue Room (No. 6) and the rooms overlooking the veranda. We found our seals intact and everything in order. We descended by the main staircase and had just reached the hall when another crash was heard and we found that a red glass candlestick, one of a pair we had just seen on the mantelpiece of the Blue Room, had been hurled down the main stairs, had struck the iron stove, and had finally disintegrated into a thousand fragments on the hall floor. Both Mr. Wall and I saw the candlestick hurtle past our heads. We at once again dashed upstairs, made another search, and found nothing. We returned to the hall. We turned out all lights, and the entire party sat on the stairs in complete darkness, just waiting. A few minutes later we heard something come rattling down the stairs and Mr. Wall said he had been hit on the hand. We then relighted the lamps and found it was a mothball which, apparently, had followed the same path as the candlestick.

In quick succession, and in full light, the following articles came tumbling down the stairs: first of all some common seashore pebbles; then a piece of slate, then some more pebbles.

During this eventful evening bells rang of their own volition. The wires could be seen moving, and even the pulls in some of the rooms could be seen swinging when we visited them. The Rev. G. E. Smith had been troubled with considerable bell-ringing, and had even cut some of the wires in an attempt to stop the nuisance. After we had consumed the excellent supper that the hospitable Mrs. Smith had provided for us, a new phenomenon occurred. The keys in the doors of the library and drawing-room fell *simultaneously* on to the hall floor. I carefully examined the keys, and the doors, and there was no sign of any thread, wire or other apparatus that could have accounted for the fall of the keys. Actually, it would require considerable mechanism to duplicate this phenomenon normally. During the occupation of the next Rector, the Rev. L. A. Foyster, every key in the house disappeared!

After our supper—or dinner—it was suggested that we should hold a séance in the Blue Room. Although it was so late, I consented.

CHAPTER VIII

A MIDNIGHT SÉANCE IN THE BLUE ROOM

THE séance began at about 1 a.m. During the latter part of the evening, two of the Misses Bull (sisters of Harry Bull) had come over from Sudbury to see me. So these ladies, Mr. and Mrs. Smith, Mr. Wall, my secretary and I adjourned to the Blue Room (No. 6) and deposited ourselves on chairs and bedsteads. A powerful duplex paraffin oil lamp was burning. There was the ordinary bedroom furniture in its usual places, including a dressing-table in front of the window. On the dressing-table stood a large, solid mahogany mirror, with a wooden back.

When we ascended to the Blue Room, we had no idea how the séance would be started. There was no medium present. In order to open the proceedings, I said—speaking to the four walls of the room—'If any entity is present here to-night, will it please make itself known?' I repeated this request two or three times. Just as we were wondering whether we were wasting our time, a faint—though sharp and decisive—tap was heard coming from, apparently, the window. We waited in silence for a few seconds and the tap was repeated, a little louder this time. All of us left our seats, and went over to the dressing-table, round which we stood in a semi-circle. Again the tap sounded, still louder, but this time it came unmistakably from the wooden back of the mirror, which acted as a sort of sounding-board. We drew our chairs up to the mirror, round which we sat as at a regular séance. Then someone suggested that the light should be extinguished. This was done, but as nothing happened, we relit it.

Then came a succession of short, quick taps or raps,

and I made a little speech to the 'entity,' thanking it for revealing its presence to us that evening, and asking whether it would answer certain questions which we would put to it. I suggested that the time-honoured 'three taps for "Yes," one tap for "No" and two taps if the answer were doubtful or unknown' should be employed. I asked the entity if it understood. Immediately, three quick, loud taps were heard from the mirror. We also suggested spelling out the alphabet, asking the entity to give a single rap at such letters as would spell coherent answers to our perfectly plain and simple questions. Again, I asked whether this was understood, and if the idea was welcome. Three raps came in reply.

As it is important that as many witnesses as possible should testify to the Borley phenomena, I will now quote Mr. Wall's words[1] as to what took place next:

'Our first attempts were naturally to ascertain the identity of the rapper. We asked if it were the nun in the old legend or one of the grooms, and a single rap denoting "no" was the reply.

'Then I suggested to Mr. Price that he should ask whether it were the Rev. H. Bull, the late Rector. I had hardly finished the name when three hurried taps came on the mirror, which meant an emphatic "yes."

'The following dialogue then took place, sometimes with the lamp lit, sometimes in darkness: "Is it your footsteps one hears in this house?"—"Yes."

' "Do you wish to worry or annoy anybody here?"—"No."

' "Do you merely wish to attract attention?"—"Yes."

' "Are you worrying about something that you should have done when you were alive?"—"No."

' "If we had a medium here, do you think you could tell us what is the matter?"—"Yes." '

At this juncture I asked the Misses Bull and Mr. and Mrs. Smith whether they would care to question the entity—the alleged Harry Bull—as to certain private affairs of the family. They said they would and for about an hour a string of questions was put to the entity. By means of the raps on the mirror, a perfectly sensible 'Yes' or 'No' was received, but great difficulty was experienced in obtaining names or

[1] *Daily Mirror*, June 15, 1929.

messages by spelling out the alphabet. At the best of times, this method is laborious, slow, and cumbersome, and whatever it was 'tapping,' it did not appear to grasp the technique of this system of 'communication.' Obviously, the questions asked by the Misses Bull cannot be printed here.

The séance lasted for about three hours, from 1 a.m. to 4 a.m., and about two o'clock in the morning we were all startled by the new cake of toilet soap *jumping out of its dish*, striking the edge of the water ewer, and bouncing on the floor. The washstand was at the far end of the room; no one was near it, as were we seated round the mirror; the wicks of the duplex lamp were raised to their full height and the room was everywhere perfectly illuminated. Everyone saw the phenomenon. Here is Mr. Wall's recording[1] of the incident, a perfect and typical *Poltergeist* manifestation:

'From one o'clock until nearly four this morning all of us, including the Rector and his wife, actually questioned the spirit or whatever it was and received at times the most emphatic answers. Finally came the most astonishing event of the night. A cake of soap on the washstand was lifted and thrown heavily on to a china jug standing on the floor with such force that the soap was deeply marked. All of us were at the other side of the room when this happened.'

And so ended this very eventful June 12, 1929. A day to be remembered, even by an experienced investigator. Although I have investigated many haunted houses, before and since, never have such phenomena so impressed me as they did on this historic day. Sixteen hours of thrills!

In spite of *Poltergeister*, rapping mirrors, and the eerie reputation of the Blue Room, I slept in this apartment in the cosy bed Mrs. Smith had had prepared for me, and was quite undisturbed. Haunted and haunters were at peace.

---

[1] *Daily Mirror*, June 14, 1929.

CHAPTER IX

THE MISSES BULL'S STORY

I HAVE mentioned that two of the Misses Bull attended the very informal séance that we held in the Blue Room in the early hours of June 13, 1929. Later in the same day, after a good night's rest, my secretary and I, at the invitation of our new friends, visited them at their old-world house, Chilton Lodge, Great Cornard, Sudbury. The Bull family are—or were—the patrons of the living at Borley.

The Misses Ethel, Freda, and Constance Bull we found very charming and cultured, and quite ready to give us any information in their possession concerning the Rectory; and willing to relate to us their personal experiences of the nun and other phenomena. They are three of the surviving sisters of the late Rev. Harry Bull, and the daughters of the Rev. Henry Bull, who built the Rectory.

The following account is a composite report, from notes, composed from information given to my secretary and me on June 13, 1929; from another interview, over a cup of tea, that Mr. Sidney H. Glanville and I had with the ladies on Wednesday, March 29, 1939; and from notes that Mr. Glanville made when he met Miss Ethel Bull and her sister at Pinner on June 25, 1938.

On July 28, 1900, the Misses Ethel, Freda, and Mabel[1] were returning home from a garden party. It was quite light, as the sun had not set. They entered their property at the postern gate at the end of the garden, in order to proceed up the lawn to the house. Immediately they had cleared the trees and shrubs and reached the open lawn, all three simultaneously saw a female figure, with bowed

[1] She died in 1936.

head. She was dressed entirely in black, in the garb of a nun. She appeared to be telling her beads, as her hands were in front of her and appeared to be clasped. Without knowing why, the three girls felt terrified. The figure was slowly gliding—rather than walking—along the Nun's Walk in the direction of the stream.

Something seemed to tell them that the nun was not normal, as she neither behaved nor progressed along the path in a normal manner. They stopped near the large summer-house and watched her. She looked intensely sad and ill. By this time they were really frightened at the strangeness of what they now took to be an apparition, and one of the girls ran into the house to fetch her sister, Miss Elsie Bull (who married shortly afterwards). When she saw the figure, she said 'A ghost? Oh, what nonsense, I'll go and speak to it!' With that, she began to run across the lawn, but she had taken hardly two steps when the figure stopped and turned towards her. She had an expression of intense grief on her face. Miss Elsie stood on the lawn terrified— and the figure vanished. The nun has been seen other years on July 28, and this fact gave rise to the tradition that she is seen *every* year on this date. I do not think this is correct.

In the November following the meeting of the nun by the four sisters, Miss Ethel Bull again saw the figure and again in the garden, but this time leaning over the garden gate. One of the maids (the cook) saw it too, simultaneously with Miss Ethel. Later, a cousin who was staying at the house, also saw it.

It is quite certain that this figure, seen first by four persons collectively, and then by two other persons simultaneously, was *objective*. It was solid, like a human being; *not* a subjective image, a phantasm, or figment of the imagination.

Miss Ethel M. Bull, with her sisters—like everyone else who has ever lived at Borley Rectory—has had some remarkable experiences. One of the typical *Poltergeist* features of the haunting is the paranormal bell-ringing. On one occasion Miss Ethel was in the house, when all the bells—of which there were about twenty—suddenly started pealing simultaneously. Immediate investigation failed to solve the mystery. This phenomenon was followed by the sound of rushing water. No explanation. A sister who was sleeping in one of the smaller bedrooms was awakened by something slapping her face. No explanation. For a long period, quite regularly every night and just before she retired to rest, a series of sharp raps was heard on her bedroom door. Later, many crashes were heard in the house. No explanation was forthcoming.

On one occasion, when in one of the upper passages, Miss Ethel saw a tall, dark man standing beside her. Before she could recover from her surprise, he vanished. Once, an uncle of the Misses Bull, who was on a visit to their home, slept in one of the rooms. He refused to say what happened, but in no circumstances, he said, would he sleep there again.

When the Misses Bull were young girls, they were leaning over the fence of their garden, looking across the fields. They were with one of the maids. They saw some young friends a few yards away, crossing the field in front of them, evidently taking a short cut to Long Melford Station, or going to the river Stour. Just a little ahead of their friends was a girl or young woman in white whom the sisters failed to recognize as one of the villagers. The Bull sisters happened to meet their friends in the evening and asked the name of the girl whom they took to the river. The young people denied that anyone had been with them; nor did they see any stranger present.

Another interesting series of phenomena occurred also during their childhood days. Every night, about 10.30, steps could be heard passing their bedroom door and upon the landing outside their room, and always stopping outside one of the night nurseries. When the sound of the footsteps ceased, three taps—and three taps only—were always heard. These footsteps and taps were heard at least a hundred times.

One night Miss Ethel awoke suddenly and found an old

man in dark, old-fashioned clothes, wearing a tall hat, standing by her bed. On another occasion, the same figure was seen sitting on the edge of the bed. This figure was seen many times. The strange footsteps heard in the Rectory have been recorded by every person who has ever resided in the place for any length of time; and, up to the period when the house was burnt, they still persisted.

Another strange phenomenon was experienced over and over again soon after the death of the Misses Bull's father (the Rev. Henry Bull) and especially when most of the members of the family were at church and when only the invalid mother and a daughter to keep her company were at home. This manifestation took the shape of sounds as if someone was entering the back door, but investigation always proved that no one was there.

Striking and independent confirmation of Miss Ethel's story of the strange footsteps of her childhood days was supplied in a letter from Mrs. E. Byford who, for a short period, was a nursemaid at Borley Rectory. This was in 1886. The letter was received on June 11, 1929. From her testimony it is quite clear that strange phenomena at the Rectory were quite openly discussed, both in the house and neighbourhood, more than fifty years ago. Mrs. Byford, writing from Parsonage Farm, Newport, Essex, says:

'Much of my youth was spent in Borley and district, with my grandparents, and it was common talk that the Rectory was haunted. Many people declared that they had seen figures walking at the bottom of the garden. I once worked at the Rectory forty-three years ago, as under-nursemaid, but I only stayed there a month, because the place was so weird. The other servants told me my bedroom was haunted, but I took little notice because I knew two of the ladies of the house had been sleeping there before me. But when I had been there a fortnight, something awakened me in the dead of night. Someone was walking down the passage towards the door of my room, and the sound they made suggested that they were wearing slippers. As the head nurse always called me at six o'clock, I thought it must be she, but nobody entered the room, and I suddenly thought of the "ghost." The next morning I asked the other four maids if they had come to my room, and they all said they had not, and tried to laugh me out of it. But I was convinced that somebody or something in slippers had been along that corridor, and finally I became so nervous that I left. My grandparents would never let me pass the building after dark, and I would never venture into the garden or the wood at dusk.

(*Signed*) '(Mrs.) E. Byford.'

If Mrs. Byford's story was not supported by the testimony of many others, I should feel inclined to think that the tales of ghosts that were current in the household had frightened the young girl, that she had become very nervous of remaining in the house, and that suggestion had done the rest. But the sounds of slippered footsteps in the passages outside the bedrooms have been heard by everyone who ever lived in the place, and Mrs. Byford's letter is just one more piece of evidence.

During my various interviews with Miss Ethel Bull and her sisters, I learnt something of the experiences that their brother, the Rev. Harry Bull, had had in the Rectory and grounds. As we have seen, Harry Bull was Rector of Borley from 1892 to 1927, having succeeded his father. For some time he lived at the Rectory with his sisters, but upon his marriage in 1911, he removed to Borley Place, near by. Later, in 1920, the ladies went to live at Chilton Lodge, and Harry returned to the Rectory with his wife.

During Harry Bull's intimate connection with the Rectory, where he lived most of his life, it is not surprising that he experienced a number of extraordinary phenomena. He made no secret of these strange manifestations, and related his adventures to his sisters and others.[1]

One day Harry was in the garden with his retriever 'Juvenal,' when the dog suddenly started howling and cowering with fright. Looking in the direction at which the dog was 'pointing,' the Rector saw the legs of a figure, the upper part of which was apparently hidden by some fruit trees. The legs moved, and when they had cleared the bushes, Harry Bull saw that they belonged to a man who

[1] See letter from Mr. J. Harley, *post*, page 50.

was *headless*. The figure went towards the postern gate—which plays a big part in the Borley drama—*through* which it passed. This gate was always kept locked. The figure disappeared in the vegetable garden, where it was lost to sight.

Upon another occasion Mr. Bull saw a little old man standing on the lawn, with one arm pointing upwards and the other down. As the Rector approached, the figure disappeared. Inquiries as to who the figure could be elicited the fact that the features were identical with those of an old gardener named Amos whom the Bulls had employed some two hundred years previously. Incidentally, the Bulls have lived in the neighbourhood for more than three hundred years. 'Old Amos' was a well-known character in the Bull family, and his traditional story had been handed down. Harry Bull was *not* afraid of ghosts. Neither was his father, Henry Bull. In addition to being an athlete, he (Henry) was also an amateur boxer, and hunted the surrounding country regularly.

More than once, Harry Bull both saw and heard the phantasmal coach with which the Borley story is so linked. The coach was drawn by two horses, and driven by a headless coachman. The whole turn-out disappeared while still in view. One night Mr. Bull was returning to the Rectory, and was in the road just outside the house. Suddenly, he heard a great clatter of hoofs on the roadway, and the rumbling as of heavy wheels. Wondering who could be in such a hurry in so deserted a spot, he stepped to the side of the road in order to let the vehicle pass.[1] The *sounds* passed him, but that was all. There was nothing tangible to be seen, and the noise gradually diminished and could be heard dying away in the distance. This account of the galloping horses is comparable with the experience of Mr. H. Mayes, the Rev. A. C. Henning's gardener, which will be recorded later. Mr. Harry Bull died in the Blue Room, in which apartment his mother and father breathed

[1] Just as Mr. Mayes did, see page 175.

E

their last. He is said to still walk down the main stairs, on his way to the library. He holds a small bag or manuscript case.

Just as Mrs. Byford confirmed the early experiences of the young Bull children, so we received a letter from a stranger, Mr. J. Harley, of Nottingham Place, W.1, whose independent testimony as to the beliefs of the Rev. Harry Bull likewise confirmed the information imparted to us by his sisters.

Mr. Harley's letter is dated June 15, 1929, and he says:

'In 1922 I resided for some weeks at the Rectory with the Rev. H. Bull, and I distinctly recall him assuring me that on many occasions he had had personal communications with spirits. In his opinion, the only way for a spirit, if ignored, to get into touch with a living person, was by means of a manifestation causing some violent physical reaction, such as the breaking of glass or the shattering of other and similar material elements. The Rector also declared that on his death, if he were discontented, he would adopt this method of communicating with the inhabitants of the Rectory.'

If there was anything in the suggestion that it was Harry Bull 'communicating' at our midnight séance in the Blue Room, Mr. Harley's evidence goes to support it. Harry spent many hours in the large summer-house, hoping to see the nun.

Other interesting incidents connected with the Borley mystery were related to us by Miss Ethel Bull. Some of the old coffins in the crypt of Borley Church have been found moved from their prescribed positions. This has occurred on several occasions and no explanation has been found for the displacements. In this connection, one cannot help recalling the famous case of the displaced coffins in the 'haunted vault' at Barbados,[1] and that of Stanton (or Staunton) in Suffolk, a few miles from Borley, in 1810.[1]

Another story is that there is church plate buried somewhere in the vicinity of the churchyard. A dowser once made an experimental investigation and, it is said, the

[1] For a concise account of this repeated phenomenon, see *Oddities*, by Rupert T. Gould, London, 1928.

whalebone 'twig' or divining-rod broke in her hands. Whether this reaction was due to water, or to a metallic lode, or if it really indicated the 'treasure' was not, apparently, ascertained. The Glanville family knew nothing about the 'lost' treasure but, very strangely, during their Planchette experiments, a perfect drawing of a chalice was produced.

Strange lights in certain rooms in the Rectory were reported by various people over a long period, but investigation invariably proved that no normal lights were present. It will be remembered that Mr. Wall saw one of these lights in Room No. 7 on the evening of June 11, 1929. I have never seen them myself.

Many people have testified to hearing footsteps in the lane outside the Rectory, when nothing tangible was visible. Mr. Walter Bull, a brother of the late Harry Bull, supplies some interesting information concerning this phenomenon. I had the pleasure of meeting this gentleman when Mr. Glanville and I called at Chilton Lodge, Sudbury (where he was living with his sisters) on March 29, 1939. Mr. Glanville had previously met him when he (Mr. Bull) called at the Rectory during an observational period when Mr. Glanville was on duty, on November 20, 1937.

As Mr. Walter Bull has spent much of his life at sea, he has had few opportunities for investigating the Borley mystery or witnessing many phenomena. Actually, he never *saw* anything unusual in the Rectory during the time he was living there, but noises were frequently heard, though they were neither loud enough nor disturbing enough to excite more than passing comment.

But, he told us, that when walking up the lane and approaching the Rectory, he, at least fifty times, heard footsteps following him. He always turned round, but never saw anyone, and could not account for them. Mr. Walter Bull was born at the Rectory. He was at home when his father died, but was away at the time of the death of his brother, Harry.

I put one last question to Miss Ethel Bull before Mr.

Glanville and I left the hospitable Chilton Lodge. I asked her whether, as a child, she and/or her sisters were frightened at what they saw and heard in their Rectory home. Miss Bull said they were not—they grew up with the 'phenomena,' of which they had little fear. But she added that nothing would now induce her to sleep at the Rectory.

CHAPTER X

THE STRANGE ADVENTURES OF
EDWARD COOPER

AFTER my secretary and I had accomplished the purpose of our visit to the Misses Bull on June 13, 1929, and had heard their evidence, we visited Mr. Edward Cooper and his wife. Miss Ethel Bull kindly gave us their address. Edward Cooper was for some years the groom-gardener at the Rectory, and he is still, I believe, employed by the Bull family in a similar capacity.

Mr. Cooper, of 'Werneth,' Broom Street, Great Cornard, Sudbury, is of the sturdy yeoman type, intelligent, hard-working, frank and downright. He and his wife live in a snug little villa on the outskirts of Sudbury.

The following story was given to us in 1929, and my secretary took copious notes, from which this report has been compiled. But nearly ten years later, that is, on March 29, 1939, the Rev. A. C. Henning and I called upon the Coopers and, for the second time, heard the account of their adventures, which they kindly permitted me to include in this monograph. When I returned home I compared the two reports, and they do not vary by a hairsbreadth. This is worthy of note, and further evidence of the integrity of the Coopers and the veridical nature of their story.

Mr. Cooper joined the staff of the Rectory in April 1916, when the Misses Bull were in residence there. He, with his wife, occupied the rooms in the cottage adjoining the Rectory. Under these rooms are stables, etc.

For more than three years during his occupation of the cottage, the Coopers, when in bed, were disturbed on most nights by the sounds of pattering which appeared to come from the adjoining living-room. It was just as if a large dog or small child had jumped from a height and was padding round the room. Naturally, at first they were somewhat concerned at what these noises could be and more than once lit the candle and explored the contiguous rooms, without success. Finally, they got used to the 'pad-pad-pad,' which usually began soon after they got into bed, between 10 and 11 o'clock, and thought nothing of it.

One night, about three years after the 'padding' sounds were first heard, and soon after the Coopers had retired to rest, the 'dog' phenomenon was again experienced. They heard the soft, but heavy pad-pad-pad in the next room when suddenly there was a terrific crash as if all the china on the kitchen dresser had fallen to the floor simultaneously. Mr. Cooper leapt out of bed and lit a candle, quite expecting to find part of his home demolished. To his astonishment, not a thing in the cottage was displaced, and no damage was done. From that night onwards they were never again disturbed. The 'dog' had gone for ever.

One early morning in 1919, when it was just getting light, the Coopers, as they lay in bed, saw a black shape, in the form of a little man, running round their bedroom. Before they could do anything about it, the form vanished. They thought the 'devil was in the house.'

The Coopers have frequently seen the 'nun,' or at least a black shape resembling a hooded figure, crossing the courtyard which is overlooked by the cottage windows. On one occasion, from their window, they saw the figure side-face, and it appeared to be the traditional nun. One bright summer's evening, about ten o'clock, when it was barely dark, they saw the figure cross the courtyard and walk towards the road. To do this in a direct line, it had to step on the cover of an inspection chamber that was flush with the ground. This cover was loose, and any normal person walking over it would rock it, thus making a clanking, metallic sound. The 'nun' stepped on the cover, but *no sound was heard.* Mr. Cooper, at the time, called his wife's attention to this fact. This figure, now seen more clearly, was dressed as a Sister of Mercy. Mr. Cooper was so struck by the life-like appearance of the nun that, next morning, he made inquiries in the neighbourhood, and at the Rectory, but no one had seen a figure such as he described.

Probably the most impressive sight that Mr. Cooper saw was the black coach. One bright, moonlight night when he and his wife were retiring to rest, he happened to look out of the window, and in the meadow by the church opposite, he saw some bright moving lights. Wondering why such lights should be present at such a time and place, he watched, and realized that the lights were approaching. As they neared the road he saw that the lights were really the head-lamps attached to a large, old-fashioned black coach which was rapidly sweeping across the hedge and road towards him and the Rectory.

He gazed in astonishment. The whole turn-out was so clear-cut that he could see the harness of the two horses glittering in the light of the head-lamps and the moon. On the box of the coach were two figures wearing high top hats. In amazement, he shouted to his wife, but she was just too late to see the extraordinary spectacle. She arrived at the window as the coach swept into the farmyard and disappeared. Mr. Cooper considers that the coach—or rather lights—were visible from first to last for a period of thirty seconds. No other person in the neighbourhood saw the coach on this occasion as far as he knew. This is not surprising when we consider the lateness of the hour, and the few people likely to be about at such a time. In answer to my question as to whether he *heard* anything, Mr. Cooper said that there was absolutely no sound at all, and not even a twig moved.

Mr. Cooper's account of the coach tallies in some respects with the story told to us by Mary Pearson. The two horses, the black coach 'like a large cab,' the passage through the trees, etc. But Mary saw no coachmen.

Mr. Cooper informed me that the road outside the

Rectory sounds hollow when a heavy vehicle passes over it. It is possible that one of the subterranean tunnels passes beneath it at this spot. Mr. Cooper and his wife left the Rectory in March 1920, when the Misses Bull went to reside at Chilton Lodge. Since leaving, he has experienced no phenomena of any kind, anywhere.

About twelve months after my first interview with the Coopers I spent a day in Sudbury in an attempt to discover those persons—workmen, servants, tradesmen, etc.—who had been in contact with the Rectory in some capacity or other. My quest was not very successful—with one exception. It was rather in the nature of a wild-goose chase, and I followed up a number of 'clues' that eventually proved valueless.

However, I did get on the track of one man, Mr. Fred Cartwright, a journeyman carpenter, who told me a most interesting story. Over a pint of ale at the 'White Horse' I heard his account of having seen the nun—or *a* nun—four times in two weeks.

Mr. Cartwright lived in lodgings in Sudbury, and he had contracted to do some repair work to farm buildings at a farm between Borley and Clare. He used to walk to his work every morning, and the shortest cut was through Borley, past the Rectory. This was in the early autumn of 1927. He believed that the Rectory was then unoccupied.

He started his first day's work on the Monday morning, and, leaving home soon after six o'clock, passed Borley Rectory just before seven. It was then barely light. On the next morning, Tuesday, he left home about the same time, passing the Rectory about 6.45. As far as he could remember, it was a fine morning. As he passed the drive gate (Plate II) nearest Sudbury (*i.e.*, the gate nearest the bricked-up dining-room window), he saw a Sister of Mercy standing quite still by the side of the gate. She looked perfectly normal, but he thought it strange that such a person should be standing at such a place so early in the morning. He concluded that she was waiting for some vehicle to pick her up (there were no

buses or public conveyances nearer than the main Sudbury-
Long Melford road). He thought that she may have been on
some errand of mercy, perhaps a case of illness, which had
detained her all night. The matter passed from his mind.

Every day he passed the same spot at about the same
hour, within a few minutes, and saw nothing of the nun
until the following Friday morning. He passed the Rectory
as usual, and noticed that the same nun—apparently—was
at the identical spot, close up to the hedge by the drive gate.
He again thought it curious that a Sister of Mercy should
have been there at such a time and, as he passed her, he
looked at her. She appeared perfectly normal, except that
she had her eyes closed. Again, the thought occurred to him
that she had been up all night tending the sick, and that she
was tired. He imagined, as he had done on the previous
Tuesday, that she was waiting for some conveyance to pick
her up.

The next, and third, time he saw the Sister of Mercy was
on the following Wednesday morning at the same hour and
place. She was standing on the identical spot as previously.
As he passed her, he looked at her intently, and saw that
she seemed pale, tired and ill, but perfectly human. Her
eyes were closed, as if asleep.

Something seemed to tell Mr. Cartwright that both the
nun and her demeanour were very unusual and he was a
little frightened, principally for her sake. As he continued
walking he could not help wondering whether she needed
assistance. He decided to offer it. He turned to walk back
and found that the nun was nowhere in sight. As he had
heard no sound of a vehicle on the road, he concluded that
she had turned into the Rectory. He therefore continued
towards Clare.

The fourth and last time that Mr. Cartwright saw the
nun was on the following Friday, at exactly the same place
and hour. It was barely light. The figure was in the
identical spot as on the three previous occasions—by the
side of the drive gate. Immediately he saw her in the

distance, he made up his mind that he would at least say 'Good morning' to her. But before he reached the drive, the nun had gone. He did *not* see her vanish, but one moment she was there; the next, she was not. Again he concluded that she had passed into the Rectory or grounds. But as he reached the drive gate he found it was tightly closed. Puzzled, and out of sheer curiosity, he opened the gate and walked the whole length of the drive from one gate to the other. Nothing was to be seen of her, and there was no sign of life in the Rectory itself, which he believed was empty—which indeed it was, as Cartwright's adventure, as we now know, occurred during the period between the death of the Rev. Harry Bull and the coming of the Rev. G. E. Smith.

When Mr. Cartwright reached home that evening, he related his strange experience to his landlord and others at Sudbury. He then heard the story of Borley Rectory, its nun, and its traditions, for the first time. Being a stranger to this part of Suffolk, he knew very little about the neighbourhood. He passed the Rectory several times during the next year or so, both at night and by day, but saw nothing further of the Sister of Mercy, though he was always on the look-out for her.

CHAPTER XI

MR. SMITH MOVES OUT

AFTER my interviews with the Misses Bull and Edward Cooper on this exciting June 13, 1929, I returned to Borley with the conviction that the story of the Rectory was one of the major problems of psychical research.

Thanks to the kindness of our hospitable friends, the Rev. G. E. Smith and his wife, I was able to continue my investigation of the Rectory for two more days on this, my first visit. I stayed at the 'Bull,' Long Melford, the pictur-esque sixteenth-century inn, itself the scene of at least one tragedy during the Civil War.[1] I had to get back to London on the following Friday, but my secretary remained at the Rectory over the week-end, in order to report progress—if any.

As a matter of fact, very little occurred during the next few days. Some inexplicable and desultory bell-ringing was recorded, but that was all.

During the next few weeks I visited the Rectory two or three times, with interesting results. One evening, a party of us was present when incessant bell-ringing occurred. This was accompanied by the usual *Poltergeist* manifestations consisting of the throwing of small pebbles, a shower of several keys (which appear to have been collected by the *Geist* and then projected into the hall); a small gilt medallion, such as are presented to Roman Catholic children on their Confirmation; and another medallion or badge, dated 'AN VIII' (*i.e.*, A.D. 1799) issued in Paris after the French Revolution. The origin of these medallions is not known,

---

[1] Richard Evered, a Melford yeoman, was murdered in the entrance hall of the 'Bull,' July, 1648.

and I will remark in passing that many of the phenomena at Borley are connected in some way with Roman Catholicism: the 'nun' and monks; the medallions; France; the 'messages' on the walls (of which I will speak later), and so on.

On July 28, 1929, the day of the year when the nun is supposed *always* to appear, a party of my friends (including the late Hon. Richard Bethell) visited the Rectory and stayed two days. Nothing of importance happened; in fact, the place seemed particularly peaceful.

Upon another visit an impressive phenomenon occurred. We had all assembled in the Blue Room, and someone remarked: 'If they want to impress us, let them give us a phenomenon *now*!' A few minutes later one of the bells on the ground floor clanged out, the noise reverberating through the house. We rushed downstairs, but could not find even the bell that was rung. Experiment proved to us that when any of these old-fashioned bells were rung, the spring and clapper did not come to rest for some minutes. But we could not discover the least movement in either spring or clapper, though we thought, from its tone, that it was the drawing-room bell that had been disturbed. I should mention that this incident occurred past midnight, when the Rector and his household had retired to rest. This 'phenomenon at request' was repeated at least three times during my investigation of the Rectory.

It was in July 1929, that the Rector and his wife thought seriously of removing from the Rectory. It was *not* the 'ghosts,' in which they did not believe, but the general unpleasantness of the place that prompted them to quit. The sanitation was bad, the water supply difficult, and the general management of the place was, as I have intimated elsewhere, impossible for a woman with a cultured and refined mind. As someone put it, trying to 'manage' Borley Rectory was as difficult as it would be to make the Roman catacombs comfortable! No, the ghosts did not frighten them as they realized that the Bull family had 'lived' with them for about seventy years, and were not afraid.

By July 15, 1929, the Rector and his wife had left Borley, though they returned on July 28 for a few hours to welcome our party. They moved to Long Melford but, of course, Mr. Smith still did duty at Borley Church and looked after the parish. It was thought that the matter could be arranged in this way. The Smiths had been in residence at the Rectory for about eighteen months. However, it was found impossible to continue this arrangement for very long and in April the Rector and his wife moved to Sheringham, Norfolk. Finally, Mr. Smith accepted a living in Kent, where he and his wife are now living in peace, both mental and physical.

One striking fact has emerged during my ten years' investigation of the Borley mystery, and that is, the phenomena are more frequent,* more varied, more convincing, more interesting, and stronger when the Rectory is occupied than when the place is unfurnished with no family in residence. Perhaps the 'ghosts' like company; or perhaps the entities, still in possession of some remnant of a persisting and very human trait, like 'showing off.' The fact remains that all the best phenomena have been recorded by families actually living in the house and not by interested investigators.

After the Smiths had removed to Long Melford, I visited the empty Rectory on two occasions. The result was almost negative, except that on the first occasion we were rewarded with a striking manifestation by one of the bells.

We first called on Mr. Smith at Long Melford and collected the keys of the Rectory. My secretary, a friend and I then made our way to Borley. We entered the building, examined all doors and windows, which we fastened. We established ourselves in the Blue Room, on an old form that we discovered in the library, and awaited events. By the light of a couple of candles, and that of our own pocket torches, we began to munch the sandwiches we had brought with us. Quite casually, my friend said: 'I *do* wish they would do something!' The words were hardly out of his mouth when one of the bells went clang-clang-clang. We dropped our sandwiches and rushed downstairs into the hall. By the light of our pocket torches we saw that the bell which was vibrating was the one formerly wired up to the dining-room. However, the wire was broken—or had been cut—so the bell itself must have received the attentions of whatever it was responsible for the ringing. We immediately examined the whole house, all doors and windows, and even went out into the drive and looked up and down the road. No one was about. The night was not a particularly dark one, and we convinced ourselves that the motive power responsible for ringing the bell came from *within* the house. The bell and spring were still vibrating when we returned.

No further demonstrations occurred that night. We remained until about 2 a.m. when, tired and rather excited, we went to claim our beds at the Long Melford 'Bull,' at which hostelry we had previously engaged rooms.

It is not much fun investigating a large and cold haunted house, with few amenities, in the winter months, unless one lays oneself out for the job—as we did when I subsequently rented the Rectory. So my visits to Borley became fewer and fewer when Mr. and Mrs. Smith quitted the Rectory. But I made arrangements for reports to be sent to me when anything of interest happened and these letters are now before me. When the Rector and his wife were packing up, prior to leaving for Long Melford, I heard (July 2, 1929) that the 'front door bell has taken to quietly ringing now and again, but this *may* be due to small boys or rats.'

Anything is, of course, possible with small boys, but as a matter of fact I have never seen one small boy in Borley since my connection with the place. And as for rats or mice, during my investigation of the Rectory, on no occasion have I seen or heard the slightest indication of these rodents. And never once has any observer, to my knowledge, mentioned rats. After all, there was little to attract a rat—or even a mouse—especially when the place was empty! And I should like to see a rat on the ceiling violently ringing a bell.

On July 10, 1929, I had a note to the effect that the small

table in the Blue Room 'had been hurled over from in front of the fireplace to the washstand in the corner, and was found lying on its side.' A few days earlier all the bells rang simultaneously. This was before the Smiths had left the Rectory, and after they had retired to rest. By this time, there were no wires intact in any part of the back of the house. In this same letter I heard that the Rectory was up for sale, or would be let.

In a letter dated July 22, 1929, I was informed that although the Rectory was locked up, on the Sunday previous it was discovered that 'the windows had been unlocked from within and one thrown up.'

On August 7, 1929, the report read: 'On going over to Borley last Sunday morning, we discovered one of the windows facing the roadway, to be ajar as if someone had been peering out. This was perplexing, as on Saturday Mrs. Smith had gone over the Rectory windows and shutters as to their fastenings, upon hearing from your secretary that on her last visit she noticed the schoolroom window open or unfastened, on the other side of the building. This window I mention is in the room in which Miss Bull experienced all those weird happenings and saw the black shape on her bed.'[1]

At this period Borley quietened down a little, and I heard no more until February 22, 1930. My informant stated: 'You will be surprised to hear that half a fireplace has been deposited on the main staircase at Borley Rectory. We went over there the other day, after an absence of over a month, and discovered the above, while every shutter and window was locked tight, as we had left them. The Rectory is up for sale by private treaty at present. Particulars from Messrs. Protheroe and Morris, 67 and 68, Cheapside, E.C.2.'

On March 14, 1930, I heard: 'Funny things are continually occurring in the Rectory, and lumps of stone are on the main stairs from whence we do not know, while some of the sounds are more than weird. By the way, the villagers are

[1] See *ante*, page 47.

emphatic that the window [of Room No. 7] still lights up at night,' though no one was residing at the Rectory.

The next report, dated March 18, 1930, said: 'It is queer to see what lumps of stone and broken glass are about the place while, recently, on entering the Rectory just at about full moon, we heard the most horrible sounds in the house. Perplexities usually occur at full moon or in its last quarter.'

In the *Journal*[1] of the American Society for Psychical Research, of which I was then Foreign Research Officer, I published a short account of the Borley phenomena. I sent a copy of the report to my correspondents at Borley, and the following, dated March 24, 1930, is the acknowledgment: 'Warm thanks for issue of the *Journal*. . . . Things are commencing again. The District Nurse had something strange occur to her near the locality, which I would rather tell you than write,[2] and the villagers still see the "light" in the Rectory. There are other things, also.'

The above was the last report of the Borley manifestations that I was destined to receive for exactly eighteen months. The Smiths had moved to Sheringham, and a cousin of the Misses Bull, the Rev. Lionel Algernon Foyster, M.A., had been appointed to the living of Borley. Mr. Foyster entered upon his new duties on October 16, 1930.

[1] Vol. XXIII, New York, August, 1929, pages 455–6.
[2] I never heard what this experience was.

Above left :   Main staircase and iron stove in hall.   PLATE III
Above right :   Corner of Base Room (study) showing observer resting.
Below left :   The " Cold Spot " (marked by white disc on floor)
outside Blue Room.
Below right :   The " Strange Coat " that mysteriously appeared in Room 6.

CHAPTER XII

A NIGHT OF 'MIRACLES'

O N September 29, 1931, I was sitting in my office at Kensington, when two ladies were announced. They were Miss Ethel Bull and her sister. As I rose to welcome them, something told me that they had interesting news of the Rectory, and so it turned out.

Miss Bull happened to be in Kensington and thought that I would like to know that the Borley *Poltergeister* were now excelling themselves, and had been ever since their cousin, the Rev. L. A. Foyster, took over his duties in October of the previous year.

The Misses Bull had an extraordinary story to tell. Not only were all the old and familiar manifestations being experienced, but the phantasm of Harry Bull had been seen; Mrs. Foyster had been somewhat seriously injured by flying missiles, and a number of remarkable—and painful— incidents had occurred. She said she thought I would like to know of these things.

I thanked her very much and said I would like to resume the investigation of the Rectory. I asked her whether she would kindly approach Mr. Foyster on my behalf, for the required permission to visit Borley again. She said she would.

In a letter dated October 1, 1931, Mr. Foyster kindly invited me to the Rectory, even suggesting that he would put me up for the period of my visit. He also offered to send me the detailed diary of events that he had carefully compiled from day to day. I replied that as I should not be alone, it was preferable—in order to give him the minimum of trouble—that my party should sleep at the 'Bull,' Long

F

65

Melford, as was our usual custom. I asked him to send me his diary, to date.

When I received the diary, a glance was enough to tell me that the most extraordinary and unpleasant things were happening in the Rectory, and I much sympathized with him. In acknowledging the document, I fixed the evening of October 13 for our first investigation.

With some impatience I awaited the day when I was again to visit Borley, and in the interval studied the record of events that Mr. Foyster had kindly sent me. It made remarkable reading. Things in the Rectory had disappeared, and some had reappeared. Others were lost for ever. Objects vanished before their eyes; and articles, previously unseen and unheard of, suddenly put in an appearance. Mrs. Foyster had been locked in her room more than once; keys had been lost; and on one occasion the Rector and his wife were locked out of their room, and had to sleep elsewhere. The little girl Adelaide, aged $3\frac{1}{2}$, whom they had adopted, was locked in her room, to which there was no key. It opened the next day after a 'relic' had been applied to it. Windows were broken; books were displaced; voices called out 'Marianne' (Mrs. Foyster's Christian name); footsteps were heard in the hall, by different people; the smell of lavender or similar faint perfume was experienced; Mrs. Foyster's bracelet disappeared; Mrs. Foyster herself was almost stunned by a blow in the eye, which bled, and which gave her a black eye for some days, and so on.

It was very evident from Mr. Foyster's diary to date that things were becoming worse at the Rectory. The *Poltergeister* were much more violent, and had started to injure people—a very unusual occurrence, by the way. I became still more impatient to see these things for myself.

We arrived at Borley on the night of October 13, 1931, as arranged. My party consisted of Mrs. Henry Richards, Mrs. A. Peel Goldney, and a Miss May Walker. The two first-named ladies were on the Council of the National Laboratory of Psychical Research, of which I was then

Director. We had previously booked rooms at the 'Bull,' Long Melford, remarking in our letter to the landlord that we might arrive 'any time' during the night, and asking him to make arrangements for our reception when we *did* arrive.

We had left London soon after tea, and travelled into Suffolk in Mrs. Richards's big Packard car, driven by her chauffeur James Ballantyne. We arrived at the Rectory just as it struck eight. As our car swept into the drive, I wondered what the evening had in store for us.

The clanging of the loud front door bell sounded very familiar to me as I rang for admittance. The door was opened by Mrs. Foyster herself, who made us welcome and ushered us into the library where her husband was sitting. We mutually introduced ourselves, and thanked our hosts for their kindness in inviting us.

We had a long chat with Mr. Foyster, and heard in detail a good deal of what had been happening there. It was an amazing story. We found Mr. Foyster a delightful, typical, cultured parson of the best type, a scholar, a Cambridge (Pembroke College) M.A., and much travelled. I believe he had done missionary work in Canada from 1910 to 1929. His wife, Marianne, was younger than he, bright, vivacious, and intelligent. It seemed strange that they should have been the focus of such unpleasant incidents as had occurred at the Rectory.

We learnt that considerable improvements had been made at the Rectory since Mr. Smith and his wife vacated it. The sanitation was better, the water system had been remodelled and the place had been put into repair. Although the amenities were now more in evidence, it was still, I thought, a difficult place in which to feel really comfortable.

With our torches, we went over the house, visiting the familiar spots, and examining all doors, windows, and fastenings. I noticed that the room over the porch (see First Floor Plan) had been turned into a Chapel, with altar, altar-rail, and stained-glass window. This was originally the old bathroom. Everything appeared normal, and the 'attics' were as dusty as ever, though I noticed that a large water cistern had been installed. We found a little girl, Adelaide, and a little boy sleeping in two of the upper rooms. They were both aged 3½ years. The girl had been adopted by the Foysters; the boy was, I think, a visitor. I shone my torch on to the children's beds, and this awoke Adelaide who just smiled sweetly and promptly went to sleep again. In Room No. 5, adjoining the Blue Room, was sleeping the maidservant employed by the Foysters, a young girl 14½ years old, who had been in the employ of the Rector for about a fortnight.

Returning to the ground floor, we prepared for supper. Though the Foysters had kindly prepared refreshments for us, we did not want to impose on their good nature too much. Mrs. Richards had generously provided a luncheon basket full of good things, including a bottle of Burgundy and a bottle of Sauterne. I asked for glasses and Mrs. Foyster fetched these from the kitchen quarters. I drew the corks of the two bottles, and handed the Burgundy to Mrs. Foyster, who poured a quantity into a glass. Consternation! Our beautiful ruby *Chambertin* had turned to jet-black ink! Immediate investigation proved that only the wine in the glass had been affected; the remainder in the bottle still possessed the bouquet it had acquired in the Côte d'Or—or whatever district gave it birth.

At almost the same moment when Mrs. Foyster was pouring out the Burgundy, Miss Walker was serving the Sauterne. Suddenly she exclaimed: 'It smells like eau de Cologne!' And sure enough it did! The proprietor of the Château Peyraguey would never have recognized it as one of his finest products, had he been present!

We then gave both bottles of wine a minute scrutiny in an effort to solve the mystery. We examined those glasses that had not been used, and they were quite normal. In short, the metamorphosis—the spirit conjuring trick, as it were—must have taken place in the glasses and not in the bottles.

I made some experiments with the household ink, mixing it with the Burgundy, and could not tell the difference between my wine and ink mixture, and the concoction supplied by the 'spirits.' Obviously, the household ink had been used. We asked for fresh glasses, resumed our supper, and drank the health of the *Poltergeister*, asking these intangible beings for further examples of their mischievous pranks. We had not very long to wait for their reply.

Mrs. Foyster, I am sorry to say, suffers, I believe, with her heart. Soon after the episode of the wine that turned to ink, Mrs. Foyster said that she felt unwell and would retire. This was about 9.30 p.m. Mrs. Goldney, who is a trained nurse, and Mr. Foyster assisted her up to bed. When they returned to the library, my fellow council members and I decided we would again examine the house. Just as we reached the door of the study a crash was heard, and we found that an empty claret bottle had been hurled down the staircase well, had struck the iron stove—just as the glass candlestick had struck it more than two years previously—and had smashed to smithereens at our feet. First the glass phenomenon, then the bottle phenomenon. At the same time, one of the bells (the pull of which was in one of the upstairs rooms) started to ring violently.

We all rushed upstairs, Mr. Foyster leading. He was anxious about his wife. Upon inquiry it was found that, of course, she had heard the smash—with which incidents she was only too familiar—and wondered what had happened. But she was snug in bed and quite all right, except for her recent indisposition.

My friends and I then examined all the upstairs rooms and found everything apparently quite normal. We opened the doors of the children's rooms, and shone our torches on their little faces as they lay in bed. Adelaide was wide awake, and had heard the noise. The boy was sound asleep. The maidservant was fast asleep in Room No. 5.

We descended to the lower floor again *via* the back staircase that leads into the kitchen (see Ground Floor Plan).

Upon our arrival at the Rectory, the chauffeur James Ballantyne had ensconced himself on a chair by the kitchen fire. As he was quietly reading the evening paper, he afterwards informed us, he happened to look up. Perhaps some sound disturbed him. His eyes travelled towards the kitchen door—the one near the dresser (see Plan)—and he was mildly surprised to see a grisly black hand move slowly up and down between the jamb and the door, and then disappear. This occurred twice. Whatever was attached to the hand, if it was attached to anything at all, was hidden by the door.

Ballantyne is a dour, unexcitable old Scotsman and a hundred 'black hands' would not move him. We asked him if he were not afraid and he said 'No.' He just went on reading. He knew that our mission concerned a haunted house, and he thought that the black hand was just part of the business. It never occurred to him to be frightened. He, too, had heard the smash made by the falling bottle, but his only comment was that he knew 'it was them ghosts larking about.'

When we all returned once more to the study, there was a further outbreak of bell-ringing and some small pebbles rattled down the stairs. Then we heard the voice of Mrs. Foyster calling out in alarm. We rushed upstairs, and found that *she had been locked in her bedroom* (Blue Room, No. 6). She said that first one door (leading into Room 5), and then the other (opening on to landing) had suddenly locked themselves. The keys to these rooms, with others, had disappeared a long time previously.

The Rector was used to this phenomenon, and knew what to do about it. He fetched a relic of the Curé d'Ars, and said that he would recite a short reliquary prayer and asked us whether we would care to join in. He and I then knelt in the passage outside, his wife also kneeling on her side of the door. He then very reverently recited a reliquary prayer, after which we all joined in saying the Lord's Prayer. We had hardly said 'Amen,' when there was a most vigorous 'click,' denoting that the door had been 'miraculously' unlocked![1] We found Mrs. Foyster a little nervous, naturally, but otherwise none the worse for her adventure. Soon after another glass object fell down the well of the stairs and was smashed against that familiar target, the iron stove in the hall. The stove and stairs are pictured in Plate III.

It was now nearly 1 a.m., and we decided we had better get some sleep. We said good night to our hosts, thanked them for the opportunity of witnessing the manifestations, and made our way to the 'Bull' for, we hoped, an undisturbed night's rest.

Having arrived at our inn we then decided to hold an informal 'council meeting.' We adjourned to my bedroom where the four of us sat on my bed and discussed the events of the evening. The question was, of course, were the phenomena genuine? If not, who or what caused them? We could at once rule out the young maidservant—who was not yet 15—and the two children, aged 3½ years. The only other person who could possibly have caused the manifestations, assuming they were *not* paranormal, was Mrs. Foyster. Preposterous as it seemed, a careful analysis of the phenomena proved that every incident—bell-ringing, throwing of objects, etc.—occurred when the Rector's wife was not within our sight or under our control.

On the other hand, every phenomenon (with the exception of the wine incident) we had witnessed that night had occurred scores of times previously, had been witnessed by many people, and had been going on for years. Was it fair, then, to our hospitable hostess to suspect her of such tricks? And what could be the motive? But we decided that we ought to tell Mr. Foyster of our doubts in the matter. We visited his home for the purpose of an impartial investigation, and we owed it to him to tell him what we thought. We decided to call at the Rectory in the morning and break the news as gently as possible.

[1] Compare Dom Richard Whitehouse's experiences with door-locking phenomena and the use of a relic, pages 96, 97, 99.

It had been our intention to return to London early on the next morning, October 14, 1931. But, as we had decided the previous night, we called on the Rector soon after 10 a.m. and, as gently as possible, informed him that his wife *could* have produced normally the manifestations that had so intrigued us. Mrs. Foyster was present, and of course stoutly denied that she was in any way responsible, and we accepted her word. The Rector pointed out that every occupant of the Rectory since the place was built had been similarly accused—which was correct.

Mr. Foyster made the suggestion that we should spend another night under their roof, confine the whole household to one room, and see what happened. We agreed to do this. So, instead of returning to London, we spent the day in Cambridge, arriving at the 'Bull,' Long Melford, in time for an early dinner. At eight o'clock we duly presented ourselves at the Rectory.

The young maidservant had been sent home (she lived in the village), so we had no need to worry about her. With screw-eyes, tapes, and seals I fastened all doors and windows that would not lock. I locked and sealed the two young children in their respective rooms, and even screw-eyed and taped the windows of their rooms. All exterior doors, and that leading to the cellar, were locked and sealed. We satisfied ourselves that we had the house under control.

By the time we had finished sealing the Rectory it was nearly half-past nine. So I assembled the incarnate occupants of the house in the kitchen (the children were, of course, in bed), at the same time calling upon the discarnate inhabitants to do their best. So our little party, consisting of the Rector and his wife, Mrs. Richards, Mrs. Goldney, Ballantyne and myself, sat round the kitchen fire and just waited for something to happen. Miss Walker had returned to London by train earlier in the day.

Everything seemed very quiet after the excitement of the previous night and we thought that our control arrangements had exorcised the *Poltergeister* for good and all. But after an hour's waiting, a bell in the hall passage suddenly rang furiously. I ran out to see if I could identify it, and found it was a bell connected with one of the upstairs rooms. From the hall I could not tell *which* room so, with our torches, we at once went to the first floor and explored. I opened up room after room and when I entered Adelaide's room, I saw the remnant of the bell wire slowly swinging. This then, was the room in which the bell-ringing had originated. Adelaide was in bed, but awake. In any case, our entry into the room, and the flashes from our torches, would have awakened her. On a previous visit to the room I had noticed that the wire of the bell-pull had been broken off close to the ceiling, and it would have been a physical impossibility, I think, for a 3½-year-old child to have pulled the wire, even if standing on a chair. And certainly I had no right to suppose that an infant so immature in both body and mind would play such a trick on us. But no other mortal person could have entered the room without disturbing our seals.

The ringing of the bell was the sum total of phenomena we heard, saw, or felt that evening. A little later some visitors arrived, which made further investigation impossible.

Mr. Foyster, in his diary, portions of which form the next chapter, very fairly and accurately refers to our visit, our doubts, and the phenomena.

We left Borley that night soon after eleven o'clock, and even our journey back to London was by no means uneventful. It was freezing hard; the car clutch burnt out near Braintree; and a police control, stopping all cars, demanded to see Ballantyne's driving licence. Stone-cold, hungry, sleepy, miserable, and crawling along at about four miles an hour, we arrived at Regent's Park at 4 o'clock in the morning. We found a good meal awaiting us and after doing justice to that, and to another bottle of *Chambertin*—which did *not* turn to ink!—we concluded that ghost-hunting was not so bad, after all. And had we not added another colourful chapter to the amazing story of 'the most haunted house'?

CHAPTER XIII

LEAVES FROM THE FOYSTER DIARY

FROM the very first day when the Rev. L. A. Foyster entered upon his duties at Borley, he kept a diary of the strange events that occurred there. Of course, he had no intention of doing such a thing before he took the living —but on this first day, October 16, 1930, such extraordinary things happened that, having an orderly mind, he decided to take careful and detailed notes of all incidents that could not be explained in terms of normality. Also, his relatives, the members of the Bull family, were both curious and concerned as to what was going on in the Rectory, and they all thought that such a record was worthy of preservation. It is worth noting that not one of the Bull family, including the Foysters, is concerned with psychical research or spiritualism, or knows anything about the subject. But Mrs. Foyster is said to come from a 'psychic' family.

After our last visit to Borley in October, 1931, I lost direct contact with the place. I do not like invading the homes and private lives of people even when they are the possessors of an interesting 'ghost.' Consequently, I did not again visit the Rectory during Mr. Foyster's occupation. But I was kept informed from time to time as to what was happening there, and it was very obvious that phenomena were of almost daily occurrence in the Foyster household over a long period of the Rector's incumbency. All the old manifestations were witnessed over and over again, and a new one, the scribbling of messages on walls and scraps of paper, developed.

Mr. Foyster very assiduously kept a record of all these strange events, and his diary finally assumed gigantic proportions. I believe that he has more than 180 typed quarto sheets of notes recording the day-to-day activities of the *Poltergeister*!

When I informed Mr. Foyster that I was compiling a monograph on the haunting of Borley Rectory, he very generously permitted me to reprint verbatim selected portions of his diary. These extracts he kindly selected himself, and wrote them out in his own hand. They follow later.

Before the reader studies these diary extracts, it should be emphasized that before taking up his residence at Borley, Mr. Foyster knew very little about the things that were alleged to be happening there. It will be recalled that he had spent several years in Canada. He knew, of course, that the Rectory was supposed to be 'haunted,' and that was all.

Mr. Foyster had been told, too, of the adventures at the Rectory during Mr. Smith's occupation, but he thought that the tales he heard were probably exaggerated, as so often happens in these cases.

When the Foysters first visited Borley, they looked at the Rectory and another house that they *could* have lived in. They decided to take up their residence in the former building. When going over the Rectory, neither Mr. nor Mrs. Foyster felt there was anything particularly uncanny about the place, or that it had a 'ghostly atmosphere.' They treated most of the stories they had heard as so much nonsense.

Here, then, are the extracts from

THE REV. L. A. FOYSTER'S DIARY[1]

OCTOBER 16, 1930. My wife, Marianne Foyster, a little girl aged 2 years 7 months (referred to as Adelaide), and myself come into residence. First experiences of anything out of the ordinary. A voice calling Marianne's name; footsteps heard by self, Marianne, Adelaide, and man working in the house. 'Harry Bull' seen at different times by Marianne between study and bedroom above. [Figure not wearing clerical dress, but a

---

[1] Interpolations of my own are in square brackets. H.P.

March 11 Two Anglican priests go thoroughly over the house with M.F. see
using incense, holy water & prayers. Presence of sort felt, but no
active demonstration. Later a stone thrown at boy from cottage.
I was out most of the remaining part of day. After my return
stone thrown at me, this as we three are standing round hall
stove, another stone fell only a few inches from my head.

" 12. Clean linen taken out of the kitchen cupboard & trailed over the floor.

" 13. M.F. hit on the head & hurt by a piece of metal thrown down back stairs.
A piece of brick dropped on suppertable close by my plate, but without
breaking or touching any crockery.

" 15 As I am typing out a diary of events in the house, first my collar, which
I had taken off for comfort, is thrown at the me; then a stick & lastly a piece
of coke thrown across the room.

" 16 M.F. in early morning finds kitchen table upside down & contents of
store cupboard partly inside & partly scattered broadcast.
In the evening, bedroom window, which had been left open, discovered
closed the wrong way round.

" 23 M.F. carrying a tray in one hand & a lamp in the other
up the front stairs, has the inside of an iron thrown at her
from a few feet ahead; it breaks the lamp chimney.

" 24 Small articles thrown at M.F. sweeping etc outside bedroom.
Harry Bull seen again by M.F. about this time, and (probably)
by cottage tenant through stairs window at night.

" 28 M.F. sees a monstrosity, (seen by her & others on other occasions)
near kitchen door. It touches her shoulder with iron like touch.

" 29 Palm Sunday till

April 11. Saturday in Easter week (when there was a small demonstration): Absolute quiet, with this one exception, during Holy week
& Easter week.

April. Milk jug is mysteriously found empty. I request a clean one and
make a rude remark about drinking after the ghosts. While we
are sitting at tea in broad daylight with doors & windows
closed missiles are thrown at me. At night I count up 12 or 13
Times I was thrown at between approximately 6 p.m & 11 p.m in
different parts of the house

May. A bad half hour in the kitchen one evening ended by my going up

FACSIMILE OF A PAGE FROM THE REV. L. A. FOYSTER'S DIARY, NOTING
APPEARANCE OF 'HARRY BULL' AND OTHER PHENOMENA.

dressing-gown of peculiar colour. Garment recognized by villagers, from description by Mrs. Foyster.]

Jugs and other utensils disappearing and coming back. Peculiar smells—especially one most nearly resembling lavender—noticeable particularly in our bedroom [Blue Room, No. 6]. Bells rung. A bracelet detached from wrist-watch while Marianne is in room only a few feet away, and no one else in the house, besides Adelaide, who was in her own room. Bracelet was taken and has never been seen since. Lavender bag, which no one has seen before, discovered on mantelpiece of Marianne's sewing-room. [Next to kitchen, see Ground Floor Plan.] Lavender bag disappears and again appears in my pocket: discovered when putting on coat one morning.

FEBRUARY 1931. Books found on window-sill of w.c. [Next to Chapel, see First Floor Plan.] As soon as one is taken away, it is replaced by another. (These books had been left by the Bulls and were stowed away on shelf in housemaid's pantry.) [Butler's pantry on Plan.] Last of these had a torn cover, which was thrown on floor.

FEBRUARY 25. A big return of crockery [that had previously unaccountably disappeared]. Marianne asks for a tea-pot: this is also returned. At my suggestion, Marianne asks for return of bracelet, but in very uncomplimentary language.

FEBRUARY 26. Books found under our bed in the morning. A consignment of hymn books, unknown of before, discovered on the rack over the kitchen range in the afternoon. In the evening Marianne is given a terrific blow in the eye—a cut under it; black eye next day—by an invisible assailant on the landing outside bedroom [No. 6, Blue Room]. She was carrying a candle.

FEBRUARY 27. Shortly after we had retired and light extinguished, first a cotton-reel and then a hammer-head with broken handle attached were thrown across our bed. Lamp lit and throwing discontinued.

FEBRUARY 28. I write a letter on the subject [of the hauntings]. Directly afterwards (the room had been empty for only a few minutes in between), two pins discovered with their points sticking upwards. One was on seat of arm-chair; the other on chair I had been sitting on. About an hour or so later an erection, composed of an old lamp and saucepan (neither of them seen before), was found outside my door. Later, the handle of a floor-polisher is put across the passage I traversed on my way to supper. Still later, a tin of bath salts placed just inside bathroom door trips up Marianne.

MARCH 5. Two articles thrown after lights were put out in our bedroom. Then, after an interval, I was aroused by a hairbrush on my head.

MARCH 6. The knob off a door thrown with some force from just behind her, at Marianne as she comes along bathroom passage.

MARCH 7. Marianne thrown at in the afternoon. In the evening, I attempt to exorcise spirits. Stone hits me on shoulder. Books thrown out of shelves in Marianne's sewing-room. Pictures in hall and on staircase are taken down and laid on ground. Things thrown in bedroom. (This night, window was closed.)

MARCH 8. At night, after carefully looking under bed, both doors in bedroom found locked. More throwing. (Window was first opened a few inches at bottom; then at top. The veranda roof [the glass roof] outside would make it very difficult for things to be thrown from outside *into* the room.)

MARCH 9. Although plumber's men were in the house thawing out pipes, stones rolled down back stairs and odd things were found in kitchen passage. In the afternoon a visitor inspects attics and is satisfied that no one could be hiding there. Hears a bell ring, and sees a big stone almost as it came to rest. We had just previously heard the stone descending back stairs. Marianne enters house just afterwards: evidence it was not she. Many incidents that afternoon and evening, amongst them one in which Marianne, hearing noise about three yards from the outside of sewing-room door (which was shut) is touched on the hair by a stone. The touch came from behind her. Later, coming again from the kitchen, she sees piece of iron coming after her (but does *not* see the being carrying it). It is thrown in behind her, just inside the sewing-room door, as she hastily dashes in and pulls the door to. As Marianne is making up fire in the kitchen, a stone flies out, crosses the room, and hits the door further from her, just as I go behind it. Two duplex lamps were burning in the room at the time.

MARCH 10. A little pile of five stones found behind Marianne's pillow when she woke in the morning. More objects carried into the house. A stone through a pane of glass in staircase window. It was thrown from *inside* while Marianne, Adelaide and myself were standing by hall stove. I think that on this night a small tin travelling trunk (not seen before) suddenly noticed in kitchen while we are sitting at supper there. This stayed in the house for some time, but eventually disappeared. China powder-box and wedding-ring discovered in bathroom. It [the ring] disappeared during the following morning. Marianne stumbles over brick placed outside bathroom door. Next morning two stones found behind my pillow.

MARCH 11. Two Anglican priests go thoroughly over the house with Marianne and myself, using incense, holy water, and prayers. A 'presence' of some sort is felt, but no active demonstration. Later, a stone is thrown at a boy from the cottage. I was out most of the remaining part of the day. After my return, a stone was thrown at me. Then, as we three were standing round the hall stove, another stone fell only a few inches from my head.

MARCH 12. Clean linen was taken out of the kitchen cupboard, and trailed over the floor.

MARCH 13. Marianne hit on the head, and hurt, by a piece of metal thrown down back stairs. A piece of brick dropped on to supper table, close to my plate, but without breaking or touching any crockery.

MARCH 15. As I am typing out a diary of events in the house, first my collar (which I had taken off for comfort) is thrown at me. Then a stick and a piece of coke were thrown across the room.

MARCH 16. Marianne in the early morning of this day finds kitchen table upside down, and the contents of a store cupboard partly inside, and partly scattered broadcast. In the evening, bedroom window which had been left open was discovered closed the wrong way round.

MARCH 23. Marianne, while carrying a tray in one hand and a lamp in the other, up the front stairs, has the inside of an iron thrown at her from a few feet ahead of her. It breaks the lamp chimney.

MARCH 24. Small articles thrown at Marianne while she is sweeping, etc. outside bedroom. 'Harry Bull' seen again by Marianne at night about this time; and, probably, by cottage tenant through stair window.

MARCH 28. Marianne sees a monstrosity (seen by her and others on other occasions) near kitchen door. It touches her shoulder with iron-like touch.

MARCH 29. Palm Sunday was still.

APRIL 11. Saturday in Easter week. A small demonstration. With this one exception, there was absolute quiet during Holy Week and Easter week.

APRIL. Milk jug is mysteriously found empty. I request a clean one and made a rude remark about 'drinking after ghosts.' While we are sitting at tea in broad daylight with doors and windows closed, missiles are thrown at me. At night, I count up 12 or 13 times I was thrown at, between approximately 6 p.m. and 11 p.m., in different parts of the house.

MAY. A bad half-hour in the kitchen one evening ended by my going upstairs to get creosote with which we fumigate the house. On my way up a lump of dried mortar hit me in the neck. On the way down a metal spanner goes through my hair. After fumigation, the trouble stops at once. Pepper, however, dropped on us in bed. Some had previously been thrown into Marianne's face in the kitchen. Next evening, Marianne does some fumigating, but is rather lenient with creosote. Bells ring; stone thrown at her, and jam-jar crashes against the kitchen door as she is returning. I go round with the creosote and trouble ceases. On the next day (Monday) I collect six articles thrown in the late afternoon and evening to show Sir George and Lady Whitehouse (who arrived about 9 p.m.), to see if anything was doing. While they are here, skirting board of unused bedroom (not entered by anyone on that day as far as we knew) discovered to be on fire.[1] Some throwing after it had been put out. We accept their invitation and stay a few days with Whitehouse. One evening, when up at Borley, Marianne sees paper in air; it at once falls to the ground. It is discovered to have some hardly decipherable writing on it. Next day when we come up, it has disappeared. Other pieces of paper with 'Marianne' written in a childish hand, were found about the house from time to time.

JUNE 6. Worst outbreak begins with a stone being thrown.

JUNE 7. Stones thrown in the evening. A chair in spare room (in which Marianne was lying in bed, very unwell) twice thrown over. Strange noises heard on landing during the night: bangs, taps on door, etc.

JUNE 8. Monday. Proceedings start soon after 10 a.m. These include a variety of things. Books, stones, clothes, suit-case, and a basket full of soiled linen were thrown over balustrade from landing to stairs and hall. The soiled linen basket was thrown twice. Marianne hears turmoil going on in what was usually our bedroom [Blue Room, No. 6]. She gets up from sick bed to see. Noise at once stops, but room found to be in confusion. Bed moved, furniture overturned. Doctor calls and witnesses some throwing. Richard Whitehouse[2] visits house and also witnesses some throwing. Marianne turned out of bed three times during the day, but each time when alone in the room. Lady Whitehouse,[3] coming up in the evening, hears more throwing. Matters are so bad that she and Sir George insist on our going down to

[1] See Lady Whitehouse's account of the incident, page 87.
[2] See his report, Chapter XV. He is a nephew of Lady Whitehouse.
[3] See her report, Chapter XIV.

their house for a time. [Mrs. Foyster does not return home until July.] During the rest of the month of June, house is empty at night except upon a few nights when I could get someone else to sleep in the house as well. On one of these evenings, when a friend was there, I heard a noise just before retiring. I went to his room to see if it came from there. I found him asleep, and an empty paint pot (which he said he knew nothing about) had been placed close up against the door inside.

AUGUST. A medium and an investigator[1] come down and hold a séance. Different spirits are tackled, among them one 'Joe Miles' who, it was declared, was responsible for the disturbances. However, it appeared subsequently that this was a mistake.

AUGUST (or perhaps September). Study attacked. Writing desk thrown on its face; chairs overturned; books pushed out of the shelves; room in confusion.

SEPTEMBER. We are locked out of our room one night. Adelaide was locked *into* hers. (All doors unlocked with help of relic of Curé d'Ars.)

On the kitchen being left empty for a few minutes, a saucepan full of potatoes, left on the stove, was found to be empty. Witnessed by Marianne and a maid. (N.B. We had no resident maid in the house from the time we arrived till September 1931.) About this time different things were moved about in the house (or disappeared altogether) to a great extent. Amongst them was a big pile of typewritten sheets, and a portable typewriter. Though money was moved, we cannot be certain that it was ever taken.

OCTOBER 13. Visit of Mr. Harry Price and three members of his council. On the first evening, the bell rang; bottle crashed on front stairs, and other things were thrown. Marianne (who, not being well, had gone to bed) had first one, and then the other door of her room locked. One came unlocked in answer to prayer. Council met next day and declared their opinion that Marianne was responsible for phenomena. She was put under surveillance, but bell from bedroom rang while she was being surveyed.[2]

OCTOBER. I am awakened one morning by having a bedroom water jug dropped on my head. I left it on the floor, and a little time afterwards it is dropped on Marianne's head.

OCTOBER–NOVEMBER. The report that a shadowy form, said by visitor to the house and by former occupants to be seen in room over kitchen [Room 3] is *true*. The story has confirmation

---

[1] I have no information concerning these people. H.P.

[2] See my account of this incident, *ante*, page 73. H.P.

from Adelaide. Being sent to lie down in that room one afternoon, she came downstairs with a bruise under her eye. On being
asked how she got it, she answered: 'A nasty thing by curtain
in my room gave it me.' This same apparition said to have been
seen also early one morning, entering our bedroom. I was up,
and Marianne was still asleep, so neither of us saw it.

NOVEMBER 13. A rather serious demonstration occurred this
evening. It was witnessed also by Richard Whitehouse and our
maid.[1] (I ceased keeping an exact diary of events in June last.
There were, therefore, various phenomena in the way of throwing,
doors being locked, etc. during these last months that are unre-
corded. But there was nothing I can think of that was very
different to what we had previously experienced, with one
exception: One evening, just after I came in, a pot of tea, apparently freshly made, but which no one would own to having made,
was placed for me in the dining-room [see Ground Floor Plan].
However, I could not be quite sure about the history of
this.)

JANUARY 1932. One night, both doors of our room [Blue
Room, No. 6] were found locked. One door was locked from the
inside. The other door, communicating with dressing-room
[Room 5] had a chest of drawers pushed right up against it
from the inside. This showed the impossibility, therefore, of the
locking having been done by a human agent. Once more we
sought admission by means of prayer. But door was still found
locked. We went into the Chapel [over porch] and while we were
there, a terrific noise started up in the hall, which we found was
due to the cat having its claw caught in the rat trap.[2] When we
returned to the Chapel, we found a key lying on the corner of the
altar. This turned out to be the key belonging to the door
between our bedroom and dressing-room.

We receive offer from Marks Tey spiritualist circle to rid the
house of ghosts for us. They come and talk it over.

JANUARY 23–24. Finally the spiritualists come with a medium
on January 23, and suggest spending the next night in the house.
Directly they came, throwing began, so I suggest their spending
that night, instead of the next, in' the house. They go to get other
members of the circle, leaving medium with us. Great demonstrations! Bottles dashed down back stairs; kitchen passage was
strewn with broken glass, etc.; bells rang. Quieted down for a
time, but racket started again when rest of circle returned.

---

[1] Mr. Foyster does not give details of this occurrence, but it is fully recorded
by Dom Richard Whitehouse, pages 97–99.
[2] I have never seen any indications of rats. H.P.

Party stayed until 5 a.m., and then left with the belief that trouble had been arrested. Next morning the house was entirely different and (with two exceptions noted below) demonstrations definitely stopped until 1935.

MAY. Some members of the Marks Tey spiritualist circle come over one afternoon. According to what they say were orders from 'the other side,' we sit in the study with room darkened and gramophone playing. Marianne, who was not at all well that day, goes off into deep sleep from which she awakens very much better. Just after this a stone is thrown down back stairs, while friend and I are passing along kitchen passage. Spiritualists attribute this to 'a little spare power floating around unused.'

JUNE. One evening two objects were thrown. On writing to inform spiritualist circle, they reply that they were told there might be some trouble in June, but that things would be quiet afterwards. They come over on three or four evenings during this month. At one of these séances, while we are sitting in the study, the spirit of well-known psychic researcher is seen by one of the spiritualists, but by no one else.

JUNE 1933. One evening I hear strange noises in the house that I cannot account for, but nothing further follows.

1935. Some indications of a little trouble starting up again. A few things disappear in unaccountable ways.

AUGUST 5. Bank Holiday. Marianne, Adelaide, self, and friend were having tea on the study veranda when noises, like a picture falling in the drawing-room, were heard. However, investigation revealed nothing out of place. These noises continued at intervals, some appearing to come from upstairs. Altogether, we heard the bangs thirteen or fourteen times.

OCTOBER. We moved out of the house.

.   .   .   .

The cause of Mr. Foyster's leaving the Rectory was *not* the ghosts, but ill-health. He is now living in retirement.

From some correspondence with Mr. Foyster we learned that the phenomena occurred both by daylight and lamplight. The Rector was never seriously hurt, but his wife was. The most severe period of frightfulness began in February 1931, and persisted until January 1932. June was undoubtedly the worst month of the year, and June 8, 1931 (the day before the anniversary of Harry Bull's death) was probably the worst day. During Church festivals the manifestations died down. Sunday was usually the quietest day of the week, and Monday the worst.

Neither Mr. nor Mrs. Foyster felt frightened during the whole period of their residence at the Rectory. If they received any 'impressions' at all, it was in the room [No. 3] over the kitchen.

Mr. Foyster thinks that phenomena are more numerous and more violent when a person possessing some psychic faculty is in the house. Mrs. Foyster comes from a psychic family.

Although the extracts from Mr. Foyster's diary quoted in this chapter give some idea of the exciting times experienced in the Rectory, properly to appreciate *how* strange their adventures were, his complete and detailed record of some 180 typed sheets should be studied. The Curé d'Ars, whose relic was used by Mr. Foyster, was Jean Baptiste Vianney (1786–1859). He led a life of extreme piety, and built homes for destitute children and friendless women. He preached that every good thing could be obtained by faith and prayer, and practised what he preached. Ars, a village near Villefranche (France), is now a pilgrim resort. The village church is built over the tomb of the good Curé.

CHAPTER XIV

PERSONAL EXPERIENCES OF SIR GEORGE AND LADY WHITEHOUSE

IN Mr. Foyster's diary the names of Sir George and Lady Whitehouse are frequently mentioned. Their home, Arthur Hall, Sudbury, is something over a mile from Borley Rectory. For many years they were friendly with the Bull family and, successively, with the various occupants of the Rectory.

When I heard that they had had personal experience of the manifestations at the Rectory, Mr. Glanville and I called on Lady Whitehouse only to learn, with regret, that Sir George had passed away. Our visit was on Wednesday, March 29, 1939.

Lady Whitehouse received us very kindly and told us some of the curious things she and her husband had witnessed at the Rectory. As both she and Mr. Foyster record, things were so bad there—and appeared so dangerous—that Lady Whitehouse insisted upon the Foysters leaving their home for a little peace and quietness at Arthur Hall.

Richard Whitehouse is Lady Whitehouse's nephew, and his report is printed as Chapter XV of this monograph. Lady Whitehouse promised to epitomize her experiences in a short protocol and she was as good as her word. In a letter dated April 2, 1939, she says: 'Herewith an account of our personal experiences at Borley. They seemed very thrilling and exciting at the time, but in the light of later happenings, fade almost into insignificance. But I do feel rather pleased that we never questioned the truth of what Mr. Bull and Mr. Foyster told us, and I think our sympathy was a great help to the Foysters.'

Here, then, is Lady Whitehouse's story, in her own words:

LADY WHITEHOUSE'S STORY

Though we had often heard from Mr. Harry Bull of the nun and the headless man, and knew that Mr. Smith and his wife had been obliged to leave the Rectory owing to unpleasant experiences;[1] and had heard a great deal from Mr. Foyster during the winter of 1931 of the terrible times he and Mrs. Foyster were having, it was not till May 4, 1931, that we had any personal manifestation of the powers at the Rectory. We went up to the Rectory on that date to meet the Rural Dean on some church matters, and, after he left, Mrs. Foyster asked me to come out to the kitchen to see what they had to put up with. The contents of the cupboard were strewn all over the place. While we were talking and wondering what could be the cause, my husband and Mr. Foyster joined us and then the row of bells began ringing and Mrs. Foyster said 'We are in for a bad time to-night. It generally starts like that.'

As we knew they were even more troubled by the unbelief in the neighbourhood than by the actual happenings, we offered to go up after dinner and see them through the evening. We arrived there about 9 o'clock. Besides Mr. and Mrs. Foyster, there were only two small children of three years old in the house, and they were both in bed and asleep. We sat in the kitchen and listened to the Foysters' weird experiences and Mr. Foyster showed us scraps of paper with mysterious writing on them, asking 'Marianne' (Mrs. Foyster) for help. They had been left about all over the house.

After a time, Mr. Foyster and my husband started to make a tour of the house and came back in a few minutes to say there was a strange smell, and went out again, only to return saying it was much stronger. So Mrs. Foyster and I went out and she at once said 'It is a fire,' and picked up the lamp and we followed her upstairs and along the

[1] The unpleasant experiences were due to the lack of amenities, rather than to the presence of the *Poltergeister*. H.P.

passage to the right, where there was a strong smell of burning. Mrs. Foyster started unlocking doors and, at the third, clouds of smoke came out and we saw that a strip of skirting board was charred, and there was a glowing hole in the middle. We set off for the bathroom at the far end of the opposite passage, filled jugs with water and came back and poured them on to the glowing woodwork. We were standing watching to see if the fire was thoroughly out, when a flint about the size of a hen's egg fell between us: the window was shut and there were no holes in the ceiling. My husband picked it up and put it in his pocket, and being satisfied that the fire was out, we went down-stairs. On the way, two more flints fell, one hitting Mr. Foyster on the shoulder, but not with any force. We got back to the kitchen and discussed what to do next.

I had brought with us a lot of dried lavender, and as the Foysters said that sometimes incense and sweet smells quietened things, I took the kitchen shovel with some glowing embers and scattered some of the lavender on them and Mr. Foyster and I started to fumigate the house. I thought I would give their bedroom a thorough doing, and had just walked slowly round the bed when there was a shower of little stones all round us. So we went back to the kitchen and my husband and Mr. Foyster went out to inspect the backyard, and the place under the room where we had seen the fire. It was full of papers and packing cases, but no sign of fire, only the water down the wall which we had poured *on* the fire. As they came in, a large flint came down the stairs by the back door. Then the bells started to ring again and we decided it was quite unfit for anyone to spend the night there and packed the whole party into our two-seater and brought them down to Arthur Hall. It was then 11.30 p.m. They stayed for a few days and then bravely went back.

My second experience was in the summer. A nephew[1] was staying with us who was very interested, and one morn-

[1] Dom Richard Whitehouse, O.S.B.

ing[1] about 11 o'clock a message came for him from Mr. Foyster, who said: 'If you want to see things, come at once.' My nephew returned about 3 p.m., saying: 'Auntie, you must go and rescue those poor people. They are having a most ghastly time!' So we went up at once. As I opened the front door, I could hear things falling, and the two little children were crouching at the dining-room door, saying: 'We don't like so many fings falling.'

I went straight up to Mrs. Foyster, who was in bed, ill, and told her they must come away again. After a little persuasion, she agreed and I put my gloves and parasol *on her bed* and went to collect some clothes for her and the children. As I left the room, she called after me: 'Your things are going!' I went back to find my gloves and parasol *on the dressing-table*. I then went to get her a cup of tea and, as I came back, a small glass bottle seemed to start from the middle of the room, and fell at my feet.

Next time I left the room, I heard a yell and found Mrs. Foyster lying on the floor, the third time she had been thrown out of bed that day. I made her as comfortable as I could, and soon had her and the children in the car and down at Arthur Hall again.

After that, though things were very active and horrible, we had no more experiences though we were often at the Rectory.

· · · · ·

It will be noted that Lady Whitehouse's testimony confirms the statements recorded in Mr. Foyster's diary, and the incidents referred to by Dom Richard Whitehouse, O.S.B., whose moving story of his experiences at the Rectory form the subject of the next chapter.

[1] June 8, 1931.

CHAPTER XV

WHAT I SAW AT BORLEY RECTORY

By Dom Richard Whitehouse, o.s.b.

[*Dom Richard Whitehouse is a nephew of Lady Whitehouse and,
as he reveals in his narrative, has been in the closest touch with
Mr. and Mrs. Foyster, the Rectory, and the manifestations. His
MS. is printed just as received. H.P.*]

IN the latter part of May 1931, I received a letter from
a relative [Lady Whitehouse] in Suffolk, describing some
unusual occurrences that she and her husband had
witnessed in what has now come to be known as the 'most
haunted house in England.' As I was in need of a holiday,
I decided to pay them a visit and took the opportunity of
discussing the subject of *Poltergeister* with a well-known
Catholic authority[1] before leaving London. He seemed
impressed by the evidence contained in the letter and asked
me to let him know the outcome of my proposed visit to
the Rectory. I had known this place since boyhood, and all
its inmates (Captain Gregson excepted) I have got to know
at some time since 1912.

It was, therefore, not surprising that I should have felt
some eagerness to visit the place again. As I was also
contemplating giving up my work in London to try my
vocation as a priest, I realized that I would have some
months of comparative leisure ahead of me before circumstances would enable me to embark upon my future work.

---

[1] The late Father Herbert Thurston, S.J. He died November 3, 1939, aged 82.
He was particularly interested in *Poltergeister*. Almost the last words he wrote
(see the *Month*, November, 1939), were to the effect that he was sorry that
he had not heard the full story of the Borley mystery. H.P.

The kindness of the Rev. Lionel Foyster and his wife made it possible for me to pay something like thirty visits to Borley Rectory between June and December 1931. The results of these visits I shall endeavour to describe as accurately as possible in the course of the following account.

My first visit to Borley Rectory during the period in question was on Saturday, June 6, 1931. I was introduced to Mr. and Mrs. Foyster and was then told something of the happenings in the house. There was no disturbance of any kind that evening, so I returned to Sudbury. On Monday morning, June 8, a boy brought a note down from Borley, asking me to go up to the Rectory at once. I hurried off and was met by Mr. Foyster at the front door. He invited me in, waving his hand in the direction of the hall in a way that suggested that this was not the first time that such things had happened.

The scene that confronted me was one of extreme disorder. Almost the entire contents of a bedroom, adjoining the Blue Room and overlooking the lawn, were scattered on the main staircase and lower floor. Shoes, bedclothes, brushes, clothes of all kinds and other odds and ends were lying about the place higgledy-piggledy. I was made to understand that there had been a loud noise and in a very short space of time the things before me had been precipitated from the bedroom in an unaccountable manner.

Needless to say, I was not going to allow this reported incident to weigh one way or the other with me. I took note of the situation, however, and while standing on the lower flight of steps opposite the study, I engaged Mr. Foyster in conversation. From this point of vantage I was able to watch both floors fairly well. Mr. Foyster then told me that the doctor had been in that morning to see his wife and had had things thrown at him. This I verified later.

While standing here, barely five minutes after my entrance into the house, my attention was suddenly diverted by hearing something drop at my feet. It proved to be a small case, apparently made to hold a watch. A minute or two later another object fell in the same manner. On picking it up and examining it, I found it to be a small metal book-rest with a picture of Abraham Lincoln engraved upon it. Both objects seem to have come from the direction of the upper landing and were recognized as household belongings. I paid no further attention to this incident. Mr. Foyster then took me upstairs to see his wife who was lying ill in bed in the Blue Room, looking, I thought, pale and anxious.

She was lying on her back, her hands under the bed-clothes, which were drawn up near her neck. Her voice was rather weak and in order to hear her speak I sat at the end of the bed on the side nearest the door. Mr. Foyster then asked me if I would mind remaining with her for a short time while he slipped across the road to the Church. I could see all round the room, which had very little furniture, and there were windows at my back and one to my left, all the latter a good distance from the bed, which had its back to the door and was only a few feet from it.

I changed over to the opposite end of the bed, keeping my eyes on Mrs. Foyster, who was still lying on her back with her hands well under the bed-clothes. We had been talking for perhaps ten minutes when I suddenly saw her start. At the same time, I felt something land lightly on my lap, coming apparently from behind me. I took hold of the object. It was a brass stiletto about eight or nine inches in length and weighing, I should imagine, not much less than eight ounces. I was told that it was a paper knife belonging to Mr. Foyster and was always kept in the study below.

Mrs. Foyster was still lying in the same position, her hands under the bed-clothes, a point I particularly noticed. I felt certain that by no possible means could she have got the object on to my lap without my detecting it. When I asked her why she started, she said that she saw the stiletto rise up from the floor behind me and then do one or two curious convolutions in the air before settling on my lap. I had no reason to doubt the statement, for I felt sure that it could not possibly have been thrown from the windows or through the door without hurting me and there was something so spontaneous and genuine in the alarm which showed itself on Mrs. Foyster's face, that I could not possibly believe she had 'manufactured' the incident. That anybody could have been hiding in the room or under the bed was out of the question. I concluded that the object had been levitated on to my lap in a supernormal manner and knowing the extent to which these incidents were upsetting the household, I asked if I might recite the Rosary and sprinkle this and other rooms with holy water, believing this might have some effect in stopping the phenomena.

Mrs. Foyster raised no objection and joined in the prayers. I had hardly finished doing this when I heard the front door open, and guessing it was Mr. Foyster, I moved out to the landing to greet him. I had only just begun to descend the staircase when I heard a piercing shriek and rushed back to find Mrs. Foyster lying face downwards on the floor with the bed-clothes and mattress on top of her. The whole thing must have happened in an instant, for I am quick on my feet and I was no distance from the room when the incident occurred. I lifted off the mattress and after a couple of minutes Mr. Foyster and I raised her back into bed. She looked very shaken and when able to get her breath, said in reply to my question, that she had felt the bed tilted and herself pushed out by something which, at the same time, gave her a blow in the body.

Shortly after, I noticed something fly across the room, which, on picking up, I found to be a small vanity case belonging to Mrs. Foyster. It came from a part of the room where nobody was standing and which was quite bare. So much for this morning's experiences. I then left the house and went home to lunch.

It is perhaps worth recording that to-day, June 8, was the fifth anniversary[1] of the Rev. H. Bull's death in the Blue Room, the very room, in fact, where I had just witnessed

[1] Mr. Harry Bull died on June 9, 1927. H.P.

such startling phenomena. I have sometimes wondered whether there was some unknown circumstai.ce connected with his life or death which is an exciting cause of the phenomena. So far as I know, nothing in the nature of what is commonly termed *Poltergeist* phenomena occurred until after his decease. Mr. Harry Bull and other members of his family often declared they had seen ghosts, but such manifestations can hardly be classed in the same category as the more violent and concrete phenomena of a later date.

I returned in the afternoon to hear that Mrs. Foyster had again been thrown out of the bed. In her weak state it seemed inadvisable for her to remain at the Rectory, so my aunt motored up at about five p.m. and took the family down to Sudbury, where they remained with us until Tuesday week. The Foysters had no servant at this period, but there were two small children of three, a boy and a girl, living in the Rectory. Fortunately, they were seldom molested.

During the next nine days while the place was vacant, I paid frequent visits to Borley, examining rooms, rafters and every corner of the house. We found Mrs. Foyster's Christian name 'Marianne' pencilled up on walls in the kind of scrawl which characterized this writing, as also on bits of newspaper which were lying about on the ground floor. In some cases there was 'please help' added.

In my notes I have recorded the fact that on one of our visits we *found a bed overturned*. These observations, I repeat, were made during the period *when the house was empty*.

The Foysters had now been in the house something like nine months and there was little sign of the manifestations abating. I suggested making a Novena[1] to ask for special guidance. We therefore recited the Rosary each day for nine days, asking our Lord and the Blessed Virgin to assist us. On the last day of the Novena, which was Tuesday, June 16, Mrs. Foyster and I walked up to the Rectory from

[1] A devotion consisting of a prayer said on nine successive days, asking for some special blessing. H.P.

Sudbury. We found some fresh writing on the wall in the kitchen passage, making the same appeal to Mrs. Foyster for help.

We then walked upstairs together and began to recite the last Rosary of the Novena on the upper landing, near, but not quite inside the small room overlooking the front entrance, a room which Mrs. Foyster had converted into a small chapel.

About half-way through the prayers a curious thing happened. The two of us became simultaneously aware of a presence near us. I am now only stating what both of us *felt*. If people conclude that this was a purely subjective experience, having no objective reality, I cannot possibly contradict them. All I can say is that that is what I felt. Mrs. Foyster seemed a bit perturbed, so I told her not to worry and continued the Rosary to the end. Neither of us could see or hear anything, although the presence seemed to be behind Mrs. Foyster and near the Blue Room.

The Novena over, Mrs. Foyster walked back towards the Blue Room to investigate and I thought I would look at the walls downstairs. I returned a couple of minutes later and Mrs. Foyster joined me on the landing. We compared notes, but neither of us had anything to report. Happening to turn my eyes towards a bit of wall that jutted out from the landing, a point directly opposite where we had been kneeling, I was surprised to notice a fresh bit of writing on an otherwise clean bit of wall. The message, which was scribbled in pencil, but quite legible, ran as follows: 'Get light mass and prayers. M.'[1] Coming at the very end of a Novena asking for guidance, it did not fail to cause me some astonishment. I should like to say that neither then nor at any other time did I ever make any attempt of any kind whatsoever to get into communication with spirits or with whatever might be causing the manifestations; nor did I in the least anticipate receiving a message of this kind and in this way. One might argue that an individual concealed

[1] See page 147.

in one of the rooms could have written it or, for that matter, that Mrs. Foyster or I had done so. To which I can only reply that, so far as I know, this was not the case. I was sorry afterwards that I did not have the writing photographed.[1]

The nature of the message perplexed me for I had had several Masses offered in connection with this house and prayers had been asked for in several quarters. I hardly knew what to make of the situation, so Mrs. Foyster and I again knelt down and, addressing the Holy Trinity, I asked where, if the message were genuine, the Mass was to be offered. We then walked away, both of us pondering over the strange occurrence.

A little later on, returning to the spot, the word 'here' was written up quite clearly under the other writing. Not knowing what to make of this, I referred the matter to a Catholic priest. He was non-committal about it and gave no particular encouragement to my request that a Mass should be said in the house. Had I known at that time that certain priests, enjoying the privilege of a portable altar, could say Mass in a private house, I might have pushed the matter further. As it was, I let the matter drop and to my knowledge no Mass has ever been said in the house by a Roman Catholic priest. The place is now burnt down.

There has recently been some correspondence in *The Times*[2] regarding the manifestations at Borley. I should like to say that I agree with Dr. Letitia Fairfield in so far as she maintains the point that there is no historical evidence for the story of the walled-up nun and the lay brother, a story that, furthermore, has nothing approaching contemporary evidence to recommend it and which obviously sprang up after people began to see ghosts in the locality, a matter of sixty years or so at the most. The bricked-up nun story, I suggest, has been concocted by the local imagination to supply a clue to the ghostly appearances of more recent times, but the proofs for supernormal phenomena do not

[1] This was done later. See pages 146, 149, 151. H.P.   [2] See *ante*, pages 28–30.

rest upon any evidence connected with ghostly appearances, even though one has every reason to believe the phantasms are genuine phenomena.

The following translation from the Latin, an extract from Dugdale's *Monasticon Anglicanum* (8 vols.) may be of interest to those who, like myself, seek to know whether a monastery ever existed at Borley: 'Edward III in the 36th year of his reign gave to the Prior and community of Christ Church, Canterbury, the Manor of Borley in the county of Essex in exchange for the customs and revenues together with all the rights which the said Prior and Community could in any way have in the town and port of Sandwich . . .' etc.

A later entry in the time of Henry VIII gives a certificate of valuation of Borley Manor amounting to £32 14s. 4d. There is thus definite evidence that Borley Manor, wherever that may have been situated, became the property of Benedictine monks in the fourteenth century.

Shortly after the events described above, I returned to London where I remained for some time. On my return, I witnessed further phenomena. On one occasion, that I can clearly recall, the Foysters and myself went upstairs and became aware of a smell of smoke. We looked around and, opening the door of a room adjacent to the children's bedroom, were surprised to see smoke issuing from the skirtingboard. This room was quite bare and was never used. The door was usually kept locked, though whether it was locked on this occasion, is a detail I cannot recall. There was a hole about the size of a child's fist burnt into the skirtingboard and I was able to pull out some fluff and other material which seemed to have been pushed into the aperture. There was no sign of a flame.

I was often a witness of the door-locking incidents. It made no difference whether you were inside or outside the room. The doors would lock and unlock themselves quite regardless of your convenience and in a manner for which none of us could account.[1] This sometimes happened to

---

[1] See Mr. Kerr-Pearse's experience, page 210.

several doors at once, the keys often being removed quite unexpectedly and as suddenly reappearing. This latter phenomenon was often repeated with other objects, such as kitchen utensils, etc.

Supernormal bell-ringing, a common feature of the Borley manifestations, was another type of phenomenon we often witnessed and, still more often, heard. More than once I have stood in the kitchen passage and watched the bells moving to and fro, the only people in the house often standing alongside of me, witnessing the same performance. The wires of these old-fashioned pull bells had all been cut in the Rev. G. E. Smith's time, as Mr. Price and others will testify. Mr. Smith was the first tenant to occupy the house after Mr. Harry Bull's death.

On other occasions, the large bell in the yard used to ring out. There was no rope attached to it and as it was high up, in an angle of the yard,[1] I hardly knew how anybody could have rung it in the daytime, without my seeing the person climbing in or out of a window. After watching these and similar manifestations over a space of six months, I must confess that I, personally, never had any occasion to suspect any member of the household of producing pheno-mena artificially or fraudulently. Books in Mr. Foyster's study were often tampered with, and on one or two occasions, we had to replace quite a number of volumes which had been flung out of the shelves.

One of the most startling series of phenomena I ever witnessed was on Friday, November 13. Mr. Foyster was obliged to go up to London on business and had asked me to stay up at the Rectory until his return late that evening.

I came up to Borley about 5.30 p.m., my arrival being greeted with a loud peal of bells in the kitchen passage. This generally heralded the outbreak of further manifestations, so we decided to put the children to bed and take refuge in the kitchen, where we could spend the evening and have our supper without being obliged to move about from room to

[1] See photograph, Plate II.

room. There was a young maid called Katie living in the house at that time who, together with Mrs. Foyster and myself, witnessed the incidents I am about to describe.

Mrs. Foyster was sitting in a small easy-chair in one corner of the kitchen. The windows and both doors were closed. Without warning of any kind, there was a sudden crash right underneath her chair, a bottle bursting into fragments on the stone floor beneath her. A quarter of an hour or so later, precisely the same thing happened to me, as I was drawing up a small chair to sit down to my supper. Katie was kept busy sweeping up the broken glass and looked quite mystified, having been in the house only a week or so. Shortly after this, all three of us witnessed another extraordinary incident. We were standing in a row with our backs to the fire, talking and looking out towards the window. Suddenly, before our very eyes, a bottle poised itself in mid-air within a foot or so of the kitchen ceiling. It remained here for a second or two and then fell with a crash on the floor before us. I repeat that all three of us witnessed this incident.

This was followed by another curious occurrence. One of the kitchen doors, which was now just ajar, adjoined a staircase leading up to the servants' quarters. We heard a noise that seemed to come from the top of these stairs, as if something was walking slowly down the steps towards us. We waited. The step got quicker and through the open door a bottle rolled into the room, circling round the floor, without breaking. There was nobody visible on the stairs or in the servants' quarters, which I examined carefully. A few other objects were thrown about and I can remember a small bit of china striking my shoulder as I walked across the kitchen floor. We had two lamps in use at the time. I had, unfortunately, forgotten to bring along my large electric torch.

Meanwhile, other phenomena began to occur outside the kitchen. The bells in the passage were ringing again and once or twice the large bell in the yard rang out sharply.

I watched the pull bells on this occasion for quite a long time. I had noticed that on some occasions when I touched the bells and locked doors with the relic of St. John Vianney, the Curé of Ars, the phenomena ceased, but this did not always happen at once, and I must acknowledge that, although manifestations seldom, if ever, occurred during the recital of prayers, they invariably broke out soon afterwards and usually with greater violence.

This confirms the opinion of a Catholic priest whom I had consulted in the matter. He had recommended me to say prayers and use holy water, but had added that in nearly all the recorded cases of *Poltergeist* phenomena, the manifestations had continued in spite of these measures. There is one Indian case recorded, however, where a Novena to St. Joseph ended the manifestations, but I have never read of a case where Mass has been said in the house actually disturbed by such phenomena.

Mr. Foyster was due back at Borley about 9.30 p.m., but owing to a bad fog, the train was very late. I was just beginning to hope I should soon be able to go home, when Mrs. Foyster said that she was tired and wanted to go upstairs to bed. It was now 11 p.m. Leaving Katie in the kitchen with one of the lamps, Mrs. Foyster and I moved off in the direction of the main staircase. She was carrying the second lamp. We had only mounted a few steps when the wick began to flicker. Looking at Mrs. Foyster, I noticed that she was staggering. I was just able to grasp the lamp in time. This went out, leaving us in complete darkness. I put the lamp down as carefully as I could on the staircase and lifting Mrs. Foyster up into my arms—she had quite collapsed—I felt my way as best I could to the top of the landing, where I laid her down outside one of the bedrooms. To my intense relief, I then heard the front door open. I called out to Mr. Foyster, who replied, and after briefly explaining what had happened, I left for Sudbury, very glad for once to be out of this extraordinary house.

On December 14, the day before I left for Sandringham, on my way to Sheringham, in Norfolk, to see the Rev. G. E. Smith and his wife in connection with their own experiences at Borley in the early part of 1929, I witnessed further phenomena at the Rectory. Mr. Foyster was ill in bed, suffering from rheumatism. He was in the room adjoining the Blue Room and which overlooks the lawn. Mrs. Foyster was standing on one side of the bed, the side nearest the door, and I was standing with my back to the window quite seven or eight feet from either of them. A tumbler of the fragile kind, usually to be found on any dinner table, suddenly dropped near my feet, circling round me and coming to rest without breaking. This certainly could not have been thrown by the Foysters without damaging the glass.

A loud noise on the ground floor, which sounded like somebody jumping and stamping in the kitchen passage, followed soon after the tumbler incident. There was nobody in the house besides us three, who were all together upstairs. On going down below, I found a jam-jar reposing outside Mr. Foyster's study [*i.e.*, the Base Room of later date] and a small tin case, which nobody recognized, lying on the floor. I have also recorded in my notes that there were two glass bottles found broken in the kitchen passage. The bottle phenomena were frequent at this period and bottles were often found lying about in odd places.

The last incident I recorded was on December 31, 1931. Mr. Foyster was in the study lying back in an arm-chair. He asked for his medicine which his wife went off to fetch. I was in the study at the time, and on her return heard her make an unflattering remark about 'the beastly things' which had removed the medicine. This form of practical joke had become as wearisome as it was annoying. Without thinking, I replied 'Perhaps if you speak nicely, they'll return.' An hour or so later, near the level crossing on the way back to Sudbury, I put on my coat. The bottle of pills was reposing in one of the pockets! It is not necessary to add that this incident,[1] in itself, is no proof of the supernormal, but when one is not acting in the strictly scientific capacity of a psychical research investigator, one does not feel obliged to regard everybody in the house, at every moment of the day, as a potential trickster. I had seen more than enough to convince me that the phenomena at Borley Rectory were preternatural and I agree with Mr. Price in asserting that this place, which is now a ruin, was once the most haunted house in England.

In conclusion, as a contributor to this book, there is one issue I should like to make clear. Although I am ready to accept the findings of Mr. Price and his colleagues regarding the manifestations, I should like it known that I do not thereby identify myself with any theories which he and others may put forward in this book to account for the phenomena. I say this because I have not had the advantage of reading the MS. of his book and wish to safeguard my freedom of view on the matter.

(*Signed*) DOM RICHARD WHITEHOUSE, O.S.B.

[1] Compare a similar incident that occurred to Dr. R. J. Tillyard, F.R.S., in his experiments with Eleonore Zugun : *Proc.*, Nat. Lab. of Psychical Research, Vol. I, Part 1, London, 1927.

CHAPTER XVI

'A RECTORY FOR SALE—CHEAP'

WITH the departure of the Rev. L. A. Foyster from 'the most haunted house,' in October 1935, Borley Rectory was destined never again to house another parson under its not too friendly roof.

I kept contact with Borley during the years 1935-6-7 and heard that the villagers occasionally saw the 'strange light' in Room No. 7, though the place was empty and deserted. Also, the rumble of an invisible coach and the clatter of phantasmal horses sometimes frightened the rustic on his homeward path along that stretch of hollow road between the two Rectory gates. The inhabitants wondered what would become of the strange building.

As a matter of fact, during the months that followed Mr. Foyster's retirement, Queen Anne's Bounty was trying its hardest to sell the Rectory, or even let it. Ten years previously, during the Rev. G. E. Smith's time, the house was also up for sale. I was told that I could buy the Rectory 'for a song.'

When I heard of the persistent efforts to sell the Rectory, I decided that I would make some inquiries as to the possibility of acquiring the place. Not only did I wish to make a prolonged investigation there, but the thought occurred to me that the house might become a sort of permanent 'psychic trust' where researchers could spend a week or two when they felt so inclined, making experiments or trying new control apparatus.

I was even approached by a man who wanted to 'go halves' with me in buying the Rectory with the idea of turning it into a sort of 'Home of Rest for Decayed Mediums,' with board and lodging at so much a week, 'phenomena included.' I pointed out that such a project would cost a fortune in order to make the place comfortable and furnish it properly. And what housekeeper would stay in the building for more than a couple of nights? As an example of what it *would* cost to furnish, Mr. Glanville once worked out how much cheap linoleum it would take to cover the rooms and passages. I forget how many square yards— or acres—would be required, but I remember that this floor covering alone would cost £80. So I turned down the 'Home of Rest' idea.

But I was still anxious to control the place in order to make some independent observations, so I decided I would at least rent the Rectory, if possible. My idea was not only to eliminate myself from the proposed scientific inquiry, but also to exclude from the investigation anyone connected in any way with the Bulls, the Smiths, or the Foysters. I wanted first-hand information and evidence from intelligent and competent persons whom I did not know, and who were in no way connected with any previous occupant of the Rectory. That is really why I wished to rent the house.

So my next move was to write to Miss Ethel Bull, asking for the name of the proper person to whom I should apply for particulars. In her reply (dated May 4, 1937) she suggested my writing to the Rev. A. C. Henning, the new Rector of Borley, who was living at Liston Rectory. By this time, the livings of Borley and Liston had been amalgamated.

So I wrote to Mr. Henning and in his reply (May 7, 1937) he not only expressed his willingness to lease me the Rectory for an unspecified period, but very kindly invited me to lunch to talk the matter over, and said he would meet me at Sudbury Station with his car.

The lunch was arranged for Wednesday, May 19, 1937, and, to the minute, Mr. Henning was waiting for me at Sudbury. As I stepped from the train and grasped his hand, a new and exciting chapter in the Borley mystery was inaugurated.

The contrast between the 'atmosphere' of Liston Rectory and that of the 'haunted house' was striking in the extreme. As Mr. Henning showed me over his warm, cosy, convenient, and comfortable home, presided over by his charming wife, I could not help comparing it with the deathly coldness of Borley Rectory. We visited the latter during the afternoon, and it was like going out of the sunshine into a mausoleum.

During lunch I heard the latest news of Borley Rectory. The situation was that the ecclesiastical authorities had decided that the place was 'unsuitable'(!) for a Rector to live in; was too large for the modern 'small family' likely to reside there; was too expensive and difficult to manage unless a Rector had private means to augment his stipend; that it was almost impossible to get servants; and that the place had had far too much publicity during recent years. As regards publicity, during the occupancy of Mr. Smith, regular motor-coach excursions, 'to see the ghost,' were run from Chelmsford, Colchester, Bury St. Edmonds and other local centres. A resident told me that there were so many headlights and hand-torches going full blast in the lanes round the Rectory one Saturday evening, that it reminded him of the Great White Way!

I then asked Mr. Henning what he thought would be a fair price for me to pay as regards rent. He said he would leave it to me. I hardly knew what price to put on the place. I realized there would be some expenditure in the way of furnishing at least one room for my observers. Then there would be travelling expenses, and so on. I thought for a moment and suggested £30 a year. Mr. Henning said that this sum was quite satisfactory and added that he would pay the rates. This was very generous of him.

After lunch, my host drove me over to Borley—some two miles away—and opened up the Rectory for my inspection. The keys were in charge of Mr. L. Arbon who, with his wife, occupied the cottage, for which they paid a small rent. Mr. Arbon was a steam-roller driver and not at all interested in 'ghosts.' His work took him away from home for long periods. I asked him whether his wife was at all nervous when in their cottage at night by herself, but he said 'No.' I wondered whether they had heard Mr. Cooper's story of the pattering 'dog'! I did not enlighten them.

Mr. Henning and I made a minute examination of the Rectory, opening up all rooms, looking in the cupboards and so on. I found the house just as cold and still as on my previous visits. I will add by way of parenthesis that Borley Rectory is the quietest and coldest house I have ever been in. Most houses, both old and new, emit *some* sounds: crepitation of the wood; changes of temperature affecting window-frames, joists and doors; air currents through chimneys and along passages, and so on. But every observer has remarked upon the stillness and coldness of the Rectory, even in the dead of night when sounds appear to be much amplified. That ancient writer on psychic phenomena, Ludvig Lavater (1527-86), when speaking of watching at midnight, recognized this aural illusion when he wrote:[1] 'If a worme which fretteth wood, or that breadeth in trees chaunce to gnawe a wall or wainscot, or other tymber, many [investigators] will judge they heare one softly knocking uppon an andvill with a sledge.' In other words, sounds appear much magnified in the still of the night, especially when one is intent upon listening for them. But if the Rectory was cold and soundless, it was also the driest house—with the exception of the cellars—that I have ever been in.

During my examination of the Rectory, I discovered nothing unusual. Mr. Henning had a number of wooden forms and books stored there, and occasionally a room was used for some parish meeting. But otherwise, the place was kept locked and visitors to the house were infrequent. Before we parted that afternoon, Mr. Henning handed to me the keys of the place, and in return I gave him a cheque for £15, six months' rent of the house in advance. I thus became the first lay tenant of Borley Rectory since it was built seventy-four years previously.

[1] *Of Ghostes and Spirites Walking by Nyght* . . . London, 1572.

CHAPTER XVII

I ACQUIRE BORLEY RECTORY

HAVING acquired the haunted Rectory, I considered how I could best carry out my plan of investigating the alleged—if I can now use such a term—phenomena that had troubled Borley for fifty years. I reiterate that I wanted, as far as possible, to eliminate myself and my friends, and all previous occupiers, from taking any active part in my proposed inquiry. I wanted *independent evidence* from intelligent, competent, and cultured strangers who were *not* spiritualists; and, if they knew nothing about psychical research, so much the better.

So I decided I would insert an advertisement in the Personal Column of *The Times* and this duly appeared on May 25, 1937. It read:

'HAUNTED HOUSE. Responsible persons of leisure and intelligence, intrepid, critical, and unbiassed, are invited to join rota of observers in a year's night and day investigation of alleged haunted house in Home Counties. Printed instructions supplied. Scientific training or ability to operate simple instruments an advantage. House situated in lonely hamlet, so own car is essential. Write Box H.989, *The Times*, E.C.4.'

The result of this advertisement was phenomenal. I anticipated replies from suitable people whose qualifications conformed to the requirements plainly set out in *The Times*. But I was *not* prepared for the spate of letters that I received from persons as far removed in the social scale as charwomen and countesses. Many of these letters were in direct answer to my advertisement, but some had been sent in by friends of the writers after the latter had communicated with me and had already studied my reply. Altogether, from first to last, some 200 applications were received, directly or indirectly, in answer to my appeal.

Some of the replies sent in were amusing in the extreme; some were ironical; some were pathetic. A few 'society women' and 'Mayfair men' must have written for the 'job' out of sheer boredom. One girl candidly admitted that ghost-hunting would be 'a thrill,' and she was sure she could 'get a kick out of it.' Many of my correspondents hoped to be paid for their services. One man modestly suggested a salary of £10 a week as 'suitable remuneration.' Half-pay army officers offered to investigate 'free of charge' if 'all expenses were paid.'

Then there were the cranks and inventors with machines to sell—pieces of apparatus guaranteed to detect a ghost a mile off. Other people had 'systems' that they wished tried out. And mediums, amateur and professional, wanted to hold séances in the house, and so did a few Pressmen and journalists who wrote, scenting some good 'copy.' Exorcisms and prayers were numerous and one kind old lady—I fancy she *must* have been old—said she would offer up a prayer for me if I would tell her the exact times when I should be in the house. A member of an occult society sent me a piece of paper in the shape of a pentagram on which were written some cabalistic characters which, if sewn in my clothing, would afford 'protection' from evil things. The aforesaid correspondents, with the many who wished to 'caretake' the place, and one or two anonymous writers who showered abuse on me, made up some 75 per cent of the 200 replies that I received. Most of these letters were at once consigned to the waste-paper basket.

But there were others. I received a sprinkling of replies from the 'right' sort of people: 'varsity graduates, scientists, doctors of medicine, consulting engineers, army men on the active list, and so on—all intelligent, all educated, all cultured, all trained, all with a scientific interest in the proposed investigation; and all willing to give their skill, time and money in the cause of psychical research. Not that I objected to paying for services rendered. But that was not the sort of testimony I required. I did not want to *buy* phenomena: I wanted the candid and accurate observations of a number of intelligent, independent, competent, and disinterested men as to whether phenomena were still occurring at Borley Rectory. I selected about forty people of the right type and I will candidly admit that were it not for the assistance these gentlemen subsequently gave me, it is very doubtful whether this monograph would have got any farther than one of my library manuscript cases.

Just by reading a letter and studying its composition I could pretty well tell whether the writer was a suitable person to take part in my inquiry. I selected a number of likely applicants and invited them to call upon me. They were all complete strangers to me. Under no circumstances would I give a person permission to visit the Rectory unless (*a*) I had had a personal interview with him; and (*b*) until he had signed the Declaration Form[1] which I *very carefully* drew up.

I had to protect myself against all sorts of possible contingencies. I had to make sure that observers would carry out my instructions. I had to be certain that they were not connected with the Press in any way and would not print or circulate a premature or garbled report of the inquiry. I had to prevent their taking unauthorized persons (*i.e.*, those who had *not* signed the Declaration Form) to the Rectory. It was important that I should extract a promise from them that they would send in a written report of their experiences —whether good, bad, or indifferent. There were other minor matters that concerned both them and me, duly set forth in the Declaration Form, which should be studied. In point of fact, as a legal document, I do not think the Declaration was worth the paper it was printed on. But it was a sort of signed 'gentleman's agreement,' and I am happy to be able to state that in no single instance was my confidence abused, or agreement violated.

For the first time in the history of psychical research, there

[1] See Appendix A.

was printed a book of instructions, with a blue cover, for the guidance of those investigating a particular haunted house. This was the Blue Book[1] that I had printed for the purpose of giving official observers some indication as to their procedure under certain specified contingencies. It was a sort of handbook to the 'ghosts' of Borley Rectory, in addition to instructions how to deal with them. It was also intended to indicate what an investigator would need in the way of such equipment as was not available in the house itself.

Observers were told what to do if they heard paranormal bell-ringing; or heard footsteps, raps, or knocks, or saw forms and apparitions. They were informed where they could get a good night's rest when 'off duty,' a square meal, the location of the nearest 'pub,' and other necessary information. A copy of the Blue Book was given to every official observer, with strict injunctions not to part with it or convey the information it contained to those who had not signed the Declaration Form. The book was considered by the Monotype Corporation (whose type was used in the printing of the brochure) to be such a novelty that they asked my permission to place a copy in their museum. Of course I consented.

Having selected my observers, my next task was to visit the Rectory and make arrangements for such comfort as I could provide for them.

[1] See Appendix B.

CHAPTER XVIII

WE ESTABLISH OUR BASE ROOM—AND
ARE DISTURBED

ON June 2, 1937, I motored to Borley. I was accompanied by a young Oxford graduate friend of mine named Ellic Howe. It was my intention to make a survey of the house with a view to establishing a Base Room or centre where my official observers could be comfortable, keep their belongings, write their reports and—occasionally —take some rest.

We arrived at the Rectory just before 12 noon and I was not long in deciding that I would choose the study or library (see Ground Floor Plan) as our Base Room. It was conveniently situated as regards the hall (where so many strange occurrences have taken place); its French windows gave easy access to the lawn, summer-house, and Nun's Walk; it was under the Blue Room, focal centre of scores of phenomena; and it was a large, comfortable sort of place —if I can possibly use the word 'comfortable' in connection with Borley—and was equipped with a large number of shelves which were permanently fixed to the walls.

Having examined all doors and windows to satisfy ourselves that they were securely fastened, we locked the two front doors, jumped into our car and sped to Sudbury in order to make the necessary purchases for equipping our Base Room. Mr. Henning had given me the names of some tradesmen in Sudbury who could probably supply us with what we required.

What we purchased was really a camper's outfit. We bought a strong metal folding camp bed, with mattress, pillows and blankets. We bought a powerful brass paraffin

PLATE IV

Right :

Italian mantelpiece in Dining room, showing marble busts recalling the monastic site on which the Rectory is said to stand.

Left :

Drawing - room with ornate mantelpiece composed of inlaid coloured marble.

Right :

Room 7. A glimpse of the main staircase can be seen through the doorway.

Left :

The Blue Room, focus of much psychic activity.

table lamp, a two-gallon can of paraffin, a bottle of methy-
lated spirits, a packet of candles, some matches, and other
odds and ends. Mr. Howe had kindly presented—and had
brought along with him—a spirit kettle, knives, forks, spoons,
plates, cups, glasses, teapot, cleaning materials, glass cloths,
etc., with a supply of tea, sugar, condensed milk and so on.
I had packed in the car about twenty readable books—*not*
on psychical research!—which, I thought, would interest
observers at the Rectory when they were resting and 'off
duty.'

We had some difficulty in packing our purchases in Mr.
Howe's small saloon car. But we managed it at last and,
after some lunch, went back to the Rectory to set out the
equipment.

Mr. Henning had told me that a large wooden table was
in the house. This we found, and installed it in the Base
Room. Then we discovered some long school forms in the
garage and these, too, we placed in the Base Room. We
erected our bed, arranged the crockery on the shelves, and
made the place a little comfortable, if not exactly home-like.
Some idea of the room can be seen from the photograph,
Plate III.

After we had made the Base Room ship-shape, Mr. Howe
and I began a tour of the Rectory and its many apartments.
We examined every room and cupboard, the cellars and,
with our powerful torches, explored the 'attics' and every
hole and corner in the house. During our tour we 'ringed'
with coloured chalks every movable object in the house.
In addition, we placed a number of small objects about the
place: match-box, cigarette carton, and small odds and
ends. These we very carefully and accurately ringed in
order to inform us, or future observers, whether any force—
normal or paranormal—had moved them.

When we came to the Blue Room, we entered and, to my
surprise, saw a long, dirty, mouldy, torn, rather moth-eaten
dark blue serge lady's coat hanging on a peg behind the
door (see Plate III). That coat was *not* there when Mr.

Henning and I examined the Rectory on May 19, 1937—
i.e., a fortnight previously. I wondered why the Rector
should have placed the coat in the house, *after* I had rented
it. It will be convenient here to give the result of my subsequent inquiries concerning this garment.

I wrote to Mr. Henning, asking why the coat, apparently
a woman's, was in the house; to whom it belonged; and if
there was a 'history' attached to it. Mr. Henning informed
me that he knew nothing about the coat, had never seen it
at the Rectory, and had no idea how it could have 'appeared'
there. Furthermore, he made inquiries in the village, and
no one had lost a coat, or knew anything about it. Mr.
Henning was certain that the coat was not in the Rectory
previous to my renting it.

I, too, made some inquiries in Sudbury as to whether
anyone had lost a coat, or had bought an old coat, but could
gain no information concerning it. I also asked Mr. Arbon,
the tenant of the cottage, and he, too, knew nothing about it.
There was no maker's name on the coat, and nothing to
identify it. And so the coat was left where I found it.
During my year's tenancy of the Rectory, it *disappeared
completely for one week*, according to our observer's report.
The tale of the coat is just one more mystery connected
with this extraordinary house.

We found nothing else of any note in our exploration of
the Rectory, and proceeded to examine the garden. We
inspected the summer-houses and fought our way through
the brambles to the stream and the cats' cemetery. We again
read the names of deceased felines on the headboards and
the place appeared as if it had not been disturbed for years,
it was so overgrown and wild.

Reversing the order of things, as new tenant of the
Rectory, I next called on the owners of Borley Place, the old
house opposite the Rectory. Mr. Howe accompanied me.
Mr. Henning had given me an introduction to Mrs. Payne,
wife of the owner. This lady insisted upon our staying to tea.
We later met Mr. Payne and had a long chat about the

Rectory, the phenomena, and the various occupiers. We found Borley Place a delightful and comfortable old house No 'manifestations' have been experienced there.

After tea we crossed over to the Rectory and again made a complete examination of the house. Nothing appeared to have happened since we left it a couple of hours previously. We had been discussing whether we should stay the night in the house, and we finally decided we would. It was a warm June evening (though quite cold in the house) and, after an hour's vigil in the large summer-house opposite the Nun's Walk, we returned to the Base Room. Here we made some tea and consumed some sandwiches we had brought with us. Then we locked up the house and walked up the village to the little licensed house where we purchased some bottles of beer with which to stock our modest larder. We returned to the Rectory and once more examined all rooms, doors, etc. We locked all external doors, fastened the windows, ended our tour of inspection at the Base Room, and prepared to settle down for the night. It was then just after 8 o'clock and, of course, quite light. There was no wind and it was a still, quiet night outside.

As I was tired, I stretched out full-length on the camp bed. Ellic Howe sat at the table, near the door, and read. We were not talking, and the house was deathly still. After about forty minutes of absolute quietness, during which period neither Howe nor I spoke a word, a series of short, sharp taps was heard in quick succession. Apparently, the sounds came from the passage just outside the door near which Howe was sitting. He said 'What's that?' I jumped off the bed and he and I went into the passage to investigate. We found nothing. All the doors were as we left them, and we saw nothing unusual.

We returned to the Base Room and, as it was now getting somewhat dark in the house, we lit our newly acquired table-lamp. I returned to my rest on the bed, and Howe continued his reading.

About fifteen minutes after we were first disturbed we

I

were again startled by hearing two loud 'thumps' that left nothing to the imagination. It was just as if someone had first thrown one boot heavily to the floor, and then the other. Before we had recovered from our surprise, we heard a door slam somewhere in the house, apparently upstairs. With the lamp and our torches we ran out of the Base Room and hurried to the first floor. There was nothing to be seen, though we once more examined all rooms, doors and windows, and shone our torches all over the attics. We found nothing that could account for the noises we had heard. None of the articles in the chalk rings had been moved. All the external doors to the house were securely fastened, just as we had left them, and the interior doors did not appear to have been moved.

We returned to the Base Room, opened the French windows, and explored the grounds. We found nothing. We watched the house from the garden for about half an hour, but saw no 'lights,' 'nun,' or anything unusual. Then we went into the road. It was now getting dark and had turned chilly. We had no firing or other means of heating the Base Room, so we decided we would get back to London.

Before returning to the house, I saw Mr. and Mrs. Arbon at the cottage, told them of my plans for investigating the Rectory and arranged with them to take charge of one set of keys. I said I would either write to Mr. Arbon, or his wife, advising them of the arrival of an observer; or I would give the person investigating a letter of introduction to him. Under no circumstances were the keys of the Rectory to be handed to any unauthorized person. This the Arbons agreed to do. Mr. Arbon told me that he became tenant of the Rectory cottage in February 1936.

After some more sandwiches and a bottle of beer, we closed and locked the Rectory and returned to London. We had had a most interesting and not uneventful day.

On June 16, 1937, Mr. Ellic Howe and I again visited the Rectory and spent the night there. After carefully locking all doors and windows, at 8.30 p.m. we went into

Sudbury for a meal. We returned at 9.15 p.m. and, during our usual patrol of the house, found that, in the Blue Room, while we had been absent, a tobacco tin had been moved three inches from its chalked outline, and a small box was seven feet from where we had left it. No explanation was forthcoming, but as we were out of the building when these movements occurred, I merely record the incident without comment.

CHAPTER XIX

ENROLLING THE OBSERVERS

BY the time the Blue Book was ready for our observers, some forty gentlemen—and one or two ladies—had been accepted as official investigators. As I have stated, they were all complete strangers to me with the exception of one B.B.C. official.

Verbal instructions were given them in addition to those printed in the Blue Book and on the Declaration Form. They were informed how to get from London to Borley by the quickest route. They were asked to 'ring' with chalk every portable object in the Rectory and to lock and seal all doors and windows when they had established themselves in the house. They were asked to complete their reports immediately after their observational period, from notes made while they were on duty, and to let me have them without delay, as they were to be used in the published report.

They were asked particularly to examine all walls and passages for pencil markings or 'messages' and ring them. Most of these messages were already on the walls when I took over the Rectory, but other markings undoubtedly appeared from time to time during the actual presence of some observers. The 'messages' to 'Marianne' appeared on the walls during Mr. Foyster's occupation of the Rectory. It says something for the observational powers of our investigators that the 'Marianne' messages were all discovered, though one might pass along the passages a thousand times without seeing the faintly scribbled pencil 'appeals.'

If all the official observers were strangers to me, they were also strangers to one another, except when two friends enrolled together. I rather encouraged this as two can

116

'work' a haunted house better than one, and they are company for each other. When two persons are on duty together, one can snatch brief periods of rest while the other is keeping watch, taking notes, etc. And sometimes it is desirable that one person should be *outside* a building, watching for a certain phenomenon, while his companion is *inside*, hoping to observe the same manifestation from his angle, as in the case of the strange light seen in the windows of various rooms.

Although all the observers (except those who were already friends) were strangers to one another at the outset of the inquiry, they occasionally met when going on duty or relieving one another, and they thus became acquainted. Sometimes a friendship sprang up in this way and they afterwards requested to be permitted to 'hunt' together. When this occurred, the reader will notice that the report of one observer sometimes contains the name of, or reference to, another official observer whose protocol is printed separately. In other words, their respective reports sometimes overlap.

It has been impossible to reproduce the reports verbatim. The reader would find the minute-to-minute protocols irksome in the extreme. And I should require a volume twice this size if I decided to print the reports in detail as set out in the official records. But extensive verbatim extracts from the original reports have been made, while the remainder have been paraphrased for economy of space. Some of the reports are very long indeed. Unfortunately, because a report is long and detailed, it does not necessarily follow that it is a 'good' one from a phenomenal point of view.

There were few entirely blank records handed in. It would serve no useful purpose to print these negative reports, so they are not included in this monograph. Some very conscientious and painstaking observers, when they had had a blank day or night wrote—very properly—pages of details of their movements, times, weather reports, and so on. It would be waste of paper to print such records. But they are preserved[1] in the vast *dossier* relating to Borley that I have accumulated.

A very few observers, after a blank day or night, became discouraged and dropped out. Others, with similar negative results, persevered, and were at length rewarded by seeing or hearing something, the result of paranormal action. I have been to Borley several times without experiencing any phenomena whatever. Especially, I was present at the Rectory on two occasions on July 28, and in neither year did I see the 'nun'—who is supposed always to manifest herself on this day—or any other phenomenon. No one can become a good investigator unless he has unlimited patience.

I found it impracticable to install instruments at the Rectory during my year's tenancy. After a careful study of the phenomena being witnessed by my observers, I came to the conclusion that I should require the most elaborate apparatus to record some of them (*e.g.*, the small pencil markings that appeared on the walls), and that would have meant my residing in the house almost permanently. I was not prepared to do this; and, as I have stated, I wished to eliminate myself from the inquiry as far as possible. However, one day early in July I did install a delicate transmitting thermograph, which was in position for twenty-four hours and it is interesting to note that the temperature (of the dining-room) measured was almost 48° Fahrenheit during practically the whole of this period. It did not vary 1.5° throughout the twenty-four hours, which proves (*a*) that although it was a normal, warm July day outside, the house itself was cold; and (*b*) that very slight variations of temperature occur in the house. Simple instruments and pieces of apparatus were used by various observers, some of whom took photographs, made drawings, or prepared plans of the Rectory.

The arrangement I have adopted for reproducing the reports of our observers is as follows: When a person visited

[1] In the Harry Price Library of Magical Literature in the University of London.

the Rectory more than once, all his records are dealt with as a group. When an observer sent in only one positive report, of no great length, it has been grouped with others in one section. A digest of all the official observers' reports is printed as Appendix C.

Usually, each observer was given a letter of introduction to Mr. Arbon, tenant of the cottage. This enabled him to obtain the keys of the Rectory. When no such letter was given, Mr. Arbon himself was advised of the impending visit of the investigator, with name and time of arrival.

CHAPTER XX

MANY MAJOR PHENOMENA CONFIRMED
BY OFFICIAL OBSERVERS

ALTHOUGH it has been found expedient to summarize the reports of the official observers in the form of a digest, printed as Appendix C, I will briefly describe, in non-technical language, the phenomena heard, seen, felt and smelt at Borley Rectory during the twelve months of my tenancy. But I urge the reader, in his own interests, to study the reports in greater detail as epitomized in the Appendix.

Forty-eight observers took part in our official investigation and nearly all reported the occurrence of phenomena. Some of the manifestations were unspectacular, but there were a few really dramatic incidents. As I have mentioned elsewhere in this work, the really exciting happenings that occurred at Borley invariably took place when the house was *occupied by a family*. But it is only a question of *degree*. The paranormal displacement of a match-box—to the extent of only a single millimetre—is just as 'miraculous,' and just as interesting, as the appearance of the 'nun' herself. But to the layman the latter phenomenon would be the more spectacular.

The official observers were very impressed with what they saw and heard. Mr. S. H. Glanville and his son were the first to do duty at the Rectory and on the evening of their arrival they heard soft taps that could not be explained. These followed a curious sharp click or crack. A later observer, who heard something similar, likened the sound to that made by an electric light tumbler switch when it is operated. But there is no electricity—and consequently no switches—within miles of Borley.

Mr. Glanville and his brother-in-law were also fortunate enough to witness the appearance of those famous wall-markings that make Borley unique in the annals of psychical research. Certainly, they did not see the pencillings form before their eyes. But happening to photograph one of those heartrending 'Marianne' messages, they noticed, an hour or so later, that other pencillings had been added! So they photographed the 'message' a second time and compared the negatives. In *one* picture only do the markings appear! If this is not *proof* of paranormal activity, I do not know the meaning of the word. The two gentlemen were alone in a locked and sealed house and always kept together. They also heard 'scrabbling' noises outside the Blue Room. Perhaps the entity was trying to write some more.

One of the minor mysteries—it may even be a major mystery if we could only appreciate its significance—was the extraordinary discovery by Mr. Glanville that someone had taken the trouble to tear his way through a bramble thicket at the bottom of the Rectory garden and dig up a cat that had been buried there for thirty years. But *was* it a cat the intruder was after? The story should be read in detail.

The other phenomena recorded by Mr. Glanville and his friends include thuds and bumps; light, tripping footsteps; movements of objects; heavy muffled footsteps, and further pencil markings. One of the most curious happenings was the pendulatory movement of the Base Room blind, which swung backwards and forwards as they watched it.

A most interesting report was sent in by Mr. M. Kerr-Pearse, one of our proconsuls at Geneva. The complete record of his many visits runs to nearly 10,000 words. Like Mr. Glanville, he heard many raps, thumps, thuds, and other sounds for which no normal explanation could be found. His carefully-placed control objects were moved by some invisible agency. And one of these objects was a bag of coal *weighing fifty pounds!* There was no explanation, except a paranormal one.

Kerr-Pearse also witnessed a number of new pencil marks

that appeared on the walls while he was actually in the house which, as usual, was locked and sealed.

Very few séances were held in the house, but an informal one which Kerr-Pearse and the Rev. A. C. Henning (the present Rector of Borley) arranged produced curious results. Mr. and Mrs. Henning and Kerr-Pearse sat round the Base Room table, on which they 'rapped' in the traditional manner. After a few minutes a most curious thumping sound was heard coming from the kitchen quarters. The thumps then proceeded along the passage towards the Base Room. Unfortunately, the little group stood up to get a better view of the passage—and the 'thumps' stopped dead. The slight noise the sitters made must have frightened—what?

Things 'appeared' while Kerr-Pearse was in the house, and these included a lump of rotten touch-wood, and a mummified frog which had been deposited in the passage. It was never discovered where the frog came from, or how it arrived.

Though Mr. Kerr-Pearse experienced no abnormal feeling of cold in the Rectory, his cousin Mr. Rupert Haig, while resting in the Base Room, was awakened by an icy cold draught playing on his face. All doors and windows were closed; a big fire was burning; and the temperature of the room measured 60° Fahrenheit. Haig's impressions are printed in full in Appendix C.

The only really disturbing incident experienced by Kerr-Pearse occurred while he was alone in the Rectory, as he was very often. He was just finishing his modest supper in the Base Room when he heard a faint but distinct 'click.' He thought it was perhaps the draught shaking the door and took little notice. When, a minute later, he proceeded to take his supper things to the pantry, he found that he *had been locked in!* What made the incident still more remarkable was the fact that—fortunately—the key was on the *inside* of the door. Had it been outside, he could have left the room only by means of the French window. Who—or what —locked the door? Whatever it was, it must have been in the Base Room while Kerr-Pearse was having his supper, and must have *remained* in the room after the door was locked. Unless it vanished through the walls. No entity of flesh and blood could have locked the Base Room on the *inside*, and remained, unseen, in the room. And the house was locked and sealed. Next day, a terrific crash was heard in the kitchen, as though a pile of pots and pans had been thrown down. But inspection proved that nothing had been disturbed. This same 'crashing' noise had been heard in the Rectory previously, by Herbert Mayes and others, and Edward Cooper recorded something similar when he was living in the Rectory cottage.

Another of our observers, Colonel F. C. Westland, had some curious adventures in the Rectory. He and Mrs. Westland found a round blue box, containing pins, which had *not* been noticed on a previous inspection. Later, it moved half an inch out of its chalked ring. No explanation. Still later, a piece of wood, origin unknown, 'appeared' on the stairs.

An interesting experiment with an electric bell contact-breaker was made by Dr. H. F. Bellamy. This apparatus was placed under a pile of books on the dining-room mantelpiece which is supported by the two strange sculptures, recalling the monastic site on which the Rectory stands. (See Plate IV.) Having carefully set the apparatus Dr. Bellamy and his friends patrolled the house, which was locked and sealed. At 12.50 a.m., while they were resting in the Blue Room, the bell started ringing. Before they could get to the dining-room, the bell had ceased. A curious sight met their eyes. All the books had been displaced, not one of them occupying its original position, and the bottom one was right off the contact-maker. At a later date, one of Dr. Bellamy's friends felt his hair ruffled, and another had his face touched by something. They were in the dark.

Several members of the British Broadcasting Corporation acted as observers at different times. Mr. de Lotbinière was the first to visit the house, and this was the occasion of one of my rare visits during my tenancy. A number of strange incidents happened. For example, as we were in the Blue Room, in the early hours of the morning, we heard a sharp click that appeared to come from the stairs. A few minutes later, Mr. de Lotbinière 'challenged' whatever it was and, before he had finished speaking, an answering crack was heard in the passage outside the Blue Room in which we were standing. We had previously heard rustling or 'scrabbling' noises coming from the Base Room.

Other members of the B.B.C. who visited the Rectory included Mr. W. S. Hammond and his friends. After sealing all doors, etc., they patrolled the Rectory at hourly intervals. Just before one of these patrols, they heard a door being closed somewhere in the building. An hour and a half later, they heard another door being gently closed. Still later, at 3.15 a.m. they heard a door being closed for the *third* time. All these incidents were investigated, without result.

The famous 'nun' put in one of her rare appearances when two members of the B.B.C., and their wives, visited Borley in February 1938. They took up their position in the large summer-house—so well known to my observers—and kept watch on the famous Nun's Walk on the far side of the lawn. The party consisted of Mr. and Mrs. C. Gordon Glover and Mr. and Mrs. Lloyd Williams.

They had been watching for about an hour when Mrs. Lloyd Williams 'distinctly saw a round, dark object,' like a short, stooping figure. The object appeared to move from a tree near the Rectory to half-way up the lawn, where it vanished. This view of the nun is comparable with what happened when Mr. V. C. Wall and I were watching from the same spot, nearly ten years previously.[1] Some little time before the vision of the nun, when the four observers were patrolling the house, a door was heard to close quietly somewhere in the building. 'It was a dead still afternoon, and all doors and windows were shut.'

[1] See page 38.

Later in the evening, when Mr. Glover and his wife were quietly standing in the doorway of the Chapel, they both heard a dull, heavy thud, followed by a short scuffle. The noises came from below stairs. Mr. Lloyd Williams and his wife were at the other end of the Chapel and heard 'nothing. Just past midnight on this same evening the whole party stationed themselves in the Blue Room and *all* heard the following sounds, which appeared to come from the kitchen quarters: Two heavy thuds, and a lighter thud; a kind of vague shuffling, 'giving an impression of general activity of some kind going on'; and a staccato and isolated crack like an electric light switch being snapped on.

Mr. M. Savage, a B.B.C. television engineer, paid two visits to the Rectory, accompanied by a friend on both occasions. During his first stay little happened except that some curious gluey substance suddenly appeared on the Chapel floor, and an extremely heavy knock occurred in the Base Room where he and his companion were resting.

On his second visit, Mr. Savage, like several other of our observers, was fortunate enough to be able to record the appearance of some of those strange wall pencillings. He and his friend made a *microscopic examination* of all the walls of the Blue Room. Every visible mark was carefully ringed. Suddenly, under their very eyes, a pencil mark appeared when they were actually gazing at the wall. They ringed it. Then *another* mark appeared, and they ringed that, too. Still *further* marks appeared, which they ringed. Then the 'appearances' ceased. But in Room 5 (the Blue Room dressing room), little drawings, like the 'Prince of Wales's feathers,' were found on the walls, after a previous very careful scrutiny. That ended their visit to this strange, 'enchanted' Rectory. Mr. Savage was the last B.B.C. official observer.

Psychical Research has always attracted members of the British universities, and at the time of writing the Perrott Studentship in Psychical Research has just been established by Trinity College, Cambridge. My own efforts to found a

Department of Psychical Research in the University of London and the sympathetic reception of the proposal by the academic authorities, are well known.[1]

It was not surprising, then, that a number of graduates and undergraduates were anxious to visit Borley for observational periods. Several of these gentlemen had interesting experiences which are detailed in Appendix C. The appearance of pencil markings was recorded by Mr. J. M. Bailey and Mr. C. V. Wintour, who thought they saw the letter 'M' grow in front of their eyes. Thinking it over afterwards, they decided it might have been an optical illusion. Which is not very surprising!

Four undergraduates from University College, Oxford, visited the Rectory in February 1938, and one of them, Mr. S. G. Welles, has recorded a phenomenon unique in the Borley annals. His long account of this incident is printed in full in Appendix C, but briefly a rectangular luminous patch, as of a lambent flame, moved slowly to and fro across the Blue Room ceiling while he was on duty there. It lasted about a minute. Numerous experiments to duplicate the phenomenon normally were afterwards made by the four men, and they utterly failed. Their report should be read in full. Later, just after midnight, the party heard footsteps in the kitchen, and a series of faint noises at regular short intervals. Other incidents which occurred that evening included the 'appearance' of a wooden lath, 42 inches long.

Mr. J. Burden and Mr. T. Stainton, two undergraduates of Christ Church, Oxford, visited Borley, and heard shuffling footsteps, swishing garments, faint whining or hooting, and a continuous wailing sound coming from the Blue Room— a sound so subtle and penetrating that it could be heard all over the house.

Do cats react to psychic influences? This question has been much debated and so Burden and Stainton thought they would try some experiments. Mr. Arbon loaned his cat for the purpose, and the animal, tempted with condensed

---

[1] See my *Fifty Years of Psychical Research*, London, 1939, pages 63-4.

milk, was gently led into the various fields of known psychic activity. The moonlight on the floor frightened her; she rubbed her back against the 'strange coat'[1] as if recognizing an old friend; and she seemed particularly interested in Room 7. The other rooms did not appear to affect her.

Soon after midnight (it is worth noting how many of the Borley phenomena occur at about this time—the traditional 'witching hour'), during Burden's watch, a noise was heard as if something were being dragged along the floor. The sounds lasted for two seconds, and were repeated at two-second intervals. The observers emphasize that the sounds were much too loud to admit of their having been mistaken. The sounds could not be accurately located, but they appeared to emanate from one of the first-floor passages. Later, fresh pencil marks were found.

Mr. Burden remained at Borley for twenty-four hours after his companion left for home and, while in the house by himself, found more new pencil marks. During his stay he 'had an uncanny sense of being watched in Room 2.'

Among the academic visitors to Borley was Dr. C. E. M. Joad who spent an observational period in the house. He was fortunate enough to witness the appearance of new wall pencillings under good conditions. His complete report should be read.

Odours, paranormally made manifest (I do not suggest that the odours themselves were paranormal) were not of frequent occurrence at Borley. But certain observers recorded such phenomena. For example, Mr. and Mrs. Foyster speak of a pleasant scent, suggestive of lavender, while Mr. Hammond mentions an unpleasant odour, 'suggestive of the lavatory.' But the most remarkable smell was, I think, the one recorded by the two flying officers, E. Carter Jonas and Caunter. On their last visit to the house they noticed an 'overpowering smell of incense.' This was the more remarkable as the Rectory was then permanently shut up, my tenancy of the place having expired eight

[1] See page 111.

months previously. They visited the place on the spur of the moment, unannounced.

Speaking of remarkable phenomena, the one recorded by Mrs. F. A. Mansbridge is almost the strangest. She had the belt of her coat lifted and dropped again by an unseen hand. The movement was quite definite.

One of the most interesting experiences was that of Mr. A. P. Drinkwater and three friends who spent a night at the Rectory in November 1937. They took extraordinary pains to close the house against any outside invasion, and very carefully examined and sealed or re-sealed all doors and windows, and checked all control objects in their ringed positions. It was a fine night, and there was no wind. The party divided themselves into two pairs, each couple taking up a different station.

Five minutes after they had taken up their respective positions, the observers in the Base Room heard two distinct percussive knocks from the room above—that is, the Blue Room. Two hours later, on their next patrol, they found that the mysterious round box in the cupboard, originally discovered by Colonel Westland, *had moved one inch* to the left of its chalked ring. They ringed it in its new position.

In the early hours of the morning, while they were resting in the Base Room, they heard a heavy thump overhead in the Blue Room. They were dozing and the noise was loud enough to awaken them to full consciousness. It was thought that the thump was the last of several heavy steps across the floor of the room above.

At 4 a.m. many new pencil marks were discovered and the party used up all their chalk in ringing them! On their next inspection patrol, they found that the blue box had *again moved*. Two paranormal displacements in one night! Later, more pencillings were found. At 8 a.m. still more wall-marks were discovered. They then went over the entire house, checked all seals, found that they were undisturbed, and left for London.

In Appendix C will also be found Mr. Henning's letter

describing how the strange light was again noticed in the
window of the Rectory while the place was unoccupied.
It was seen by four people, including Mr. Henning's man-
servant, Herbert Mayes, who also describes his own adventures in the house. These included many strange noises and
the familiar 'crash' of crockery or saucepans, a phenomenon
experienced by Mr. and Mrs. Foyster, Mr. and Mrs.
Edward Cooper, and Kerr-Pearse. How a clergyman heard
'furniture being thrown about' in the Rectory is also
described in Appendix C which, I reiterate, *should be read in
full.*

I think it will here be appropriate for me to say a few
words about the *evidential value* of our observers' reports, and
the methods of precision employed in investigating the
phenomena.

What *is* evidence? The word (from the Latin *evidentia,
evideri*, 'to appear clearly') has been defined as 'denoting
the facts presented to the mind of a person for the purpose
of enabling him to decide a disputed question.' Evidence
includes all such facts. Evidence has also been defined as
'the testimony of others touching their observation and
experience.' And, as St. George Jackson Mivart, the
biologist, remarks in *Nature and Thought*,[1] 'evidence is and
must be the test of truth, and is, I suppose, the ultimate
ground on which we believe anything.'

I submit that our forty-eight official observers and their
friends have furnished such evidence (as is defined in the
above explanations of the term) for paranormal happenings
in Borley Rectory. As regards the evidence itself, both in
quantity and quality it is far superior to any testimony ever
previously submitted in support of alleged supranormal
phenomena. That is partly why the Borley case is unique
in the annals of psychical research.

The evidence submitted by our witnesses for the haunting
of Borley Rectory would be acceptable in a court of law in

[1] London, 1882, p. 133.

K

consideration of their number, their integrity, their unemo-
tionalism, their disinterestedness, and their skill. And
especially it is this disinterestedness that makes their testimony more valuable—in a legal sense—than those observers
(including myself) who, without being the least aware of
the fact, must be subconsciously *ex parte* to a greater or lesser
extent. All those who have resided in the Rectory, or who
have been intimately connected with the place, were quickly
convinced of the abnormality of certain incidents that came
under their notice. A recurrence of these phenomena would
increase their belief in the certainty that the place was
haunted; and the psychologists would insist that their later
experiences might be coloured by their earlier convictions.
I reiterate that this same argument can be applied to myself,
as I have been connected with the investigation for ten years.
That was the main reason why I decided to eliminate myself
as far as possible from the official inquiry.

But with the official observers it was different. They were
strangers to me; they were strangers to the Rectory and all
of its occupants; they were strangers to psychical research,
and they had never heard of the Borley mystery. And they
were sceptical. Some of our witnesses were even sceptical
as to the *possibility* of such phenomena happening. And they
had no *a priori* convictions.

Another advantage our observers possessed was that they
were able to bring fresh minds and fresh methods to bear
on the mystery. And as each investigator or group used a
different method of investigation—at any rate in detail—the
cumulative effect of this varied and independent testimony
is of immense evidential value.

A still further advantage our witnesses had over the non-
official observers was that the former were able to view the
phenomena under conditions of *control* not possible with
residents and others connected with the house. Of course,
that is why they were enrolled. The systematic and scientific
methods employed by the visitors could not easily have
been applied by any of the Rectors or their households. Nor

could these gentlemen have expended the time and care
necessary in preparing those exact protocols that are so vital
when dealing with the so-called 'supernatural.' But our
own observers' reports are merely complementary to the
extremely valuable evidence supplied by the Rectory residents and others.   In fact, without this firm basis of what
I will call the 'local testimony,' no outside or independent
investigation would have been possible.

The phenomena our observers were able to confirm
included footsteps and similar sounds; raps, taps and
knockings; displacement of objects; 'clicks' and 'cracks';
sounds as of door closing; knocks, bumps, thuds, jumping or
stamping; dragging noise; wailing sounds; rustling or
scrabbling noises; 'metallic' sounds; crashing, as of crockery
falling; wall-pencillings; 'appearance' of objects; luminous
phenomenon; odours, pleasant and unpleasant; sensation
of coldness; tactual phenomena; sensation of a 'presence';
and a fulfilled prediction.   One observer says she saw the
'nun.' The complete list of those who experienced the above
phenomena is printed as Appendix D.

CHAPTER XXI

MRS. WILSON'S EXTRAORDINARY INSECT

AS the dispassionate chronicler of the Borley drama, romance, or mystery—call it what we will—it is my duty to record any unusual incident that has been reported to me by a responsible person. And certainly one of the most 'unusual'—if I can use such a mild term in this connection—stories in the Borley *dossier* is that concerning the strange 'insect' that much alarmed a well-known artist.

Early in August 1938 I was rung up on the telephone by a lady. She had read about Borley Rectory, and approached me for permission to visit the place as she wished to paint a picture of the house. She said her name was Mrs. Margaret E. Wilson. Though I had never met the lady, or corresponded with her, I knew Mrs. Wilson by repute as a painter and exhibitor. She said she had no interest in Borley from the 'psychic' point of view. She was not a spiritualist; she knew nothing about psychical research or 'ghosts,' and her concern with the Rectory was purely artistic and æsthetic. She was interested in painting old and picturesque houses, and she was certain that Borley Rectory *must* be old *and* picturesque.

I pointed out to Mrs. Wilson, as gently as I could, that Borley Rectory was *not* old; that it was ugly; that it reminded me of the red bricks of suburbia, and that it was as much unlike the typical old country rectory, as chalk is to cheese. Mrs. Wilson was disappointed, but still asked for permission to paint the place as a documentary contribution to the history of the Rectory, which I told her I was preparing.

I informed Mrs. Wilson that, as far as I was concerned, she could paint the house, but that she would have to get permission from the Rev. A. C. Henning, as my tenancy of the Rectory was ended, and my authority had ceased. I gave her Mr. Henning's address. She duly wrote to this gentleman, obtained the necessary sanction, and eventually painted the Rectory. In the light of after events, it was very fortunate she did this, as her oil painting of 'the most haunted house' cleverly and faithfully executed, is the only coloured picture of the Rectory extant. It is now preserved with the Borley records.

Armed with Mr. Henning's authority, she visited Borley on August 22, 1938. She arrived at Sudbury just before midday and at once proceeded to the Rectory. She had no occasion to enter the house—as she was *not* interested in the phenomenal happenings there—so she did not apply for the keys. She made straight for the garden, had a good look at the exterior of the house from every angle, and decided to paint the back—which is really the front—of the building, the only elevation really worth painting. She took up her position on the lawn, under one of the large Cedars of Lebanon, near the summer-house (see Plate I), opposite the Nun's Walk. She erected her easel, unfolded her camp-stool, and began to work. No one was about on this hot August morning; the place was deadly quiet; and she thought she could work in peace, undisturbed.

In her subsequent report Mrs. Wilson stated that: 'As the hours passed and I was quite alone, the forbidding silence seemed to envelop everything with apprehension and I felt conscious of time and invisible watchers near me and around me. A neglected garden can present a cheerful appearance, but here one feels the very weeds do not wish to flourish—or cannot—and lack the joy which most growing plants have. Or so it appeared to me in the Rectory grounds.' The reader may think that these sombre thoughts were due to auto-suggestion, as of course she knew a little of the history of the place. But as I got to know Mrs. Wilson better, I found her particularly unemotional and, if I may say so, a very hard-headed business woman, in addition to being an artist.

She sat there painting the Rectory when she was disturbed in a very curious manner. I will quote from her report:

'While I was painting, and about 3 o'clock in the afternoon, I suddenly noticed a sound, such as of approaching wings or rushing wind coming towards me. Looking up, I saw the queerest object with impelling eyes advancing towards me at about eye level. It seemed to be coming out of a mist. It was accompanied by a wasp on its left, and this must have been the wings I heard. I had just time to jump up and as they were quite near my face, which seemed to be the objective, I struck at it with my mahlstick, and seemed to hit the big object into the grass. The wasp seemed to go off on its own. With alarm I searched for the nameless object I had struck, as if I had not killed it, I thought it was possible it might attack me. I searched, but was unable to trace it and eventually gave up looking. Gradually, the unusualness of the creature dawned upon me and the more I thought of it, the less I could understand what it was.

'Certainly, I had never seen anything like it before, and should describe it as being quite three inches in length, the body entirely black and composed of sections enabling it to bend and expand with ease. Its eyes were large and the colour of bloomy black grapes. The object was flattish. It was so real, that in jumping up, I had no time to put my palette down, and this resulted in upsetting medium on my skirt and ruining it. I had grasped the palette in my left hand.

'As time elapsed I gathered myself together, mentally realizing that I had to catch a train and that it was useless to go on thinking as every moment was precious if I hoped to obtain what I was down here for—that is, to paint the Rectory—and I worked with renewed speed to recover lost time.'

When Mrs. Wilson arrived home, she at once painted the strange, articulated creature with large goggle eyes, while its appearance was still fresh in her memory. Later, Mrs. Wilson asked her friend, Miss Joyce Mercer, to re-draw the creature in black and white, more suitable for reproduction. This is printed on page 135.

No wonder Mrs. Wilson was startled! I have shown her sketch to several naturalists and entomologists and they all declare that it is like 'nothing on earth'! Mrs. Wilson's testimony is valuable because she happens to be well

IMPRESSION OF THE 'STRANGE INSECT,' WITH 'LARGE GOGGLE EYES,' SEEN BY MRS. MARGARET E. WILSON IN THE GARDEN OF BORLEY RECTORY. DRAWN BY MISS JOYCE MERCER FROM A SKETCH BY MRS. WILSON, MADE A FEW HOURS AFTER THE INCIDENT.

acquainted with insects. She is well known for her studies of insects and still life, and spends much of her time out of doors, painting such things. 'Impossible' as this insect appeared, it is just one of the many 'impossible' things that have happened in this 'enchanted' Rectory.

Above left : The Hall.   PLATE V
Above right : The Kitchen passage and back stairs from the Dining-room.
Below left : Kitchen passage from the Kitchen.
Below right : The Bathroom passage from Room 5.

CHAPTER XXII

WHAT THE MEDIUMS SAID

MANY mediums, amateur and professional, tried their hardest to solve the Borley mystery. In home and public spiritualist circles the 'spirits' were asked to give *their* version of the Rectory phenomena. Very few of their 'answers' have reached me, but I have records of a few séances at which the Borley manifestations were discussed.

On Sunday, June 16, 1929, Mr. C. Glover Botham and Mr. Harry Collard, two London mediums, held a séance in the Rectory without result. They sat by lamplight, and also in darkness, but the 'spirits' were silent. Later, as we have seen from the Rev. L. A. Foyster's diary,[1] the Marks Tey spiritualist circle held some meetings in the Rectory, and claimed to have quietened the entities—at least for a time.

But an interesting—if not very successful—attempt to throw light on the previous history of the Rectory was made by 'Marion' (*i.e.*, Josef Kraus) the well-known vaudeville telepathist, hyperæsthete, and psychometrist. As a hyperæsthete, Marion has been brilliantly successful. Mr. S. G. Soal and I conducted many experiments with excellent results.[2]

When Kerr-Pearse discovered the touchwood 'apport,'[3] on July 18, 1937, he sent a portion of it to me. I happened to show it to Mr. S. H. Glanville, who made the suggestion that Marion should be allowed to psychometrize it. An appointment was accordingly made with Marion, Mr.

---

[1] Page 82.
[2] See *Preliminary Studies of a Vaudeville Telepathist*, by S. G. Soal, London 1937. (*Bulletin III*, University of London Council for Psychical Investigation.)
[3] See page 206.

Glanville conducting the inquiry. I was not present. The séance was held on November 9, 1938. It is important to note that Marion had never met Mr. Glanville; knew nothing of the history of the Rectory except what he might have seen in the papers; did not know that Glanville was in any way connected with me or the Rectory; and, when handed the piece of rotten wood, did *not* know that it had any connection with Borley. Mr. Glanville did not speak during the first part of the séance. This is what Marion said:

'It does not come from one place, but went through many places: it goes rather far. It does not start in this country at all; it has been brought from another continent and later wandered about. It went to different places. I do not know which place to say at the outset, or how to describe the sort of country. It is a place rather on its own without any surrounding. It is a sort of old-fashioned building with small buildings adjoining. A small island. The people who live here are coming and going. There is no peace or rest. There is a sort of feud or quarrel between two families—two sorts of ideas. They are not enemies, but have a quarrel between each other, not for something but for ideas or ideals. . . . Their lives did not touch.

'One of the last owners was a very tall man, he is dead. He was a public man who played a big part in public life. . . . He worked to a certain point and became very disappointed— died a lonely man and not appreciated. They tried to blame him for many things and, during the last few years of his life, he became very queer. He was disappointed with life and his work.'

At this point, Mr. Glanville gave Marion some general information concerning the Rectory and its history. Marion remarked that 'the building was connected with a church— a general association with a church. But people in the church were enemies to him.'

I have not reproduced all that Marion said, as a great deal of it was very wide of the mark. But there was more than a germ of truth in some of his utterances. Unfortunately, as there are many people living who might object to my elucidation of Marion's remarks, I must refrain.

Like a bolt from the blue, a Major G. Huth, a man I do not know, wrote me from Breslau, Germany, to the effect that he had been having sittings with an 'apport' medium named Frau Sadler. In his letter he said that this woman had been getting 'apports' purporting to come from Borley Rectory! He asked for a photograph of the Rectory, as that might 'help' the medium. I sent him a small picture.

In reply, Major Huth wrote (November 1, 1938): 'Thanks for the photograph of the Rectory. Frau Sadler has already got in touch with the entities causing the disturbances in the place. Their number is 14 at the present stage (13 men and a spectacled woman), but their number seems to be increasing, as it is rather a complicated affair. It takes a little time. But you can assure the owner that there will be no further disturbance in the place as soon as the cause of the disturbance has been removed from the house.'

In a second letter, dated January 2, 1939, Major Huth said: 'You would do me a great favour to write and tell me whether a book *Praise and Principle*, by McIntosh (London: George Routledge & Sons) belongs to the library in the Rectory. It has a grey mottled cover.'

I did not recognize the book, of which I had never heard. It was *not* one of the books I placed in Borley library—none of which was missing. I suggest that Frau Sadler had been reading accounts of the Rectory in the German papers, and claimed that one of her literary 'apports' had come from that place.

I am afraid that the professional mediums threw little light on the Borley drama. Mr. Glanville, his family, and friends were much more successful—or at least more entertaining—in their amateur table-tipping séances and Planchette writing, accounts of which are printed in Chapters XXV, XXVI, and XXVII.

CHAPTER XXIII

'MOVING DAY'—AND A GOLDEN APPORT

M Y tenancy of Borley Rectory expired on May 19, 1938. On May 9, 1938, I visited Borley officially for the last time as tenant and handed over the keys of the Rectory to Mr. Henning.

On this day Mr. Geoffrey H. Motion—a neighbour of mine—and I travelled down by car, arriving at the Rectory about four o'clock in the afternoon. We went in his car, because it is a particularly large and roomy one and I wanted to collect my belongings that I had installed at the Rectory, tidy up the place, and so on. It was my first visit for many weeks.

After a walk round the garden, examining all the old familiar spots such as the summer-houses, Nun's Walk, the cats' cemetery, and the pond, we entered the Rectory and inspected the place from top to bottom. We entered every room, peered—with our torches—into all the cupboards. Noted that most of the portable objects—but not all—were ringed in their familiar places, and scrutinized the walls. We were sorry for the person who was to rent the Rectory after me. The walls were simply covered with multi-coloured chalk rings and squares, enclosing the large and small pencillings, and we wondered how much it would cost to re-distemper them. Most of the marks had, in addition to their control rings, the date of finding, and the initials of the finders.

We checked up all the Marianne 'messages,' found there were no additions, and then climbed to the attics. Everything was in order, and the place was as dusty as ever. We then once more descended into the habitable portions of the house, again visited each room, and collected most of the odds and ends that various observers had left—and ringed —there in order to tempt the 'entities.'

By the time we had reached the ground floor again, we had an armful of oddments which we placed in the Base Room. After some tea and sandwiches in the Base Room, and a rest, we made another tour of the house, again examining all rooms, cupboards, walls *and floors*. For example, our scrutiny was so complete that on the floor of the Blue Room we found a solitary wooden match-stick that someone had very carefully enclosed in its appropriate chalked rectangle. Then we journeyed to the cellar and examined it. There were the same old empty bottles and other rubbish, but no live things. The frogs, toads, and lizards had disappeared. The reason for this was, I think, that during the repairs to the house, that had recently been carried out, the cellar had received some attention from the workmen and they, probably, had temporarily frightened the animals away. I looked in the well, and that, too, was devoid of livestock. We left the cellar, locking the door behind us. It was then about 6.30 p.m. We then went to Sudbury for some dinner, after very carefully locking the place up. We returned to the Rectory about 7.30, found everything normal and called at the cottage to see Arbon, whom we heard pumping in the courtyard (the same pump supplied both the Rectory and his cottage) and gave him a bottle of beer. We heard the latest news of the village, and learned that determined efforts were being made to sell the Rectory.

At 8 p.m. we again made a complete tour of the house in order to see whether anything had happened while we were at dinner. Everything was as we had left it. We then checked every seal and locked all doors, except the front one.

Then we began packing up our belongings into Mr. Motion's car. The camp-bed, china, cutlery, books, stove, coffee percolator, and the many odds and ends that had accumulated were all finally stowed away and we returned to the Base Room to have another rest. It was now getting dark, especially in the Rectory. We had refrained from packing the paraffin lamp in the car as we intended staying at the house until the early morning, and in any case I had told Arbon that he could have it as a 'souvenir' of our year's investigation.

At ten o'clock, we made another tour of the house: all was quiet and normal.

At midnight, or a few minutes before, we made another tour of the house. I had the paraffin lamp in my hand, Mr. Motion carried his powerful pocket torch. As we entered the door of the Blue Room, our lights lit up something on the far side of the room, in the opening between the Blue Room and the dressing-room (Room 5) adjoining. Both Motion and I simultaneously saw the glint as we entered the room. Motion ran across the room and picked it up: *it was a lady's 22-carat gold wedding-ring.*

We had entered both Blue Room and dressing-room several times during the evening, and it is *unthinkable* that we should not have seen it or trodden on it. It will be remembered that we found a solitary match-stick on the Blue Room floor, so good was our search. So where did the ring come from?

Upon our return to London early next day—or rather the same day—I made inquiries about the ring and found it was an ordinary wedding-ring, not very much worn and made—according to the hall-mark—at Birmingham in 1864—the year after the Rectory was first occupied. Another strange coincidence! I could have found the name of the maker of the ring, but as he must have turned out thousands bearing the same mark, I thought it useless to trouble myself in the matter. In any case, the maker himself must be dead. It was—and is—if it has not disappeared from my desk drawer!—just an ordinary wedding-ring.

I not only made inquiries about the ring, but I asked our observers whether they had lost such an article of jewellery. I had heard of no such loss, and it is unlikely that a woman, after losing her wedding-ring, would not make some inquiries about it. She would be very concerned. And very few women had visited the Rectory, and it is unlikely that any of our visitors would have worn such an old ring. But I could find no one who had lost a ring, and heard nothing further about it, in spite of some trouble I took in the matter.

But was that the *first* time that this same ring had been found in the Rectory? If the reader will glance at Mr. Foyster's diary,[1] he will find that on March 10, 1931, 'a wedding-ring was discovered in the bathroom.' *The ring disappeared the following morning* (March 11, 1931) and was never seen again. Is it possible that the ring that was picked up by Mr. Motion was the *same* ring that Mr. Foyster discovered? I am afraid that there is now no means of finding out. One gold wedding-ring looks very like another and it is very difficult to identify any particular specimen. I should add that I knew nothing of Mr. Foyster finding a ring until I read the selected extracts from his voluminous diary which he sent me seven years later. Of course, it is possible that the ring found its way into the Blue Room in a perfectly normal manner.

Mr. Motion and I made another minute search for other 'apports,' and found none. Actually, the house seemed deadly still and quiet during my last night there. No noises, no pencilled 'squiggles'—as Dr. Joad calls them—no footsteps or banging of doors, no strange smells. The night was particularly peaceful. Motion and I left Borley soon after 4 a.m., arriving in London at about six o'clock. I little thought that my next visit to the Rectory would be to clamber over, at some risk to my personal safety, the blackened and crumbling rafters of what once supported the Blue Room, where we found our golden 'apport,' and the passages where the 'Marianne' messages so mysteriously appeared. It is now time for me to say something about the messages themselves.

[1] See page 78 of this work.

CHAPTER XXIV

THE 'MARIANNE' MESSAGES

ONE of the most striking—if not *the* most striking—aspects of the haunting of Borley Rectory is the writing on the walls. I think I am right in saying that this phenomenon is unique in the annals of psychical research.

Of course, 'spirit writing'—real or alleged—is well known. At séances, I have received written 'messages' on slates or papers, purporting to have been written by spirit entities. I think it can safely be assumed that all these writings were produced by the mediums concerned. The slate messages undoubtedly were. And this form of 'manifestation' is no longer fashionable—at least in this country. But the very curious pencil markings that so many observers have recorded at Borley over a period of years are in a class by themselves and are one of the major puzzles connected with this extraordinary case.

It is a fact that no *messages* appeared after the Rev. and Mrs. Foyster left the Rectory. Those cryptic and rather pathetic appeals that successive observers discovered on the walls all 'appeared' during their occupation of the house. Mr. Foyster, in his diary (Chapter XIII of this monograph), under date May 1931, mentions that messages were appearing on pieces of paper, found lying about the house, though one piece, bearing the word 'Marianne,' was seen fluttering in the air and was caught by Mrs. Foyster. 'Marianne' is, of course, Mrs. Foyster's Christian name. The messages seemed to be appeals directed to her, and to no one else. That may have been because she was young and sympathetic, and most likely to help—whoever wanted help.

Those markings that *did* appear after the Foysters left

were apparently meaningless. They have been described as 'jabs,' scribbles, 'squiggles,' etc. Occasionally, the markings appeared to be in the form of the letter 'M.' All the messages had a Roman Catholic flavour. There were references to 'Mass,' prayers, lights, and so on. This suggestion of the Roman Church is compatible with the early tradition of a Benedictine monastery on the site of the present Rectory, and fits in with the legend of the nun and the lay brothers. It also fits in with the fact that the services at Borley Church have, at least during recent years, been 'high.' I will now describe the 'messages' themselves. I will take the ground floor first, and will number the writings as they appear on the Ground Floor Plan (see Page 16). I will first take message No. 4, which reads:

'MARIANNE LIGHT MASS PRAYERS.'

This message (see Plate VI) was on the wall of the kitchen passage, opposite the Sewing-Room. It was 4 feet, 4 inches from the ground.

The second writing was merely the letters 'Ma' (reproduced herewith):

and was found also in the kitchen passage, under the barred window opposite cellar stairs. The word suggests that it was merely the *beginning* of a message, or at least the beginning of the word 'Marianne.' Perhaps the writer was disturbed when about to produce the complete word. It was 2 feet 6 inches from the floor, very scrawly, and looks as if the entity were left-handed.

We will now mount to the upper storey of the Rectory, where the messages were more numerous and more interesting. The first writing, 'Marianne' (marked No. 1 on First Floor Plan) was found on the wall by the stairs leading to the bathroom passage. It was $4\frac{1}{2}$ inches in length, and 4 feet 6 inches from the floor. It is reproduced in Plate VI.

L

The next message we found was on the outside wall of the bathroom (it is marked No. 2 on Plan) and reads:

'MARIANNE PLEASE HELP GET.'

I have reproduced it photographically in Plate VI. Its height was 4 feet 3 inches from the ground, and the length of the message was $3\frac{3}{8}$ inches, its total depth being $1\frac{3}{4}$ inches.

No. 3 message (see Plan) was the longest of them all and read:

'MARIANNE AT GET HELP
—ENTANT BOTTOM ME.'

It was discovered on the outside wall of the bathroom, near the door, 4 feet 7 inches from the ground. (See Plate VI.) It is partly meaningless, and one word suggests 'repentant.' Underneath the message is printed in capitals 'I cannot understand, tell me more.' These words were written by Mrs. Foyster, hoping that a second 'message' would elucidate the first. An answer eventually appeared. Mrs. Foyster has signed her request 'Marianne.'

The answering message (Plate VI) that appeared at some period—not stated—was written *under* the first 'appeal' and Mrs. Foyster's request. It was almost undecipherable, but the following words or letters can be made out:

'LIGHT IN **** WRITE PRAYER AND O ****.'

Underneath this 'message' Mr. Kerr-Pearse—emulating Mrs. Foyster—wrote in capitals 'I still cannot understand. Please tell me more.' There was *no* answer to his request.

No. 6 marking on First Floor Plan is the solitary word 'Edwin,' one inch long, reproduced herewith:

It was found on the exterior wall of the bathroom near the staircase to the attics. 'Edwin,' by the way, was a friend of the Foysters.

The last, and one of the most interesting messages, was

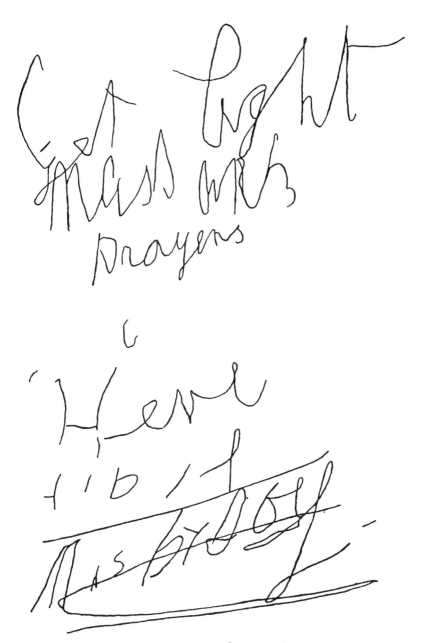

TRACING OF A PENCILLED WALL 'MESSAGE' THAT APPEARED
NEAR THE BLUE ROOM DURING THE PRESENCE OF MRS.
FOYSTER AND DOM RICHARD WHITEHOUSE, O.S.B., JUNE
16, 1931.

found on the landing archway near the Chapel, 4 feet 8 inches from the floor. It appeared during the presence of Dom Richard Whitehouse and Mrs. Foyster.[1] It is marked No. 7 on Plan. It read:

'GET LIGHT MASS AND PRAYERS HERE.'

Underneath were some—apparently—meaningless letters or symbols. The writing was too faint to photograph satisfactorily for purposes of reproduction as a half-tone block, so it was very carefully traced, and is illustrated on page 147 in facsimile.

I have now described and illustrated the principal messages and markings, but there were many more than are mentioned above. For example, there was a large inverted 'M' on the foot of attic stairs; a 'W' (or inverted 'M') on the wall of Room No. 2, 3 feet 10 inches from floor; a similar marking, 2 feet 3 inches from floor, on the wall outside Sewing-Room; another 'lower-case' 'm' (below) on passage wall near kitchen, 2 feet 6 inches from floor; the letters

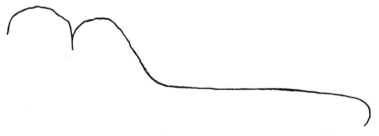

'Ma,' 5 feet 1 inch from floor, on wall opposite Sewing-Room; a spiral, 2 feet 6 inches from floor, on wall outside scullery; a similar mark, 4 feet 4 inches from floor, on the wall of back staircase; and a letter like a 'G', 4 feet 2 inches from floor, also by back staircase. In addition, there were literally hundreds of marks, mostly small, scattered all over the rooms and passages. Some of these have been described by our observers. Mr. S. H. Glanville, Colonel Westland, and Mr. Kerr-Pearse spent an enormous amount of time

[1] See page 94.

and trouble in photographing, tracing, and recording the Borley pencil markings.

The markings were made undoubtedly with some substance that cannot be distinguished from the ordinary 'lead' (*i.e.*, graphite) used in a lead pencil. I took samples of the markings and, under the microscope, compared them with powdered graphite from an ordinary pencil. I could see no difference between the samples. Some of the markings are fine and some are coarse, and apparently both hard and soft leads have been used. The grains were quite distinct under the microscope.

Certain of the detached letters appear to have been made by a left-handed person; or, more probably, by a right-handed person using his left hand. The suggestion has been made that a child did them. With the exception, perhaps, of some of the jabs and 'squiggles,' I am certain that this was not the case. Those 'Marianne-get-Mass-prayer-light' concepts never originated in the brain of a child.

And the height of the writings from the floor, mostly from about 5 feet to 4 feet 2 inches, precludes any possibility of a child having done them, unless a chair was used—which is most unlikely. The one or two markings (mostly the letter 'M') that appeared about two feet or so above the floor, *might* have been done by a child.

A man, 5 feet 11 inches in height, when normally writing on a wall, and if standing, uses his pencil at a height of 5 feet $2\frac{1}{2}$ inches from the ground, a little below eye level. Only one marking, the letters 'Ma,' was found above the five-foot limit. The remainder of the wordings were at a height of from 4 feet 2 inches to 4 feet 8 inches from the floor. Taking the average, I consider that they were made by a person about 5 feet 2 inches or 3 inches in height.

But I am sure that all the 'messages' were not written by the same hand. I have shown the photographs of the writings to several people (including a bank manager) whose duty it is to study hand-writings on documents, and they all agree that at least two 'entities' were operating. Some of the scribbles (from 2 feet 3 inches to 2 feet 6 inches) might have been produced by a child.

The mechanics and construction of the messages suggest a foreign origin. The appeal 'Marianne please help get' is the phrasing of a person who does not properly understand the English language. I should probably make the same blunders if I were trying to write a similar message in, say, Italian. I think it is some proof of the authenticity of the messages, and additional evidence for the theory that they were written by a foreigner. But the calligraphy is entirely British and entirely modern. It is all very complicated!

Mr. S. J. de Lotbinière, in the report of his second visit to the Rectory on December 14, 1937, mentions that he found a number of small marks 'evidently made by someone measuring up the walls, probably for some such purpose as redecoration.' I quite agree. These marks were in straight lines, rather like those on a graduated measure, and have not been taken into account in this monograph. But similar marks—hundreds of them—are peppered all over the walls, and they vary in length from one millimetre to several inches.

It can hardly be doubted that some of the marks, especially the smaller ones, appeared paranormally. Many observers have testified to this effect. For example, Mr. Kerr-Pearse, at 7.25 p.m. on July 13, 1937, 'examined every inch' of a certain wall. At 8.30 p.m.—*i.e.*, an hour later—he found two small marks which were *not* there before. Many other marks appeared while he was there. On July 18, 1937, during another visit, six marks appeared in the Chapel after he had 'examined it very closely.' Mr. M. Savage, of the B.B.C. on May 7, 1938, found a new pencilling in the Blue Room. He says: 'We are as definite as one can be that it was not there on any of our previous inspections.' A moment later, *another* mark appeared four inches below the first one. Then other marks appeared! Another B.B.C. official, Mr. C. Gordon Glover, also found a new mark while he and his friends were in the house.

Mr. Glanville and his friends, on August 14, 1937,

photographed one of the 'Marianne' messages. Although the house was locked and sealed, *another* mark appeared by the side of the message an hour or so later. The message was again photographed, and the new mark can be seen in one photograph, but *not* in the other. If this is not evidence for a paranormal pencil mark, I do not know what is. Many other marks were discovered in the same way.

Mr. Drinkwater found so many new marks that his chalk was used up before he could ring them all! This was on December 14, 1937. During the visit of Mr. Bailey and Mr. Wintour in July 1937, 'three circles' appeared behind a door at 11.23 a.m. after a thorough inspection of the wall. 'We are both certain that they were not there at 11.15 a.m.' Then a new 'M' appeared and they 'thought they saw it grow under their eyes.' Dr. Joad, after examining the walls, 'found another pencil squiggle' which it was 'inconceivable' that he and his friend could have missed on their previous inspection. I could go on multiplying such examples, but the reader will find many similar ones scattered throughout this monograph. And, as we know, a complete 'message' appeared within a few yards of Mrs. Foyster and Dom Richard Whitehouse, in answer to their Novena.

Both Dr. C. E. M. Joad and Mr. Elliot Smith raise the question as to whether a ghost, a discarnate spirit, or a 'psychic factor' can sharpen a lead pencil. But surely, using a lead pencil—even using it intelligently—is not a more wonderful phenomenon than Kerr-Pearse being locked in the Base Room while he was having his supper; or the lifting up of Mrs. Mansbridge's coat belt; or the filling of the room with incense for Flight-Lieutenant Jonas's delectation. If a ghost can, in true *Poltergeist* fashion, pick up a glass candlestick and hurl it down the well of the stairs—and I saw this at Borley with my own eyes—then it can pick up a lead-pencil and use it. Mr. Elliot Smith says: 'Where does it get the material lead?' Well, lead pencils are plentiful, and a *Poltergeist* would not have to go far in order to find one. I do not suggest that—assuming these markings are paranormal—the *Geist* would resharpen the pencil it was using. It would probably find another pencil! There was evidence that more than one pencil was used in the scribblings.

I agree with Dr. Joad that the idea of a *Poltergeist* 'apporting' a pencil from somewhere and then materializing fingers with which to use it, is 'incredible.' But *everything* is incredible connected with Borley Rectory. My task has been to collect and present the evidence—of which there is more than ample—for paranormal pencillings. And I do not think that this evidence can be shaken. If the whole thing had been a hoax from beginning to end, and if a number of silly people had set out to fool us—and themselves—I think these practical jokers would not have been content to make mere lines, dots, and half-formed letters on the walls. I think they could not have resisted the temptation of writing more messages, amusing or facetious. The fact that only scrawly marks or lines appeared goes far, I think, to prove their genuineness.

PLATE VI

The pencilled wall "appeals" to
Marianne. The block letters in
bottom specimen were written by
Mrs. Foyster and Kerr-Pearse
respectively (see text).

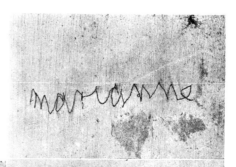

CHAPTER XXV

'TRY THE SPIRITS'

MR. S. H. GLANVILLE is neither a spiritualist nor a 'believer.' He knows nothing about spiritualism and, until he joined our official observers, took only an academic interest in psychical research. His son, Mr. R. H. Glanville, is likewise a sceptic, though he—like his father—has become convinced, through personal experience, of the paranormal happenings at Borley Rectory.

As the Rectory was supposed to be full of spirits, Mr. Glanville thought that he would like to 'try them.' Incidentally, he is a collateral descendant of the famous Joseph Glanvill (of the 'Drummer of Tedworth' fame), so perhaps his interest in *Poltergeister* and the occult generally is slightly inherited. Anyway, he thought he would organize a few séances in the Rectory, which he did, with very curious results. His records—or protocols—are at least much more interesting—if no more veridical—than those of the professional mediums who also tried their hand at 'trying the spirits.'

Mr. Glanville was sufficiently acquainted with séance technique to know that for table-tipping or table-talking, a table was the first requisite. So he built one specially—a very light affair weighing two or three pounds. He took it to Borley.

He was unable to be present at the first séances, but his son Roger, Mr. A. J. Cuthbert, and Mr. Kerr-Pearse started the ball rolling as it were, and the extracts from the records that form this chapter are taken verbatim from the excellent bound record-book of everything that took place at the Rectory during Mr. Glanville's investigations at the place.

The following informative extracts were obtained at a number of séances held at the Rectory between October 23 and 25, 1937. A great deal of the information dealt with private matters connected with past Rectors and their living friends. For obvious reasons, these intimate 'revelations' have not been included. The séances were held in various parts of the house: passages, kitchen, Base Room, etc.

At the first séance on October 23, 1937, the table 'felt alive' immediately they started, and within two minutes was rocking backwards and forwards. During the sitting 'we all experienced an ice-cold draught which was generally most noticeable when the table was rocking violently. A. J. Cuthbert noticed an icy draught behind his ears and Kerr-Pearse got the impression that there was a presence behind Cuthbert's right shoulder. R. H. Glanville had the feeling that we were being watched.' The code used was: one rock of the table for 'No'; two for 'Uncertain'; and three for 'Yes.' When a word was to be spelled out the table started rocking and the sitters went through the alphabet in time with it, the table stopping at the letter to be indicated. Almost without exception they went through the complete alphabet once before arriving at the letter wanted, and on some occasions, twice. This made the spelling of words a slow and laborious procedure, as they found it was necessary to check up continually. At times the rocking was slow and deliberate and, at others, so fast that it was almost impossible to keep pace with it. The table stood 2 feet 2 inches high, and was 12 inches square.

Here are some of their records:

THE STORY OF THE NUN

Are you Harry Bull? *Yes.*
Did you write the messages? *No.*
Does the 'strange coat' belong to someone you know? *Yes.*
To a woman? *Yes.*
To a friend? *Yes.*
Is she alive? *Yes.*
Does she live near here? *Yes.*
Has she been in the house lately? *No.*

Will she come again? *No.*
Do you know the Rev. Henning? *Yes.*
Does he come here? *Yes.*
Could he help you? *Yes.*
By saying and having 'light, Mass, prayers,' etc.? *Yes.*
In your room? *No.*
In the passage here? *No.*
In the Chapel? *No.*
In the village church? *No.*
In the house? *No.*
In the kitchen? *Yes.*
Has the kitchen anything to do with your death? *No.*
Has the kitchen anything to do with the misfortune in this house? *Yes.*
Has there been any other cause for the trouble? *Yes.*
Concerning yourself? *Yes.*
Concerning the story of the 'nun'? *No.*
Did the 'nun' die violently here? *No.*
Did the present trouble start with your father? *No.*
Was it before his time? *Yes.*
Was it long before his time? *No.*
A previous Rector? *Yes.*
In a previous house? *No.*
In this house? *Yes.*
Did your father build this house? *Yes.*
This house is supposed to be haunted. Was it haunted before your father's time? [No reply.]
Was it haunted during his time? *Yes.*
Did your father see the 'nun'? *Yes.*
Has the 'nun' left here? *No.*
Is she happy now? *No.*
Can we help her? *Yes.*
By a service? *No.*
By a Christian burial? *Yes.*
Is she in the garden? *Yes.* [Very definite.]
Shall we see her? *No.*
Is she near the house? *Yes.*
Is anyone buried in the garden? *Yes.* [Definite.]
Was there a burial in the garden during your time? *No.*
Has anyone been buried in the garden? *Yes.*
Only the 'nun'? *Yes.*
No one else? *No.*
Is she buried under the house? *No.*
Near the house? *Yes.*

Could we find her? *Yes.*
Is she deeply buried? *No.*
Is she buried near the summer house? *No.*
On the east of the house? *No.*
On the north of the house? *No.*
On the south of the house? *Yes.*
On the west of the house? *Yes.*
On the south-west of the house? *Yes.* [Definite.]
Is she buried under trees? *Yes.*
Is she buried in a coffin? *No.*
Is she buried under a stone? *No.*
Is she buried under a cedar-tree? *No.*
Is she buried near the path by the south-west of the house? *Yes.*
Is she buried near the path? *Yes.*
Has she ever been found? *No.*
Is she buried within two yards of the path? *Yes.*
Is she buried near the greenhouse? *No.*
Is she buried by the stables? *No.*
Is she buried by the small pond? *No.*
Is she buried under a tree within two yards of the path? *Yes.*
Is she buried under a large tree? *Yes.*
Can you spell the name of the tree? *Yes.*
Do you know the kind of tree? *Yes.*
Can you spell its name? *Fi.*
Is 'fir' correct? *Yes.*
Within two yards of a fir-tree? *Yes.*
Is the fir-tree a large one? *Yes.*
Is the fir-tree near the vine by the corner of the house? *Yes.*
Are you certain? *Yes.* [Definite.]
Has it been cut down? [No reply.]
Would she like us to look for her? *Yes.*
If we look, can we find her? *Yes.*
Is she buried in the garden? *Yes.* [Definite.]
Is she buried fairly near the greenhouse? *Yes.*
Is she buried more than three feet deep? *No.*
Is she buried under a small stone with 'B' on it in the path? *Yes.*
Are you certain she is under the stone? *Yes.* [Definite.]
Is the house still haunted? *Yes.* [Definite.]
Is the movement of things part of the haunting? [No reply.]
Do you know what moves them? *Yes.*
Spell it. [No reply.]
Do you move things? *Yes.*

Did you move the tobacco tin from the drawing-room? *No.*
Do you know when you move things? *No.*
Does cold interfere with your power? *No.*
Does light interfere with your power? *No.*
Does heat help you? *Yes.*
Would it help if we arranged for Mass to be sung in the kitchen? *Yes.*
Can you spell the nun's name? [No reply.]
Is it a Biblical name? [No reply.]
Do you know who wrote the wall messages? *Yes.*
Did you write them? *No.*
Did a human write them? *No.*
Did a man write them? *No.*
Did a woman write them? *No.*
Did a child write them? *No.*
Is it a type of being we do not understand? [Indefinite.]
Are you often in the house? *Yes.*
Are you often on the landing? *Yes.*
Do you go up and down the stairs? *Yes.*
In your library and old study? *No.*
Are you tired? *Yes.*
Shall we stop? *Yes.*
　[Later, when another entity 'came through']:
Is anyone buried in the garden? *Yes.*
Who is it? *Fadenoch.*
Was he a member of the monastery? *Yes.*
Was he prior? *No.*
Was he a lay brother? *No.*
Was he a monk? *Yes.*
Was he a novice? [No reply.]
Was he a friend of the nun? [No reply.]
Had the burial been made before your lifetime? *Yes.*
Is there evil in this house? *No.*
Was there evil in this house? *Yes.*
Is there now only good in this house? *Yes.*
Should the house be destroyed? *No.*
Are we wrong in asking these questions? *No.*
Do you know who wrote the messages on the walls? *Yes.*
Did you? *No.*
Will there be more messages? *Yes.*
Shall we see them? *Yes.*

So now the reader knows exactly where the 'nun' is buried; who 'moved' things in the Rectory; some informa-

tion about the 'messages'; and that a monk named 'Fadenoch'[1] is also interred in the Rectory grounds. It is interesting to note that some of the table-tipping answers corresponded very closely with the replies given to the same
questions of a private nature that we asked when we had our
séance in the Blue Room in the early morning of June 13,
1929. (See Chapter VIII.) I have explained why this
intimate 'conversation' cannot be given. I need hardly
warn the reader not to take this séance 'information' too
seriously.

[1] Or perhaps 'Father Enoch' was meant.

CHAPTER XXVI

THE VOICE OF PLANCHETTE

FROM table-tipping Mr. Glanville turned his attention to Planchette writing. In his record book, he tells us: 'We had, some years ago, obtained a Planchette with a view to carrying out some experiments. These did not materialize, however, as the board persistently refused to move, and at none of the sittings did it write a single word. It was stored away and not used again until it was taken to Borley where it at once became extremely active.'

A 'Planchette' is a heart-shaped piece of wood at the apex of which a sharpened lead pencil is inserted at right-angles. At the other end of the board are two small pentagraph wheels or castors in order that it can be made to move easily over a sheet of paper when hands are rested lightly on it. It is believed by some to write independently of the volition of the person or persons touching it. Planchette writing is in the same category as automatic writing. There is no doubt that some of these 'automatisms' are genuine, but are the result of subconscious activity of the mind, and nothing to do with spirits. Many otherwise normal persons are automatists. The Planchette, ouija board, and similar contrivances merely take the place of the hand in automatic writing. If the reader is a spiritualist, he may think differently.

The first Planchette writings were produced (October 25, 1937) by Roger Glanville, Kerr-Pearse and A. J. Cuthbert. The results were not very encouraging. Then Mr. Glanville showed these scripts to his daughter (his children are, of course, grown up), Miss Helen Glanville, who had never used a Planchette. *No details of the previous writings had been given her.* Alone, Miss Glanville, at her Streatham home, on October 28, 1937, produced a number of scripts, from which the following are extracts. The 'questions' were asked aloud:

[No question asked, but the name *Marianne* was written.]
Is it someone using this name? [Indistinct.]
Could you tell me your own name? [Indistinct.]
Are you buried in the garden? *Yes.*
Can you tell us where? *Der re Ind.*
Do you mean under the fir-tree? *No.*
Near a tree? *Yes.*
Is there anything to tell us where? *Stone.*
Can you tell me the rest of your name? *La....* [then indistinct.]
Are the first two letters 'La'? *irre.*
Do you mean 'Lairre'? *Yes.*
Can we help? Are you unhappy? *Yes.*
Can we do anything to help you? *Mass.*
[No question asked.] *Prayers aness.*
It is 'Mass,' isn't it? *Yes.*
Can you tell me, are you buried in the garden? *Yes.*
Do you want Mass said in the house? *Yes.*
In any special room? *No.*
Upstairs? [No reply.]
Downstairs? [No reply.]
Do you mean it does not matter where? *Yes.*
If you still want to talk, say 'yes.' *Yes.*
Can you tell me the name of your nunnery? *Larire.*
Do you mean 'Lar'? *arre.*
Is it the name of your nunnery that you are trying to write? *Yes.*
Can you tell me how far away? Two miles or more? *Yes.*
Was it Bures? *Yes.*
Do you mean it was Bures? *Yes.*
It is your own name you are trying to write, isn't it? *Yes.*
Can you tell me the name of the Monk? [Indistinct.]
Is he unhappy? *Yes.*
Can you tell me when you passed over? *1667.*
The month? *May.*
The day? *17.*
Can you tell us why you passed over? *Yes.*
Did they hurt you? *Yes.*
Was there something you wanted very much before you passed over? *Water.*

Do you mean water? *Yes.*
Can you try to spell the name of the Nunnery? [After several attempts *Haiv* was written.]
Is it 'Haiv'? *Yes.*
Was it a closed order? *Yes.*
Do you want more questions? *Yes.*
Was the monk's order that of St. Benedict? *Yes.*
Is the monk buried at Borley? *Yes.*
Do you know where? *Yes.*
In the garden or under the house? [No reply.]

(On October 31, 1937, at Streatham, Miss Helen Glanville, Mr. S. H. Glanville and his son, and Mr. Kerr-Pearse had a Planchette séance, the fingers of each person being placed lightly on the board):

Who is there? [Indistinct, then] *Mary.*
What is your name? *Mary Lairre.*
How old were you when you passed over? *19.*
Were you a novice? *Yes.*
Why did you pass over? [No reply.]
Are you under the wall? *No.*
Are you at the end of the wall? *Yes.*
Where did you hear Mass? [Indistinct.]
Will you please spell each letter? *B-o-r-l-e-y.*
Did you know Father Enoch? [Indistinct.]
Will you repeat your last answer letter by letter? *J-e-s-u-s.*
Have you a message? *Chant light Mass.*
Do you want it for yourself? *Yes.*
Why? *I am unha* . . . [three letters indistinct.]
Is it your own fault? *No.*
Whose fault? *Waldegrave.*
Were you murdered? *Yes.*
When? *1667.*
How? *Stran* . . . [last letters indistinct.]
Were you strangled? *Yes.*
Will our Mass be sufficient? *No.*
What Mass do you want? *Requiem.*
Must it be by a Roman Catholic priest? [Indistinct.]
Are you French? *Yes.*
Where did you come from? *Havre.*
Is it 'Havre'? *Yes.*
What was the name of your nunnery or convent? *Bure.*
Did Waldegrave take you from Bures? *Yes.*

M

Do you want burial as well as Mass? *Yes.*
Are we speaking to Mary Lairre? *Yes.*
Do you want water? *Yes.*
What kind of water? *Holy.*
What else do you want? *Incense.*
Are you ever in Borley house? *Yes.*

At the above and other Planchette séances, many private questions were discussed, and the operating entities made some startling 'disclosures' concerning a number of tragic incidents alleged to have occurred at Borley. These records have been carefully preserved. The value of these Planchette writings must be assessed by the reader himself. But they are very interesting.

CHAPTER XXVII

'SUNEX AMURES' SAYS HE WILL BURN
THE RECTORY

THOUGH the Planchette writings recorded in the last
chapter have a great interest—perhaps a psychological
one—for students of the Borley problem, they contain
little or nothing that can be easily proved or disproved; no
predictions that can be verified; and no very startling disclosures—even if the script statements are true. Certainly,
we might begin to dig up the Rectory lawn for the nun,
'Mary Lairre', and 'Father Fadenoch' the monk who,
Planchette says, are buried there. It is a fact that let into
the garden of the Rectory is a large stone with 'B' on it, and
it is under this stone that the nun is alleged to lie. Perhaps
some day it would be worth while digging for the remains
of the two lovers. And this thought suggests to me that the
molestation of the cats' cemetery[1] may have been the work
of someone who obtained a 'clue'—perhaps at a séance—
as to where 'Mary Lairre' was buried. The bones dug up
by Mr. Glanville certainly belonged to no nun!

But one startling piece of information or prediction—fulfilled to the letter—*was* obtained at a Planchette séance at
Streatham, under the following circumstances.

It will be remembered that Miss Helen Glanville had had
no previous experience with the Planchette until her father
experimented with it, and her, in October 1937. Then the
family more or less forgot about it. But exactly five
months later—on March 27, 1938, to be precise—something
prompted Miss Glanville to get out the little heart-shaped

[1] See page 199.

163

contrivance and again try it. As her brother Roger happened to be at home, she invited him to join her.

They spread a piece of white paper on the table and placed the tips of their fingers lightly on the polished surface of the Planchette. Miss Glanville said: 'Does anyone want to speak to us?' *Immediately*, the word '*yes*' was written. Then Miss Glanville said 'Who are you?' She had hardly finished speaking when Planchette wrote in a large scrawly hand:

'*Sunex Amures and one of his men* [indistinct] MEAN TO BURN THE RECTORY *to-night at 9 o'clock end of the haunting go to the rectory and you will be able to see us enter into our own and under the ruins you will find bone of murdered* [indistinct] *wardens* [not clear] *under the ruins mean you to have proof of haunting of the rectory at Borley* [indistinct] *the understanding of which* [indistinct] *tells the story of murder which happened there.*'

Miss Glanville then asked: 'In which room will the fire start?' Immediately Planchette wrote: '*Over the hall. Yes yes you must go if you want proof.*'

'Why cannot you give us proof here?' was asked. '*We will*' said Planchette. And that was all. Other questions were asked, but Planchette was dumb.

The above promise—or threat—by 'Sunex Amures' is quite definite. He said he would 'Burn the rectory'—and burnt it was! Eleven months later, to the day, Borley Rectory was gutted by fire!

Not only did 'Sunex Amures' say that the Rectory would be burnt, but he said that it would start 'over the hall.' That is *exactly* where it *did* start. The lamp that caused the blaze was upset in the hall, but the first part of the house to burn was immediately *over* the hall—exactly at midnight on February 27, 1939.

I must emphasize that all these Planchette scripts and séance records were—and are—carefully preserved. Actually, the script bearing the threat to 'burn the rectory' was sent to my office at the time. Needless to say, neither Mr. Glanville nor his family were greatly perturbed by the threat to burn the Rectory, and did *not* travel to Borley on the night of the séance in order to see 'Sunex Amures' and his merry men start the blaze. In other words, they did *not* take the threat seriously. Speaking of Planchette scripts, Mr. Glanville and his friends used up so much paper that he finally bought lengths of white wall-paper on which to record the 'messages.'

CHAPTER XXVIII

THE RECTORY'S NEW OWNER

ON November 1, 1938, I broadcast from London on haunted houses. I did not mention Borley Rectory by name, but detailed certain incidents that had occurred there, knowing that those of my hearers who knew anything at all about the 'most haunted house' would recognize the place to which I was referring.

Amongst the letters from listeners that the British Broadcasting Corporation forwarded to me after my talk was one (dated November 2, 1938) from Captain W. H. Gregson, R.E. (Ret.) of Maldon, Essex. He said: 'I was greatly interested in hearing your broadcast talk on ghosts last night, as I have recently purchased Borley Rectory wherein you conducted some of the investigations of which you spoke. I should be so very interested to hear from you concerning your stay in Borley Rectory, as to any strange or inexplicable occurrences which you noted during your stay. We shall take up residence at the Rectory early in December, and are naturally very interested in the rumours concerning it—though without, I must admit, any degree of nervousness with regard to them.'

So Captain Gregson was the new owner! I knew from the letter[1] that Miss Ethel Bull sent to Mr. Glanville that the Rectory had been sold, but it was a curious coincidence that the new owner should reveal himself to me through my wireless talk.

In my reply to Captain Gregson I mentioned that I was preparing a monograph on the psychic history of the Rectory and hoped he would let me know should any

[1] See page 237.

untoward incident or inexplicable happening occur there. I told him that there was nothing to be nervous about. I also said that if I lived in Essex—as he did—instead of in Sussex, I would have bought the house myself as a sort of week-end place where I could do some occasional investigating.

In his second letter to me, Captain Gregson mentioned that curiosity concerning the place was drawing crowds of people to the Rectory. These 'sight-seers' (though it is difficult to imagine what they expected to see) were very annoying. On one evening when the Captain happened to be there, a whole string of cars was in the road—the occupants of which had come to see the 'haunted house.' One man was so very persistent that the Captain took compassion on him, and invited him into the house and showed him round.

The letter continues: 'In the library [our old Base Room] he began to collapse, because of the malevolent influence which he said existed just there. I certainly did not feel anything myself, but I liked to think that there was really something eerie. It adds charm to the place.'

The return of the 'rubber-necks' to Borley was curious, as nothing like it had happened since the Rev. Eric Smith was driven almost frantic by gangs of sightseers who invaded the Rectory and grounds. I might have mentioned before that during my tenancy only once (when I was not present) were our observers disturbed by strangers. The exception was when a party of young fools of both sexes (who were old enough, and presumably educated enough to know better) from a house a few miles away drove over to Borley one night and created a disturbance at the Rectory. I hope they read what I think of them. During my tenancy I never once saw even a single villager, and no one called on me.

Captain Gregson moved to Borley early in December 1938, and I heard indirectly that he had renamed the Rectory 'Borley Priory.' I believe there was some clause in the conditions of sale that precluded his calling his house

Borley Rectory on account of possible confusion. I do not know who suggested 'The Priory,' but it was a very happy choice and a most appropriate name.

I also learnt that Captain Gregson was living in the Rectory cottage with his two young sons, Alan, aged eighteen, and Andrew, aged fourteen, while he was gradually 'moving in' his furniture into the big house and getting ship-shape at leisure: an excellent arrangement. I never knew whether he was disturbed by the 'padding dog' that so troubled Edward Cooper. Probably not, or I should have heard of it. Arbon, of course, had moved out of the Rectory cottage, and was living in Brook Hall Lane, Borley.

I had no further occasion to correspond with Captain Gregson during 1938, and waited patiently for news of any 'happenings.' When next I *did* write, it was to commiserate with him over the tragic disaster that had befallen him and the Rectory.

PLATE VII

Right :

After the fire. Gutted Rectory showing first floor burnt out. Photographed from the lawn. Compare with photograph on Plate I.

Left :

Burnt-out brick gable-ends.

Below left :

The " Cold Spot " outside the Blue Room (compare photograph on Plate III).

Below right :

All that remains of the burnt-out Chapel.

CHAPTER XXIX

THE RECTORY DESTROYED BY FIRE

O N the stroke of midnight, February 27, 1939, Borley
Rectory caught fire, and in a few minutes was a
blazing inferno. (See Plate VII). Thus was the
prophecy, threat, or promise of 'Sunex Amures,' Miss
Glanville's Planchette entity, fulfilled!

By a strange coincidence—everything connected with
Borley was strange!—I learnt of the fiery end of the Rectory
in exactly the same way as, in 1929, I first heard of the
manifestations that were taking place there. On the afternoon of Tuesday, February 28, 1939, the editor of one of
the great London dailies rang me up and broke the news.
The story he had received was to the effect that the fire had
started in some miraculous manner.

As my Press cuttings began to come in, I saw such headings
as 'Most Haunted House on Fire,' 'Rectory Ghost Goes
West,' 'Ghosts Burnt Out,' and so on, and the actual
account of the burning was appropriately dramatized. Of
the more serious reports of the fire, I take the following from
the *Suffolk and Essex Free Press*, in the issue of March 2, 1939:

'It appears that Captain Gregson was sorting out some books
when a paraffin lamp overturned and the room speedily caught
fire. Captain Gregson was in serious difficulty, because water
had to be pumped before any could be had for use. The Sudbury
Fire Brigade was called about 12.15 a.m., and Second Officer
H. Rogers arrived at 12.30, with several firemen and the Merry-
weather pump. On arrival they found that the roof had collapsed
immediately over the room in which ghosts had been reputed to
appear. The interior of the upper room was well alight and
another part of the roof had caught, also the staircase. A plentiful supply of water was obtained from a pond fifty yards away,

and the firemen, who promptly got to work, mastered the outbreak after an hour and a quarter's work. They left about
8.15 a.m. after clearing the débris and making all safe.'

Another account, from the *East Anglian Daily Times*
(March 1, 1939) says:

'Captain Gregson, with the aid of an oil-lamp, was sorting
out library books in the main hall when the lamp overturned and
burst. The burning oil spread among the packages and he rushed
to the cottage to rouse his sons. In a few minutes the hall was a
mass of flames. Sudbury Fire Brigade arrived and found the
front ground-floor rooms, and the bedrooms above, already
involved. Before the Brigade had obtained control, a portion of
the roof fell in.'

From a witness who saw the fire, whom I subsequently
interviewed, I heard the following account. He said: 'I was
returning home late from Sudbury on Monday evening,
February 27, when, as I approached Borley Church, I saw a
red glow in the sky. Wondering what it could be, I hastened
my steps and, as I neared the Rectory, I found it was
ablaze. It was as light as day. A column of flames and
sparks was shooting up into the sky and the top of the
Rectory reminded me of the blast furnaces I have seen in the
Midlands. Then I heard a crash as the roof fell in. The far
side of the house [*i.e.*, the rooms overlooking the lawn,
including the Blue Room] seemed to be burning most
fiercely, and the flames were streaming out of the windows.
The firemen were pumping water on to the building. It was
the fiercest fire I have seen in these parts.' Neither the cottage nor outbuildings were damaged by fire or water.

Of course I wrote to Captain Gregson, sympathizing with
him in his loss, and hoping that the damage to his personal
property was not too great. I said I was not particularly
surprised that the place had been burnt down, as one or two
outbreaks of fire had occurred there in previous years. It
will be remembered that the Rev. L. A. Foyster speaks of
fire in his diary, and Lady Whitehouse actually saw the
skirting-board ablaze. Dom Richard Whitehouse also saw
'smoke issuing from the skirting-board' on one occasion.

In my letter to Captain Gregson I asked him to let me know exactly how the fire started and what had taken place at the Rectory since I last wrote him in the previous November. From a long and detailed reply (dated March 2, 1939) which he kindly sent me, I will quote the following verbatim:

'Thank you so much for your kind letter of sympathy. You will have seen in various papers an account of the fire, and so far as I have studied the reports, they give the full account of what occurred. We had not actually established ourselves in the Rectory (which I have renamed The Priory) but were still camping-out, so to speak, in the Cottage. But all our stuff was in the Rectory, and has been destroyed.

'The fire was caused through a big pile of books (which I was dusting and sorting out in the Main Hall) falling over on to a lamp and upsetting it. The only suggestion of any mysterious influence lies in the fact that I had stacked the books quite carefully, and that in ordinary commonsense, they should have remained in their stack without falling over at all. The Sudbury Brigade (which I got at once) were extremely good, very prompt, and most efficient, but the place is practically ruined, and all my things (including my books, which I valued very greatly) are destroyed.

'During my ownership of the Rectory, one or two rather unaccountable things have certainly happened. Of these, the most curious was in connection with the well in the cellar. It was open when we took possession, and sometimes the boys used to go down the cellar to see how the toads were getting on. I was afraid that the boys might fall down the well, so I placed a heavy hatch-cover over the top one afternoon, to safeguard them. They had been a little nervous of the open well themselves, and appreciated it being securely covered up. But the next morning, they went down the cellar and came rushing back to ask me why I had removed the cover without letting them know. The cover had been thrown off, and lay some distance away on the floor. As the whole place had been securely locked, and certainly no one had entered in the meanwhile, this has struck us all as definitely weird, and I cannot see any normal explanation.

'Then, last week, while the boys and I were busy in the Hall with book sorting, my elder boy was thirsty, and fetched a glass of water from the cottage. He placed the glass (from which he had taken only a sip) on the bracket table in the Hall, so as to be handy when he wanted another drink. We were very busy and interested over the books, and he forgot about his thirst. Later on, we all came in together to the cottage, leaving the glass (practically still full of water) on the hall table. The following morning, when I unlocked the Rectory and went in with my elder son, we found the glass still on the corner of the hall table, but in four or five pieces, quite dry, and not a trace of moisture either on the table (which was a polished mahogany one) nor on the floor beneath. Again, we know definitely that no one but ourselves had been in the place.

'Then (and this happened within a day or two of our first taking possession of the Rectory), we lost our dog in a strange way. He was a black cocker spaniel, and the most sane and shrewd dog possible. I took him out with me one night to get some water from the big wheel pump in the courtyard (which, as you will remember, is a narrow passage between the two wings of the Rectory), I distinctly heard footsteps at the far end of the courtyard, as though something was treading over the wooden trap-door leading down to the cellars. I paused, and my dog stopped dead, and positively went mad. He shrieked, and tore away, still shrieking, and we have not seen or heard of him since. I searched the yard, but no one was there.

'Another day (this time in broad daylight, about two in the afternoon), as I was in the courtyard, I heard most human-sounding footsteps in the kitchen wing. So definite and real were they that I called to my son, whom I supposed had gone in and was walking about. But both the sons were in the cottage, and the doors had not even been unlocked. I got the back-door key instantly, and we all went in and made a thorough search—with no result.

'Numerous small things have been upset or moved. Usually we have had family arguments as to who had been "messing about," but generally without coming to any satisfactory conclusion.'

There were phenomena even while the Rectory was blazing. During my last visit to Borley in June 1939, I met two persons who said they saw 'figures moving amongst the flames, near the Blue Room window' while the fire was at its height. And a constable saw 'a woman in grey and a man wearing a bowler hat' in front of Captain Gregson as he crossed the courtyard during the fire. This incident is recorded by Captain Gregson in an interview[1] he gave a Pressman:

'About four o'clock in the morning a police constable asked me who were the lady and gentleman who had just preceded me in passing over the courtyard. I told him there was no woman on the premises.'

When next I saw Captain Gregson, he confirmed in greater detail all the strange incidents connected with his short residence at the Rectory that I have related above. He said that the two figures seen coming out of the Rectory during the fire were 'cloaked.' There were no people in the house when it caught alight: he was quite alone. There were two figures seen at the upper windows while the place was blazing. One appeared to be that of a girl, the other was merely a 'formless figure.' They were seen by several villagers.

---

[1] *Sunday Graphic*, March 5, 1939.

CHAPTER XXX

THE GHOSTS SURVIVE

THE Borley ghosts are fire-proof. These psychic sala-
manders did not, apparently, perish under the incan-
descent ruins of the Rectory, but became if anything
more active.

On Saturday, April 15, 1939, Captain Gregson related
some of his experiences at the Rectory in the B.B.C. 'In Town
To-night' series. He told how he heard invisible footsteps
in the courtyard; how the well hatch-cover was thrown;
the story of the shattered glass and the disappearing water;
and detailed how figures were seen wandering about the
flames while the house was burning. The reader is acquainted
with these stories.

But one or two strange incidents related by Captain
Gregson I had not heard, as they apparently happened after
he wrote to me on March 2, 1939.

After he lost his cocker spaniel in December 1938 he purchased another one. It, too, was a spaniel puppy. Going
through the courtyard one day with the animal, it behaved
exactly as its predecessor did. It saw something that Captain
Gregson could not see, began whining and shrieking—and
bolted. It has not been seen since.

One day Captain Gregson found a toad in the cellar. He
thought it was a pity to let it lie there, so he picked it up
and, making a bag out of a piece of cloth, placed it inside.
He took the four corners of the cloth and tied them into two
knots, very tightly, making it impossible for the toad to
escape. I am not sure whether he intended to put the toad
back into the cellar, or to place it in the garden. Anyway,
a minute later, when he went to remove the toad, it was

gone! The knots were still tied tightly, and there was no visible means of escape.

Another strange story related by Captain Gregson in his broadcast described how he found some imprints in the snow which were made neither by a human being nor by any animal known to him. Coming down one morning, he happened to go into the garden. Snow had been falling and lay thick and white. Stretching diagonally from one corner of the main lawn to the other was a series of impressions in the snow. For a moment he wondered who could have been trespassing during the night. Then he realized that they were not a bit like imprints that could possibly have been made by a human foot. Nor were they like the imprints of any animal with which he was acquainted. They appeared to be almost formless, and yet quite distinct. Moreover, the track was in one direction only, and seemed to disappear at the wall which runs parallel to the Nun's Walk. *They did not return.* The mystery was never solved. These footprints are reminiscent of the famous 'Devil's hoof-marks' which were found one morning stretching across Devonshire, from Totnes to Exmouth, on February 8, 1855, after a heavy fall of snow. The tracks covered 100 miles, and the footprints —unlike those of any animal known to naturalists—were to be seen even on the roofs of houses and the tops of high walls, and on both sides of the estuary of the River Exe. The mystery was never solved.[1]

One of the strangest stories told me after the Rectory fire was by Herbert Mayes, chauffeur to the Rev. A. C. Henning. The incident occurred to him while he was cycling home from Borley on the night of Thursday, March 16, 1939, exactly two weeks before I interviewed him. It was a dark night, and there was no moon. As he was cycling past the Rectory—or rather the ruins of it, because it had by then been gutted by fire—he heard what sounded like horses stampeding. They appeared to be coming towards him.

[1] See *The Times*, February 16, 1855, and *Illustrated London News*, February 24 and March 3, 1855.

The first thought that occurred to him was that the horses belonged to Mr. Payne, of Borley Place, and that they had broken loose.

As a safety measure, Mayes jumped off his bicycle and, with it, stood flat against the fence and hedge in order to allow the horses to pass him. He turned his lamp towards the direction of the horses. The sounds came nearer and nearer, and finally passed him. *But there were no horses!* The galloping hoofs could still be heard dying away in the distance, but never a sign of an animal—human or equine—did he see. From first to last, he estimates that he heard the 'horses' for three or four minutes. Mr. Mayes's experience is comparable with that of Mr. Harry Bull and others who also heard the clatter of hoofs on that hollow road outside the Rectory. At the same time, Mr. Mayes also saw 'lights,' but it is possible that these came from the window of the Rectory cottage, in which Captain Gregson and his two sons were then residing.

If any further evidence is required for the haunting of Borley Rectory—or its ruins—*after* the fire, it is supplied by Mr. Charles Graham Browne, of Pound Hall, Melford; and Miss Rosemary M. Williams, daughter of Captain Williams, of Borley Lodge, near Sudbury.

Mr. Browne and some friends thought they would like to see the burnt-out Rectory, so they visited the ruins on Sunday night, March 26, 1939, a month after the conflagration. It was a bright, clear starlight night and the moon was in its first quarter. After inspecting the front of what remains of the building, they went on to the lawn and the Nun's Walk to get a better view of that side of the house overlooking the lawn and summer-house. As they gazed at the gable walls, all that remains of the upper storey of the Rectory, a girl in white suddenly appeared at the aperture of the burnt-out window of the Blue Room. Her figure was outlined in the moonlight. She appeared to be standing on nothing; in fact, there was nothing to stand on except the charred and crumbling rafters that once supported the Blue

Room and other apartments on the first floor. The figure appeared to be small, but quite distinct. The 'girl' was visible for several seconds and then fall back into the burnt débris behind her, or vanished through the wall. Mr. Browne saw her only as she disappeared from the window.

Mr. Browne, whom Mr. Henning and I interviewed on March 29, 1939, kindly supplied the above particulars. He was quite definite about the appearance of the figure. No human being could have climbed up to that window, under the existing conditions. When I visited Borley on March 28, 29 and 30, 1939, I tried to reach the burnt-through rafters by climbing over the débris, but I could not reach the Blue Room window aperture, because, as Miss Williams emphasizes, there was nothing to stand on, and with every step I took I was afraid of being precipitated into the rooms below.

Miss Rosemary Williams had a better and longer view of the figure, as she saw it before Mr. Browne did. She thought the girl's dress was light blue, but the moonlight might have given it this tint. I wrote to Miss Williams and received the following signed report:

MISS WILLIAMS'S STATEMENT

'On the evening of Sunday, March 26, 1939, Captain Gregson gave permission to a party of us to visit Borley Rectory. At about 10.30 p.m. we all met at the Rectory gates. It was a cold night. The moon was only in its first quarter, but shone sufficiently brightly to illuminate the ruined building.

'We were most anxious to investigate inside the house, but Captain Gregson asked us not to walk among the wreckage, as he would feel responsible should some of the charred rafters fall upon one of us and cause an injury.

'For about half an hour we wandered round the house in small groups. Someone had a camera and hoped to get a photo of the alleged "nun."

'It was while I was standing on the path [the Nun's Walk] that runs parallel with the large lawn, looking up at the house, that I saw a small woman in the upstairs room (which you term the Blue Room). I had the impression of someone in a light buff-coloured coat, but as the figure approached the window,

N

I could see that it was a woman clothed in blue. She remained for several seconds and then turned towards the wall and, as it seemed, walked through it.

'I will draw a diagram of her movements:

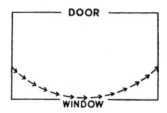

'None of the others would believe me when I called out that I had seen her. Those near me admitted that they were not looking up at the window at the time, except Mr. Browne, who said he saw, for a flash, something resembling a figure of a woman disappearing from the window.

'I was convinced I had seen her, while the others tried to prove that it was a trick of the moon on a piece of glass or that someone was actually in the building. The former suggestion was dis-proved as all the window panes had been smashed;[1] and in the latter case, we found that the floor boards were burned, so that no human person could have been at the window.

'The most extraordinary part to me, was that the apparition should seem so natural and unfrightening. I had often visited Borley Rectory before, spending many hours watching and listening.

[Signed] '[Miss] ROSEMARY M. WILLIAMS.'

When I was at Borley, exactly a month after the fire, I made a thorough examination of the damage. I found that the entire first floor and attics of the Rectory had been con-sumed. The brick gable-ends were still standing and, if one stood on the lawn and looked through the apertures formerly containing the window-frames of the Blue Room and Rooms Nos. 4, 5 and 7, one could see right through the house to the trees bordering the road in front of the Rectory.

The chapel was a mass of charred woodwork and I could not reach what was once the stained window because it had

[1] The window-frame had been burnt right out, leaving the bare brick aper-ture, as can be seen from the photographs (Plate VII), taken thirty-six hours after Miss Williams's visit.

been blown out. Also, the floor had been burnt away. The 'cold spot' on the landing outside the Blue Room must have become a very hot spot, as it no longer existed! The 'tower' was gutted, as can be seen from the photographs that I took on my visit. These are reproduced on Plate VII.

The lower portion of the house did not suffer so badly as the first floor, but of course it was ruined. The main staircase—down which so many bottles, pebbles, and china ornaments had been precipitated during the palmy days of the haunting—had gone; in fact, it was the first to go. All the windows of the lower rooms had been blown out or burnt out, and everywhere there was charred wood, desolation and ruin. Some of the walls looked as if they might topple over at any moment. In fact, notices had been put up warning persons that they entered the ruins at their peril. Since I took the photographs which are reproduced in this work, portions of the walls *have* collapsed owing to the high winds.

The last Borley phenomenon—or alleged phenomenon—brought to my notice related to, of all things, a camera. Mr. W. Davey, of Whitton Church Lane, Ipswich, visited Borley Rectory on Easter Monday, April 10, 1939, in order to see the ruins. He took his camera with him. When he got there (he tells me in a letter dated April 11, 1939), the place seemed placid and peaceful enough. He went on to the lawn to take a few photographs—and then something curious happened. He stood in front of the ruins and took a photograph of them. Then he closed his camera, which 'immediately flew open with a smart click'—of course spoiling the latent picture. Again, he took a picture of the Rectory, and *again* the camera flew open after he had pressed the button. Mr. Davey mentioned that he had had the camera for five years, and never before had the camera behaved like it. He decided he would give up the photographic part of his visit as a bad job. He had just made this mental resolution when he 'noticed something at the very spot where Captain Gregson lost his dog.' The 'something' he could not define.

My next visit to Borley was on Wednesday, June 21, 1939. The occasion was a 'psychic fête' organized by the Rev. A. C. Henning and his Church Council for raising funds for the restoration of Borley Church. I promised I would take a number of the London Ghost Club members with me.

The day—the longest day of the year, by the way—duly arrived and we all spent a jolly time on the Rectory lawn and amongst the ruins over—or through—which Captain Gregson and his sons had arranged 'personally conducted tours.' On the lawn were skittles and clock-golf. A 'white elephant' stall and pig-pelting competition spread itself along the Nun's Walk, and coco-nuts were flying hither and thither. These unusual 'movements' were not, however, due to *Poltergeist* activity, but were the result of the well-directed shies of the local rustics who had assembled to make merry. After a charming speech of welcome by Mrs. R. A. Butler, the wife of the Under-Secretary of State for Foreign Affairs, we all had tea. 'Ghosts were our hosts,' as some one said, but to quote the account of the fête that appeared in *The Times*:

'No ghosts were seen. No bricks were hurled at visitors, and no one received a black eye. There were no psychic manifestations or strange phenomena. . . . Still, it was a pleasant day, even for those enthusiasts who braved the stinging nettles and briars and brambles to trace out the Nun's Walk and find the haunted pond almost hidden by an overgrowth of rank weeds. Since this former rectory was gutted by fire last February the cellars have been open to daylight, so that this afternoon even they offered little satisfaction to the inquiring Ghost Club. There was therefore little to do but turn to the coconut-shy and so replenish the funds of Borley Church.'[1]

Yes, it was a pleasant day, and I could not help wondering, as I stood in the shelter of the summer-house and watched the animated scene, whether my observers would ever again keep their nightly vigil among the Cedars of Lebanon

[1] *The Times*, June 22, 1939.

around which throngs of merry-makers were so joyfully disporting themselves. As for myself, it would probably be my last visit to Borley Rectory. And it was exactly ten years (less nine days) since first I set foot in what was subsequently to become known as 'the most haunted house in England' —a well-earned title indeed!

CHAPTER XXXI

CAN THE PHENOMENA BE EXPLAINED?

IS it possible, on any hypothesis, to explain the amazing events that have occurred at Borley during the past seventy years? Personally, I do not believe that any one theory will cover all the observed facts. Undoubtedly, the major and most spectacular of the Borley phenomena (excluding the appearances of the 'nun' and other phantasms) were—or are—the work of *Poltergeister*, those mischievous entities whose pranks are usually as noisy as they are senseless. The throwing or displacement of articles are common manifestations. The word *Poltergeist* comes from the German verb *poltern*, to rattle, and *Geist*, a spirit. The term is a very appropriate one.

The evidence for *Poltergeister* in the annals of psychical research is as impressive as it is voluminous, and very many cases have been fully authenticated. To take a famous case (and a rather appropriate one, as this monograph concerns a rectory), that of the Parsonage at Epworth, the birthplace of John Wesley (1703–1791), is worth citing. The *Poltergeist* disturbances in this house during the months of December and January, 1716–17 were, until the record of the Borley manifestations came to be written, the most fully authenticated in the history of the subject. I will not describe this most interesting case, but will refer the reader to Joseph Priestly's *Original Letters by the Rev. John Wesley and his Friends*,[1] where he will find the fullest account of the phenomena.

But if the Borley stone-throwing, furniture-moving, bottle-dropping, hair-ruffling, bell-ringing, belt-raising, soap-

[1] London, 1791.

pitching, and door-locking annoyances were due to *Poltergeister*, as I am certain they were, I doubt if these playful little fellows were responsible for the shufflings, scrabblings, thumps, thuds, footsteps, swishings of clothing, code-tapping, wall-writings, and similar phenomena. I believe that they were caused by the persisting remnants of the egos or personalities (the reader can call them spirits, if he pleases), with some portions of intelligence still retained, of persons who once were associated with the Rectory, or with some building formerly on the same site. The Rectory I think is —or was up to the time of its destruction by fire—saturated with such emanations.

I do not pretend to understand the mechanism of how a 'persisting ego' can so adjust its immaterial elements as to write a message on a wall or lean over a gate in the guise of a nun. Several years ago Professor C. D. Broad postulated a theory[1] that some part of us may survive the dissolution of our body for a limited period. He termed this 'something' the 'psychic factor' which, under certain conditions, may unite itself with another person and produce another mind, the active portion of which belongs to the dead person. I have tried to apply this hypothesis to the Borley phenomena. But as these are mostly of a physical nature, I am afraid that Dr. Broad's theory does not help us much in our present inquiry.

The spirit hypothesis, that is, the continuity of personality and the power to communicate after death, covers many of the facts connected with Borley. The spirit hypothesis, plus the assumption that *Poltergeister* are responsible for some of the phenomena, cover *most* of the facts. The 'forms,' the 'nun,' the 'shadows,' and other figures seen at Borley by so many people at different times perhaps once belonged to living, incarnate beings. But if I am asked how I can 'explain' the coach, the noise of galloping hoofs, the appearance of the bay horses, the 'glittering harness' (seen by Edward Cooper), the 'light in the window' (seen by many

[1] See his *The Mind and Its Place in Nature*, London, 1925.

people), the odours, the sensation of an invisible presence, the feeling of coldness (which might have been only a physiological reaction to some subconscious and repressed fear), and the many bizarre phenomena (*e.g.*, the gluey substance found on floor of Chapel), I can only say that I do not know. But I will also add that *no one knows*.

The suggestion has been made that the various forms seen at Borley are mere subjective hallucinations. But this argument will not stand the simplest analysis. The 'nun,' for example, has been seen by the four Misses Bull at one and the same time, and again by Mr. and Mrs. Edward Cooper simultaneously. Undoubtedly, these phantasms were objective, were real external entities, and were visible to the human eye. In the same category as the 'subjective hallucination' theory is the suggestion that living persons—with certain powers—can telepathically convey apparitions of the dead to other living persons.

Neither are the auditory phenomena recorded at Borley hallucinatory in any sense of the word. For example, Mr. Glover and his party heard two 'heavy thuds' and then one of a lighter character. Four persons heard it plainly, at one and the same time. Again, the Rev. and Mrs. A. C. Henning, and Mr. Kerr-Pearse, at an informal séance, actually *induced* a 'most extraordinary noise' and they heard its progress down the kitchen passage. This was not hallucinatory!

Another suggested explanation of the phenomena is the diabolic theory of the old Roman Catholic theologians. It is useless to speculate about this until we know more about the entities themselves and understand the meaning of the manifestations that they produce. One does not hear much these days about evil spirits, devils, and 'elementals' in connection with psychical research. I think that the experience of most of the Borley investigators is that the entities concerned in the haunting are benevolent, rather than malevolent. Certainly, the Rev. L. A. Foyster had his head whacked with a hair-brush as he lay in bed, and his wife once received a black eye; but these manifestations were probably the work of a too-playful *Poltergeist* with an exuberance of spirits.

Although it would be irksome to the reader for me to detail particulars here, a curious discovery I made during an analysis of the Borley phenomena was to the effect that they are—or were—cyclic and recurrent. I found that in very many cases, the manifestations had a definite and determinable periodicity: that is, they recurred at definite intervals. Not only did they recur at definite intervals of time, but they became gradually weaker at each recurrence. And the intervals may be long or short, though they are always approximately the same.[1] I have not been able to verify that—according to the Borley legends, in which I do *not* believe—the 'nun' always manifests herself on July 28 of each year. But I *have* found that she appears at definite intervals, apparently earth-bound, as an objective entity perceptible to the sensory organs.

To sum up, amongst the many suggested explanations, some of which I have outlined above, the spirit hypothesis is the one that best covers many of the observed phenomena at Borley Rectory. If this is admitted, then that hypothesis is immensely strengthened by these phenomena, if they are genuine.

---

[1] I have developed this theory in my *Fifty Years of Psychical Research*, Longmans, London, 1939.

CHAPTER XXXII

THE CASE FOR THE JURY

READERS of this monograph are now in possession of all the evidence I have accumulated for the alleged haunting of Borley Rectory, and it is for them to decide —as the jury—whether in fact the place *is* haunted, or not. It is all a question of evidence. As the dispassionate narrator of the Borley story, I have been very careful not to make overstatements, and I have avoided the dramatization of incidents—not an easy matter when dealing with the amazing happenings that have occurred there almost since the place was built.

Most of the evidence for the haunting of Borley is not only personal and first-hand, but it is also documentary, as the reader has by now realized. And no case in the annals of psychical research is so *fully* documented.

And who are our witnesses? They are, first of all, *every person who has ever resided in the Rectory* for any length of time. They are the patrons of the living, five Rectors and their families, and their servants. There is the testimony of the present owner of the Rectory—or the ruins—Captain Gregson; there is the evidence of our official observers and myself; and there is the confirmation of this evidence by many complete strangers. My own observers were specially chosen for their intelligence, ability, culture and independence of thought. They included doctors, university men, engineers, army officers, and level-headed business men— none of whom had any bias towards psychical research or spiritualism, and none of whom had ever heard of Borley Rectory before they began their investigation.

In all, there are no fewer than 100 witnesses, most of

whom are still living and available. If half the number of these witnesses was eliminated, the evidence of the remainder would still be sufficient, I think, to prove up to the hilt that manifestations have occurred at Borley to which no laws known to physical science can be applied. Take away fifty per cent of the Rectory witnesses, and the Borley mystery would *still* be the most remarkable in the history of psychical research.

Can *all* these 100 witnesses be mistaken? Is it possible that *all* these 100 people, over a period of sixty years, have been the victims of visual and aural illusions? Can *all* have been hallucinated? I do *not* think that this is possible. 'Suggestion' could *not* account for most of the phenomena seen and heard at Borley. When Mr. Kerr-Pearse was having his supper and was locked in the Base Room, investigation proved that the door *was* locked—although he was alone in a house, every entrance to which was sealed. There could be no suggestion about *that*. That door-locking phenomenon *happened*. When Mrs. Foyster, Dom Richard Whitehouse, and the maidservant were together in the kitchen, with doors and windows closed, and bottle after bottle materialized and crashed under their very eyes, there could be no suggestion about *that!* And it could not have been a case of mal-observation. When the Misses Ethel, Freda, Mabel, and Elsie Bull saw the 'nun' on their lawn on that bright summer's evening, they could *not* have been mistaken. And they could *not* have been mistaken when the figure vanished. Neither 'suggestion' nor collective hallucination could account for what these four young women saw. When Mr. Motion and I picked up the gold ring off the Blue Room floor on our last visit, after we had thoroughly searched the room several times, *that* was an abnormality, not suggestion. There is nothing abnormal in the ring itself, it was the finding of it that was so strange.

Of course, it is possible that people said they saw or heard things when they *knew* they did not. But would *all* of our 100 witnesses lie? Would 100 people tell the same or similar lie, in the same way, and with the same wealth of detail, over a period of sixty years? I am quite certain they would not. That would be a phenomenon as remarkable as any seen at Borley, and of the greatest psychological importance. But I am certain our witnesses were *not* lying, and that the things they say they heard and saw really happened in the way they say they did.

It has been seriously suggested that Borley is a sort of enchanted village. The argument is that when a person crosses its boundaries, he steps into a strange, new, four-dimensional world, and that his normal sensory organs are put out of gear, as it were. This theory is even more fantastic than that ghosts inhabit the Rectory and that objects move of their own volition. And yet it was put forward by a mathematician who does *not* believe in 'ghosts'!

The suggestion has also been made that a person must be, if not exactly a medium, at least 'psychic' to the extent of being able to experience and appreciate the strange occurrences that take place at Borley Rectory and its vicinity. If that indeed be the case, then the great majority of those—including 95 per cent of our observers—who have ever been to the Rectory are singularly gifted 'sensitives.' Of course, the exact reverse is the case: the very worst results have been achieved by the professional mediums. But because a person is a professional medium, that is no guarantee that he is gifted.

Another suggestion has been made that some person or persons—unnamed—have encouraged the belief that Borley Rectory was haunted in order to benefit themselves in some way. There is not the slightest foundation for such an argument. Every person—including all the Rectors—who was in any way intimately connected with the house, has been put to considerable annoyance, trouble, and pecuniary loss, directly traceable to the manifestations. Not only did their pockets suffer, but in some cases their health was also affected. Every occupant of the Rectory during recent years has had a miserable time there, and no one has made a penny-piece out of Borley, in any shape or form. Everyone —including the present writer—has been put to considerable expense in trying to solve the mystery.

An attempt has been made to analyse the phenomena and to determine the locations or areas affected, and the times of occurrence. We have already seen[1] that the Rev. L. A. Foyster states definitely that there was 'absolute quiet' in Holy Week and Easter Week. June was the worst month of the year. Sunday was usually the quietest day of the week, and Monday the worst.

Mr. S. H. Glanville made an analysis of the phenomena that occurred at Borley during a period of less than twelve months during Mr. Foyster's occupancy of the Rectory. Of the forty-five separate major manifestations, it was noted that 80 per cent occurred during the hours of darkness. On the ground floor, the great majority were observed within an area covered by the Sewing-Room, the kitchen, the passage between the Sewing-Room and the kitchen, and on the back stairs. A considerably lesser number occurred in the library [Base Room]. On the first floor, phenomena were confined to an equivalent area as observed on the ground floor [see Plans, pages 16, 22].

During my own investigations, I found that the principal focal centres of disturbance were in the kitchen passage, kitchen, Sewing-Room, large cupboard, Base Room, and hall. Upstairs, the phenomena were confined principally to the Blue Room and landing outside ('cold spot'), and the Chapel. Most of the appealing 'Marianne' messages appeared in the passage between Room 5 and the bathroom. These writings, and the hundreds of small pencil marks that appeared all over the house, are of great interest to psychical researchers. They are very unusual. Another unusual feature, even for a haunted house, is that the place was so soundless and cold.

I must say a word about those who visited the Rectory and neither saw nor heard anything worth recording.

[1] Page 79.

Actually, only three such reports were received—a very small percentage compared with the number of reports sent in. The reports contained nothing of value—just the plain statements that nothing happened. Occasionally, a friend would call at the Rectory to see whether anything was occurring there. He would stay a short while and would probably see nothing. I think it would have been extraordinary had he done so. I, too, have paid several visits to Borley without results worth mentioning. To be impressed by the Borley phenomena, one has to stay at the Rectory day after day—or at least hour after hour, in perfect quietness, and be prepared to keep watch both day and night. In other words, one has to employ a certain technique, familiar to investigators, in order properly to carry out a prolonged inquiry. A person might call at the Rectory fifty times without seeing or hearing anything. One cannot, I am afraid, walk into a haunted house and ask to see a phenomenon, like going into a shop for a pound of tea. One has to *wait* for it. But, as regards Borley, the phenomena are stronger and more frequent when the place is occupied by a family.

During the preparation of this work I received a number of letters from persons who were interested in Borley Rectory or its phenomena. One of these communications came from Mr. W. S. Pennefather, of Walton-on-Thames. He says:

'My father, a clergyman, rented this house [Borley Rectory] for his six weeks' holiday one summer, previous to 1896. To the best of my knowledge, no incidents occurred during our stay, and it is unlikely that the then incumbent said anything to my father, as he was desirous of letting the house.'

In replying, I asked Mr. Pennefather whether he could fix the exact year of his father's visit. He could not, but his father, he told me, was appointed Vicar of Kensington in 1896, and it was *before* that date that the Pennefather family spent their vacation at Borley. If we assume that the year of their visit was 1895, that would be during the incumbency of the Rev. Harry Bull, who succeeded his father as Rector in 1892. Of course, I do not for one moment question Mr. Pennefather's assertion that there were 'no incidents' during their stay at Borley, but after forty-five years it would be difficult to remember trivial, but unusual happenings, had they occurred.

Several attempts at exorcizing the ghosts at Borley have been made by various people, with negative results. I understand—though I have no first-hand evidence—that a well-known bishop carried out a rite of exorcism at some period in the history of Borley, without positive or lasting results. The Rev. L. A. Foyster was more successful with his creosote, and Dom Richard Whitehouse's Novena produced a 'message.' One would have thought that the fire which so completely gutted the Rectory would have been both exorcism and purification in one—if the disturbing entities are evil. But we have no evidence that they *are* evil. On the contrary, all the records go to prove rather that the 'spirits' —if they be spirits—are more troubled than troubling.

Speaking of exorcisms, a correspondent, the Rector of a Hertfordshire parish, makes the interesting suggestion that if some scandal connected with a religious really occurred at the monastery at Borley, no matter how long ago, we ought to communicate with the Mother Houses of the Order, acquaint them with the facts, and ask them to undertake a Novena of Reparation. It will be remembered that Dom Richard Whitehouse made a Novena near the Chapel in the Rectory, with interesting results. As I have remarked before in this monograph, there is a strong Roman Catholic element in the Borley mystery.

I now come to the point where I must ask my readers— the 'jury'—whether, on the evidence submitted, and the evidence alone, the Rectory is haunted, or not. Have phenomena occurred at Borley Rectory that cannot be explained in terms of our known physical laws? In other words, are the phenomena—or some of them—genuine? Are all the 100 witnesses mad, lying, or were they hallucinated immediately they crossed the 'enchanted boundary' of Borley village?

I put it to that great tribunal, the public, is Borley Rectory haunted, or is it not?

My answer to my own question is 'Yes, decidedly!' It is difficult to put into cold print the enthusiasm with which I record my affirmation. But then the reader has *not* had a glass candlestick hurled at him from above when he knew there was no one above to hurl it! The reader has *not* seen two keys fall from two doors simultaneously, when he was looking at them, knowing that no mortal hand supplied the energy. The reader has *not* interviewed about 100 people, as I have, who have experienced similar manifestations. So I will not ask him to share my enthusiasm. But I *will* ask him to weigh very carefully all the evidence submitted in this monograph before he hastily gives his verdict.

For a hundred years a few scientists, rather half-heartedly, have been trying to find out these things—without success. Even the 'spirit hypothesis' does not cover the 'appearance' of a psychic coach-and-pair! These are things that we do not understand, and Science, to its eternal shame, is making little attempt to understand them. I trust that at least this monograph will advance the time slightly when Orthodoxy will be compelled, by force of public opinion, to do so.[1] And with that rather forlorn hope I will leave my jury to consider their verdict.

---

[1] Since the above was written, there has been established (January 1940) at Trinity College, Cambridge, a Studentship in Psychical Research, out of a bequest left to the College by Mr. Frank Duerdin Perrott as a memorial to F. W. H. Myers. The value of the Studentship is £300 per annum, and is the first of its kind in any British university. My twenty-years' fight for academic recognition is at last bearing fruit. H.P.

APPENDIX A

'HAUNTED HOUSE'—DECLARATION FORM

I, the Undersigned, in consideration of having had my services accepted as an Official Observer, make the following Declaration :

1. I will fulfil all conditions and instructions, verbal and written, which are given me.
2. I will pay my own expenses connected with the investigation.
3. I am not connected with the Press in any way.
4. I will not convey to any person the name or location of the alleged Haunted House.
5. I will not write, or cause to be written, any account of my visit/s to the Haunted House, and will not lecture on my experiences there.
6. I will not photograph or sketch any part of the Haunted House or grounds without written permission.
7. I will not allow any person to accompany me on my Investigation, who has not signed the Declaration Form.
8. I will fulfil my obligations as regards Observational Periods, at the times and on the dates as arranged.
9. I will furnish a Report after each Observational Period.
10. I will not use the Telephone[1] installed in the House except for the purpose of reporting phenomena to the person or persons whose names have been given me, or for requesting assistance from those persons.
11. I will lock all doors and fasten all windows on my leaving the House, and will deposit key/s to person as directed.

Date..................................... *Signed*.............................

[1] The telephone was *not* installed, as originally intended.

APPENDIX B

THE BLUE BOOK

INSTRUCTIONS FOR OBSERVERS

PRIVATE AND CONFIDENTIAL

1. Attend carefully to all written and verbal instructions, and carry out to the letter.
2. Each Observer should provide himself with the following articles, in addition to night clothes, etc.: Note-block, pencils, good watch with seconds hand, candle and matches, pocket electric torch, brandy flask, sandwiches, etc. If he possesses a camera, this can be used. Rubber- or felt-soled shoes should be worn.
3. When going on duty, search the house thoroughly, close and fasten all doors and windows. If thought necessary, these can be sealed.
4. Visit all rooms, etc., at intervals of about one hour, unless circumstances call for your presence in any particular part of the house or grounds. Before going on duty at each period, inspect grounds.
5. Occasionally extinguish all lights, and wait in complete darkness (varying your observation post), remaining perfectly quiet.
6. Make a point of taking meals at same times each day or night. Depart from this rule if circumstances warrant.
7. Make the fullest notes of the slightest unusual sound or occurrence.
8. Take exact times of all sounds or happenings; also make notes of your own movements, with exact times. Record weather conditions.
9. Frequently examine grounds, and, occasionally, watch windows of house from exterior of building.
10. If with companion, both he and you should act in unison (in order to have a witness), unless circumstances determine otherwise. If several Observers present, party can be divided between house and grounds.

194

11. For one half-hour before, and half-hour after dusk, take up position in Summer-house. Remain perfectly quiet, and watch the 'Nun's Walk' on far side of lawn. It is this path that a black, draped figure is said to frequent.

12. If phenomena appear strong, or if experiencing a succession of unusual events, immediately communicate with one of the persons whose telephone numbers have been handed to you. Detail exact happenings. Expert assistance, or further instructions, will be sent you.

13. Establish your base in one room, and keep all your equipment, etc., at this post. This will prevent your hunting for an article when wanted in an emergency.

14. Keep the electric torch *in your pocket always*, whether in or out of the house. Be careful with all lights, matches, cigarette ends, etc.

15. Should strangers call, be courteous to them. Do not permit them to enter the house; do not encourage them to remain; *on no account give them information or opinions* of any sort. This applies to villagers, hotel staff, etc., equally.

16. *Re* meals. You should come provided each day with sandwiches, etc., and hot drinks in a vacuum flask. Rest can be obtained on the camp bed provided, but excellent meals and beds can be procured at 'The Bull,' L——¹ (2½ miles), or at S——² (2¼ miles). It should be possible to obtain sufficient rest during the 24 hours, but if two are on duty, take turns at resting, and wake your companion if anything unusual occurs. Leave your car in the appointed place, screened from the road.

17. When asked to take charge of instruments, examine them regularly with torch, and record readings and times in note book. Carefully note anything which may appear unusual. Change charts when necessary, marking on each the time it was changed, and date.

18. Spend at least a portion of the day and night (in complete darkness) in the Blue Room.

19. No Observer is permitted to take a friend to the house, unless permission has been given, and the necessary Declaration Form signed.

20. Your report and notes should be posted to the Honorary Secretary, University of London Council for Psychical Investigation, 19 Berkeley Street, Mayfair, W.1, as soon as possible after you have completed your 'watch.'

¹ [Long Melford.]   ² [Sudbury.]

Possible phenomena which may be experienced. There is some evidence for all of these alleged manifestations during the past forty years.

BELL-RINGING. If a bell rings, immediately ascertain which bell, and from what room or place the 'pull' was operated. Note if bell-pull is in motion, and record duration of ringing, and exact time.

MOVEMENT OF OBJECTS. When going on duty, see that objects are on chalked outlines, and check frequently. When an object is heard to fall, immediately ascertain in which room object has fallen, and draw rough plan of room, showing the direction of flight. Estimate approximate force expended, and, if object *seen* in flight, note speed, course, force, and trajectory. Examine object and restore to chalked outline.

FOOTSTEPS. If footsteps are heard, try to judge direction, note duration, and record type (heavy, soft, pattering, shuffling, etc.), and at what time they were heard.

FORMS OR APPARITIONS. If seen, *do not move and on no account approach the figure.* Note exact method of appearance. Observe figure carefully, watch all movements, rate and manner of progression, etc. Note duration of appearance, colour, form, size, how dressed, and whether solid or transparent. If carrying camera with film ready for exposing, quietly 'snap' the figure, but make no sound and do not move. If figure speaks, *do not approach*, but ascertain name, age, sex, origin, cause of visit, if in trouble, and possible alleviation. Inquire if it is a spirit. Ask figure to return, suggesting exact time and place. Do not move until figure disappears. Note exact method of vanishing. If through an open door, quietly follow. If through solid object (such as wall), ascertain if still visible on other side. Make the very fullest notes of the incident. The 'nun' is alleged to walk regularly along the 'Nun's Walk' in grounds. (See Instruction No. 11.)

RAPS OR KNOCKS. Ascertain exact location and intensity, and whether soft or percussive. Imitate knocks with knuckles or foot, and note whether your signals are duplicated. If so, say aloud that you would like a number of questions answered, and that the 'entity' can reply by giving one rap for 'yes', two for 'no', and three for 'doubtful or unknown.' Endeavour by these means to ascertain name, age, sex, condition, etc. Ask 'entity' to knock at a letter while you call over the alphabet. Information can thus be conveyed, and intelligent sentences formed. Ask entity to return, making definite appointment. It is alleged that knocks can frequently be heard in the Blue Room. (See Instruction No. 18.)

PERFUMES. If air becomes scented, try to identify perfume, and ascertain whether it is general or localized. Look for any dampness.

LIGHTS. If lights are seen, note mode of appearance, judge exact position in room or grounds, size, shape, height from ground, duration, colour, and whether lambent or percussive. If travelling, direction and trajectory, and method of disappearance. Note whether odour accompanies lights.

APPORTS. (Objects abnormally brought or precipitated into house.) Note exact time of arrival, if possible, and endeavour to ascertain their origin. Carefully preserve and continue inquiries.

DISAPPEARANCES. Note under what conditions the object disappeared, exact time of disappearance, and if accompanied by sounds of any sort. Search for object and note if, how, and when it makes its reappearance.

THERMAL VARIATIONS. Transmitting thermographs are used for recording changes of temperature. These should be read frequently. (See Instruction No. 17.)

EXTERIOR OF HOUSE

The above suggestions apply equally in the case of phenomena occurring *outside* the house. But *Poltergeist* phenomena (such as stone-throwing) outside the house may be observed from within the building. The fullest particulars concerning such phenomena should be recorded.

IMPORTANT NOTE

Although some—or all—of the above phenomena may be observed, it is very important that the greatest effort should be made to ascertain whether such manifestations are due to normal causes, such as rats, small boys, the villagers, the wind, wood shrinking, the Death Watch beetle, farm animals nosing the doors, etc., trees brushing against the windows, birds in the chimney-stack or between double walls, etc.

APPENDIX C

DIGEST OF OFFICIAL OBSERVERS' REPORTS

MR. SIDNEY H. GLANVILLE was our first official observer. By profession he is a consulting engineer, but he is also a clever draftsman, photographer and inventor of gadgets for trapping ghosts! And he is an ideal investigator.

Immediately my *Times* advertisement appeared, he wrote for an interview, was gladly accepted, and his first observational period began on June 19, 1937. His son, Mr. Roger H. Glanville, accompanied him.

In his first report, Mr. Glanville stated that he made a minute examination of the house and grounds, took full measurements of all the rooms, etc., and subsequently prepared the plans of the Rectory which are reproduced in this volume. [Pages 16, 22.]

He also devised something that would have told us, had it been used, of the path taken by any ghost curious enough to pick up—literally and metaphorically—the idea.

The appliance in question was an aluminium container partially filled with fine corundum grain. In the bottom of the container was a tiny hole. This container or cup, weighing five ounces, was placed on the sill of the Blue Room window, and ringed with chalk. If any entity—incarnate or discarnate—had picked up or carried the container, a trail of corundum powder would have informed us of the path taken. Alas! no ghost was curious enough to interfere with it.

In his first report, Mr. Glanville says that 'the house is the coldest and most silent I have ever experienced.'

Actually, the day was a quiet one. The Glanvilles arrived on Saturday, June 19, at 9.35 a.m. and left the following morning at 7.30 a.m. But they were able to record two incidents which could not be explained in terms of normality. At 11.29 p.m. 'a short, clear, sharp click or crack was heard,' but exact location of sound could not be determined. At 1.58 a.m. 'two soft taps were heard.' They came from the direction of the upper rooms. Both sounds were investigated without result. It is interesting to note that a 'thump' emanating from the same direction was heard at almost the same time (1.41 a.m.) by Mr. A. P. Drinkwater and his friends on November 14, 1937.[1]

On Saturday, August 14, 1937, Mr. Glanville and his brother-in-law, Captain H. G. Harrison visited the Rectory. All doors and windows were fastened and sealed. During their tours of the house they photographed the 'Marianne get help' message.[2] An hour or so later, when on their next routine visit to the rooms, *several new markings were found.* One of these was close to the 'Marianne' message they had previously photographed. This message was again photographed and the two prints compared. The new pencil markings are in *one* photograph only—proof positive that they were added while they were in the house. They were duly ringed. In a covering letter to his report, Mr.

Glanville says: 'These pencil markings were well worth the whole trip.'

The only unusual noises that were heard included a sharp 'crack' near the front door; and, while they were sitting in the Blue Room in semi-darkness, they heard faint 'scrabbling' sounds outside.

I have already mentioned[1] that there is a cats' cemetery at the end of the Nun's Walk. It is much overgrown and difficult of access owing to brambles, etc. The Glanvilles had, of course, noticed the 'cemetery' and the headboards on a previous visit.

During their tour of inspection of the garden on August 14, Glanville noticed with surprise that the grave of the cat 'Gem' had been considerably disturbed. The headboard had been flung into a near-by bush, and an area, the size of a small room, had been dug—as if a large hole had been excavated and then filled in, leaving a quantity of loose earth spread around.

When next he saw me, Mr. Glanville asked me whether I could tell him who disturbed the cats, and for what purpose. I certainly could *not!* The garden had not been touched since Mr. Foyster left. And *why* should any person take the trouble to go to a remote and overgrown part of the garden, and dig up a cat's grave that had remained unmolested for many years? But was it really a cat buried there? The same idea occurred to both Mr. Glanville and me that something else may have been buried there, and that some person, for reasons best known to himself had, through prudence or fear, decided to disinter it. What man in his right senses would take the trouble to fight his way through a thicket of brambles and spend time and energy in digging up a cat's grave? But that someone *had* done this was evident, and had taken a considerable amount of trouble over it, too.

A fortnight later, on their next visit, Mr. Glanville and his son took a couple of spades with them and decided to do a little digging themselves. They re-dug the cat's grave over the same area as was indicated by the freshly dug earth. After considerable digging they turned up a lot of large bones that certainly never formed part of the anatomy of a cat. They appeared to have once belonged to the local butcher, but one or two of them they could not identify. On my next visit to Borley I asked the tenant of the cottage (Mr. Arbon) if he could throw any light on the mystery of the cats' cemetery. But he knew nothing about it. So the mystery still remains: *Who* disturbed the cats, and *why*?

On Saturday, August 28, 1937, Mr. Glanville, his son, Captain H. G. Harrison, and Squadron-Leader Horniman spent the night

[1] See page 25.

at the Rectory. Between 11 p.m. and 4 a.m. (on the Sunday) they 'all heard several light thuds or bumps,' but could not locate them. When Glanville and his son were out for a meal, their colleagues, remaining on duty, 'at 8.24 p.m. clearly heard the sound of light tripping footsteps coming down the main stairs.' Nothing was visible. Also, 'a few very small, light and apparently new pencil marks have been made on some of the walls.'

Mr. Glanville and his son visited the Rectory again on September 18 and October 2, 1937. The only phenomena heard occurred on the former date: 'At 10.30 p.m. a solitary tap was heard, at 10.34 another single tap. Both these apparently came from the dining-room wall.' Every window and door in the house (except those of the Base Room and front doors, near which they were watching) had been sealed with thread and wax.

On September 24, 1937, Mr. Glanville received a letter from his brother-in-law, Captain H. G. Harrison. His (Harrison's) friend, Squadron-Leader Horniman had been to the Rectory on the previous Monday with a friend. Horniman made the following report: 'What is interesting is that, without any previous information, this friend came over desperately cold in the identical spot on the landing [outside Blue Room], where Kerr-Pearse's friend did.[1] Kerr-Pearse [who was on duty at the Rectory] felt his hands, and confirmed that they were much below normal temperature.'

This 'cold spot' outside the Blue Room [see Plate III and + on First Floor Plan] is very interesting. At least three persons, at different times, and complete strangers to one another, have 'come over cold' on this identical spot, which is *exactly* above the subsidence in the cellar, already commented upon. Also, this is the exact spot where the Rev. G. Eric Smith heard 'sibilant whisperings' and Mrs. Foyster was given a black eye by an invisible assailant on February 26, 1931. When Mr. Glanville realized the importance of this position on the Blue Room landing, he marked the spot by pencilling a tiny cross, almost invisible, on the floor. Only he, his son Roger, and Dr. Bellamy knew of this. On their next visit to the Rectory (on September 18, 1937), Mr. Glanville and his son discovered that a flat tobacco tin that he, and other observers, had left as a 'control' on the drawing-room mantelpiece, had been moved from its chalked position and had been carried upstairs and placed, with mathematical precision, exactly over the tiny pencilled cross. Mr. Kerr-Pearse had been the last to visit the house, and had left the

[1] See Kerr-Pearse's testimony, *post.*

tobacco tin within its prescribed markings. Mr. Arbon informed Mr. Glanville that no one had been in the house since Kerr-Pearse's visit, and the keys had never left his possession.

The next report from Mr. Glanville is dated October 28, 1937. He and his son Roger, and a friend named Alan Cuthbert, visited the Rectory on the previous Saturday. Mr. Mark Kerr-Pearse, whose experiences form the next section of this monograph, was also on duty. Glanville says:

'At about 2 a.m. Cuthbert was sound asleep in the Base Room. Kerr-Pearse, Roger and I were sitting on the landing, in the dark, when *we all heard heavy muffled footsteps walk across the hall,* just under us. They were quite distinct and no mistake was possible. There were accompanying sounds of general movement of a body. We went down almost immediately but found nothing but Cuthbert, still soundly sleeping in the Base Room. During the night there were sundry taps and thuds which I will leave to Kerr-Pearse to report.[1]

On Saturday, November 20, 1937, Mr. Glanville, his son Roger, Captain H. G. Harrison and Dr. H. F. Bellamy visited the Rectory for an observational period. Their report says:

'At 8.25 p.m. we were all in the Base Room and noticed that the blind, which had been lowered earlier in the evening, was moving at the sides. The movement is not easy to describe. The edges of both sides were waving regularly, a sort of palpitating action as though being blown. We all watched closely for several moments and, thinking there must be a draught, applied our eyes to the gap between the blind and the window frames, but none could be traced. We then slowly released a cloud of cigarette smoke directed to the narrow space between the blind and the frame. This was not dispersed immediately as it would have been, had it been a draught. The Base Room glass doors and the doors of the hall were all closed at the time. The incident lasted about five minutes. We can offer no explanation. At 7.30 a.m. on the next [Sunday] morning a single sharp rap was heard, coming from the corner of the Base Room, over the table.'

When Mr. Glanville and his party arrived on the Saturday morning, they found the painters at work on the outside of the house. I had given permission to the Chelmsford Diocesan Dilapidations Board to make a survey under the Ecclesiastical Dilapidation Measures, and the outside of the Rectory was being redecorated.

The name of the foreman painter was Mr. Hardy. He was

[1] See *post*, page 210.

born in Borley and has lived there all his life. He has worked at the Rectory on many occasions. Some years before his interview with Mr. Glanville, Mr. Hardy was working in the Rectory. It was on a bright summer's afternoon. Suddenly a fellow workman called him into the library and pointed to a column of smoke rising vertically from the centre of the lawn. The phenomenon lasted for one or two minutes. Immediate investigation provided no clue to the mystery and no explanation was ever forthcoming.

About a fortnight before Mr. Glanville's visit, Mr. Hardy's son, aged nineteen, when returning from work at night, heard singing or chanting coming from the church as he passed. The church was closed at the time. He did not stop to investigate. Mr. Hardy remarked that Borley Rectory had had the reputation of being haunted as long as he could remember, and that some years ago the villagers were afraid to pass it at night if they were alone.

Mr. Glanville and Alan Cuthbert paid another visit to the Rectory on March 12, 1938. Mr. M. Savage and his friend, Mr. Bridgewater, were also present. After a thorough examination of the house, they began their usual routine patrols. At ten o'clock in the evening they found some fresh, dark sticky stains, of the consistency of glycerine, on the floor of the chapel. They were *not* there during previous patrols. They scraped up some of the fluid, but could not obtain sufficient for purposes of analysis. At 1.45 a.m. they all heard a 'sharp, hard sound sufficiently loud to make us jump.' It came from the top, middle shelf of the bookcase in the Base Room. The thermometer on the bookcase showed that the temperature had varied only 1° Fahrenheit during the previous ten hours, so it could not have been due to any crepitation of the wood. Immediately preceding the sound from the bookcase was heard another noise from the Blue Room above. It was as if a chair leg had been scraped along the floor.

In addition to his reports, abstracts of which appear above, Mr. Glanville and his friends made a number of experiments with table-tipping and the Planchette, with curious results. They are described in Chapters XXV, XXVI, and XXVII.

THE ADVENTURES OF A PROCONSUL

Mr. Mark Kerr-Pearse is on the staff of the British Legation at Geneva. In the latter part of 1937, he was on holiday in England and, seeing my *Times* advertisement asking for observers, he 'joined up' early in June. He thought that ghost-hunting would be a pleasant way of spending part of his vacation.

Actually, Mr. Kerr-Pearse spent more time at Borley Rectory than any other official observer. Altogether, he was present in the house for some weeks. Often he was alone; sometimes he was joined by a friend; occasionally, other of our investigators spent their observational periods while he was 'residing' in the house.

If the weather was fine, Mr. Kerr-Pearse would remove the camp bed from the Base Room and place it in the large summer-house, where he would spend part of the night. This intrepid young man spent many such nights reclining on the bed, with eyes fixed on the Nun's Walk, hoping to see the figure before he dropped off to sleep. If the weather was inclement, he would rest in the Base Room. He was the only investigator who spent any time in the house entirely by himself, with the exception of Mr. J. W. Burden, who spent the night of December 18–19, 1937, alone in the Rectory.[1]

Mr. Kerr-Pearse is a very shrewd observer and a model of what a psychical researcher should be. His very long and detailed routine reports were prepared with meticulous care, and occasionally they are literally minute-by-minute records of what was taking place in the house or grounds and his own actions at the time, weather conditions, etc. His analyses of the phenomena and conditions under which they were experienced were most helpful.

Mr. Kerr-Pearse's first visit to Borley was on June 26, 1937. After a very careful examination of the place from cellars to attics, and the sealing up of all windows and other entrances, he began his watch, spending some time in each apartment.

At 7.50 p.m., when in the Blue Room, he 'heard two distinct raps in quick succession' which appeared to come from the direction of the attic stairs. He at once investigated, but could find no cause for the knocks. He then 'asked if anyone was there; or, if they wished to speak to me, to tap. No reply.'

After more routine patrols of the house, which occupied him until nearly three o'clock the next morning, he took an hour's rest in the summer-house. At 4.30 a.m. he made another inspection of the grounds, and at 5.50 a.m. made a thorough search of the house. Everything was in order. Then he went into the garden again. As he was passing the French windows of the Base Room (which, of course, were closed), he heard a 'thump' which obviously came from inside the room. He immediately entered and found that one of the books on the mantelpiece had fallen down. No one was there. The book had been in position all night. He spent some time in the room, but nothing further occurred.

He spent the whole of the next day and night in the Rectory,

[1] See *post*.

sleeping in the summer-house for an hour or so during the small hours. On the morning of June 28, at 11.40 a.m. he placed a screw on the mantelpiece of the Base Room, very carefully ringing it with chalk. At 11.45 he happened to glance at the mantelpiece and found that the *screw had been moved* to one side of the chalk ring. This must have occurred while he was actually in the room, a few yards away from the screw.

His experiences, unexciting as they were, impressed and interested him, and a few days later (July 3 and 4) Kerr-Pearse again visited the Rectory. Nothing whatever occurred to warrant comment, except that under one of the 'Marianne' messages [see Plate VII] he added the words: 'I still cannot understand. Please tell me more.' This was a sort of supplementary request to the one that Mrs. Foyster (Marianne) had previously written under another message asking for help.

On July 10, 1937, Mr. Kerr-Pearse visited the Rectory and remained there until the 19th, with the exception of July 12, when he was away. During this long period he carried out a microscopic scrutiny of the house, the walls, and everything visible. He tabulated and numbered every portable object in the rooms and noted, on paper, every pencil mark, however tiny, on the walls and passages. He also made plans of the house, marking on them the various objects that had been placed in the rooms for control purposes. A complete inventory of these articles was made.

Observers had been instructed to *ring* with chalk every pencil mark seen on the walls, and to put a date against it—the date of discovery. Mr. Kerr-Pearse checked these, marked others that had not been so treated (the very tiny pencil marks), and made a list of them.

And yet, in spite of his scientific control methods, pencil markings appeared during his visit—almost under his eyes. For example, at 7.25 p.m. on July 13 he checked up the marks on the staircase. But 'at 8.30 p.m. I found two more pencil marks, which I chalked and numbered 1 and 2. These were *not* here at 7.25, as I re-examined every inch of the wall'. At 8.35 a.m. on July 14, he found *another* pencil mark on staircase wall, and this he numbered 3. *At the same time, the wicket gate at the top of the back stairs opened.* He heard it open, investigated, and found it ajar. It had been firmly latched. He reclosed it. No explanation.

On this same day (at 7.15 p.m.) Mr. Kerr-Pearse discovered a pencil line a foot long in passage under 'Marianne-Light-Mass-Prayers' message. He also found various groups of markings on the left-hand side of kitchen wall. They were *not* there earlier in the day. He ringed them with chalk.

On July 15 I visited Borley for a few hours in order to see if everything was all right. I arrived at 8.25 p.m. and left three hours later at 11.25. Mr. Kerr-Pearse showed me the new marks that had been found. During a routine examination of the house we found five new marks in Room 2. One, which could not possibly have been overlooked on previous examinations, was very conspicuous.

On the next morning at 9.45 a.m. Kerr-Pearse found more marks. One was discovered in passage between butler's pantry and the small staircase. It was in the shape of the letter 'c' and was nine inches long. The second was six inches long and re-sembled the letters 'Ma.' The third marking also resembled 'Ma'—both pencillings suggestive of an attempt to write 'Mari-anne.' Heavy pressure had been applied with, apparently, the same soft pencil. The handwriting was similar to that of the other 'Marianne' messages. These last two markings were near the window in passage: one was two feet from the ground, under window; the other was five feet from the floor, by the side of the window. The pencil with which the marks were made had, Kerr-Pearse thought, broken while the letters were being formed. He minutely searched the floor for a possible detached point, without result.

On this same morning, July 16, at 11.30 a.m., the Rev. A. C. Henning called on Mr. Kerr-Pearse. With him was his gardener, Herbert Mayes. The subject of the 'strange coat'[1] was raised, and Mayes confirmed the fact that when he went over the Rectory on June 1 previously, the coat was *not* in the house, and he knew nothing about it. He searched the place very carefully, looking behind all doors. As we have seen,[2] the coat *was* there when Mr. Ellic Howe and I visited the Rectory on June 2. Therefore the coat *must* have 'appeared' in the Blue Room some time between the afternoon of June 1 and that of June 2.

Kerr-Pearse's protocol continues:

'July 16, 7.5 p.m. Discovered a further small pencil mark in same passage about one foot to right of scrawled "Ma." Made with sharp, soft pencil. Definitely was *not* there this morn-ing.'

Kerr-Pearse dined with the Hennings on the evening of this day (July 16) and they all returned to the Rectory at 9.30 p.m. They thought they would try an interesting experiment, the

---

[1] See page 111. [2] See page 111.

account of which I will quote verbatim from Kerr-Pearse's
report:

'Returned with Rev. and Mrs. Henning. As an experiment
we hung up the coat[1] in Blue Room, placed two night-lights in
Chapel and one in ground-floor passage opposite Sewing-Room.
We then sat in Base Room and rapped table. After about fourth
attempt, *a most extraordinary noise was heard as though coming from
the kitchen, and slowly moving down passage* towards us. It lasted
fully a minute and ceased abruptly when we stood up—unfortunately making a noise in doing so—to get a better view of
passage. We could not account for this noise, as the evening was
very quiet and the night-light burned without even a flicker. We
returned the coat to Room 7.'

On July 17, two pencil lines were discovered at 5.45 p.m.
They were not there in the morning as Kerr-Pearse scrutinized
each wall morning and evening, ringing every new mark.

A piece of rotten wood, like touch-wood, was found on the
hearth in the Sewing Room at 9.45 a.m. on July 18. It was
roughly three feet square. It could not have fallen down chimney,
which needed cleaning very badly, as there was no soot on it.
The wood was *not* there the previous evening on his 11 o'clock
patrol, and Kerr-Pearse did not leave the house. Later in the
same day, at 6.20 p.m., he discovered two fresh pencil marks on
open door of scullery.

Still later in the day of July 18, *more* pencil marks appeared.
I will quote verbatim from Kerr-Pearse's log:

'9.45 p.m. The following pencil marks have appeared since
my morning inspection: Six marks in chapel which I am certain
were not there previously as I had examined it very closely.
Also a mark by kitchen door in passage opposite Sewing-Room
about two feet from floor. So much pressure had been applied
that the distemper and part of the plaster of wall had been
scratched away.'

Mr. Kerr-Pearse left for London at 9.50 the next morning,
July 19, 1937.

He returned to Borley on July 24, 1937, and stayed until
August 7. He was away on business in London for one day
(July 27). On the next day (July 28) he did *not* see the 'nun,'
as he should have done, according to tradition.

During his absence from Borley between July 19 and 24, other
observers had been in the house and had marked and ringed
some fine cracks in the wall plaster, obviously mistaking them for

[1] The 'strange coat.'

pencil lines, or perhaps merely drawing attention to them. But when Kerr-Pearse made his first inspection on July 24, the first thing he noticed was an unringed 'W'—or inverted 'M'—on window ledge in passage opposite Sewing-Room, and another mark on staircase wall. These were duly ringed and dated.

After a quiet day or so, more pencillings appeared on wall of kitchen. Nothing of importance happened for some days, so Kerr-Pearse thought he would examine the two wells. He cleared out the one in the cellar, and found that it was very shallow with a smooth concrete bottom. It is really a tank, but at one time it was a deep well, and was filled in for safety's sake. He cleaned it out, hoping for something interesting, but found only some old tins, half a brick, a broken tumbler and so on. It is possible to enter the cellar from the courtyard *via* this tank, though it would be an unpleasant business. Observers were warned against this and so kept cellar door (leading into house) locked, or sealed, or both.

Kerr-Pearse next examined the main well in the courtyard[1] and actually descended to the first platform, eight feet down, by means of the supply pipe. However, this pipe was so slippery that further descent would have been dangerous, if not fatal. He found the platform very rotten and makes the suggestion that the touch-wood found in the Sewing-Room came from the well platform. Personally, I doubt this, as the piece I saw was as dry as tinder. Anyway, the mystery as to *how* the wood got into the Sewing-Room was not solved.

At 9.10 a.m. on August 5, Kerr-Pearse found a petrified frog, with dust and fluff sticking to its hind legs, in the passage outside the drawing-room. It was *not* there overnight, and every door and window in the house was closed. He suggests that it was due to *Poltergeist* activity. It is possible that a live frog—or a frog that had just died—might have come up from the cellar. But the frog in the passage was dry, flat, and petrified. How did it get into the house?

Kerr-Pearse left for London on August 7, as no further incidents occurred.

Kerr-Pearse was again at the Rectory from August 23 to 28. No phenomena were noted, and the house appeared even quieter than usual. But one day the Rev. A. C. Henning called at the Rectory, accompanied by his wife and a Miss Reid. The following is from the official report:

'While inspecting the house with the Rev. and Mrs. Henning

[1] See my account, page 21.

and their friend Miss Reid, the latter had a curious experience
outside the Blue Room. She had a feeling of terror, a sensation
of "pins and needles" all over, and felt very cold although it
was a warm evening. We felt her hands, which were indeed icy.
On leaving that part of the house, she became more at ease but,
when we returned about fifteen minutes later, the same thing
happened again. I would add, that no one else had any similar
feeling. Miss Reid is a very level-headed person and does not
in any way pretend to be psychic.'

This is the second person to be affected by the 'cold spot'
outside the Blue Room [See Plate III]. It will be remembered
that the friend who accompanied Squadron-Leader Horniman
to the Rectory on September 20 was similarly affected.[1]

Mr. Kerr-Pearse did not again visit Borley until September 21,
1937. He was accompanied by his cousin, Mr. Rupert Haig,
aged about 33, a barrister-at-law in the Colonial Legal Service.
I will now quote Kerr-Pearse's notes verbatim:

'Sept. 21, 1 p.m. A single, but distinct rap on door of Base
Room. Went out, but neither saw nor heard anything.
'Sept. 21, 8.30 p.m. While standing with my cousin on landing
outside Blue Room, we heard a rustling noise below. This must
have been caused *by the moving of a sack of coal (weighing about
50 pounds) by about 18 inches*. This sack was lying on its side against
Base Room wall in passage. I had noticed its position by a stain
on the floor.
'Sept. 22, 2.30 a.m. A single rap on window of Base Room.
(May have been a moth.)
'Sept. 22, 3.40 a.m. My cousin was awakened by icy draught
on his face. This was odd, as both doors and windows were
closed and the fire had been burning for at least 12 hours. The
temperature of room was 60° Fahrenheit by the thermometer.
'Sept. 22, 4.30 p.m. Was sitting in Base Room, when I heard
a heavy "thud" in Blue Room overhead as though a small
packing-case had been dropped. Went up, but found nothing.
All objects in marked places.'

When later Mr. Kerr-Pearse and I discussed the sack of coal
incident, he told me that the phenomenon was very impressive.
The weather was rather cold and they had bought a 56-lb. bag of
coal locally. About six pounds had been used on the Base Room
fire, and the bag placed outside the door. He had *very carefully*
noted its position by a stain on the floor. His cousin, too, noted
the position. No normal explanation was forthcoming for the
'telekinetic' movement of the bag. Both Kerr-Pearse and his

[1] See page 200.

cousin heard the movement from their position outside the Blue Room.

Mr. Haig left England shortly after his visit to Borley and, later, sent his cousin the following letter:

> 'P. & O. *Ranchi,*
> '(Posted Port Said),
> 'October 2, 1937.

'My dear Mark,

'If I did not enjoy my visit to your haunted house, I at least found it most interesting. I entered it with a completely open mind, but left it with the firm conviction that it *is* haunted.

'You will recollect that I woke you up in the middle of the night and offered no explanation. . . .

'Immediately before waking you, I had been awake for a considerable time. I cannot say how long, but it must have been at least half an hour. To begin with, I was certainly in a jumpy state. I was expecting footsteps, thumps, knocks, and even to see something, but as time went on and nothing happened I became calmer. Everything was perfectly still and I saw and heard nothing, but suddenly the air surrounding me became ice cold, my hands became icy, and in fact I became cold all over and my hair stood on end. I was rigid. The sensation lasted as nearly as I can judge about 20 seconds, and then passed off. It was so unpleasant that . . . . I was compelled eventually to awake you.

'You can make of that exactly what you please. It may well have been nothing but nerves and fright. But of what was I frightened? I had seen or heard nothing; and remember that I had been awake for nearly half an hour; was quite calm and was lying in a room which was occupied by another person, and was lighted by a lamp and a fire which still burned brightly only a few feet from me. The sensation was completely sudden.

'I am myself convinced that the experience was not natural; but of course I do not in the least expect anybody else to be so. I am sorry that I missed the dropping of the packing case in the Blue Room. At 4.30 p.m., I think I could have stood that with comparative equanimity. I am most interested in the house.

> 'Yours affectionately,
> (*Signed*) 'RUPERT [HAIG].'

Mr. Kerr-Pearse was due in Geneva in November 1937, and he visited Borley for the last time from October 23 to November 1, 1937. During part of this period, Mr. S. H .Glanville, his son Roger, and Mr. Alan Cuthbert, were at the Rectory.[1]

His last visit proved both interesting and exciting. On the day he arrived, at 3.45 p.m., he heard a distinct rap in hall corridor. A few minutes later a loud creak came from the back

---
[1] See their report, *ante*, page 201.

staircase 'as of a heavy footstep on a loose board.' Next day, at
4.30 p.m., the brass ring attached to shutter of Base Room
windows rattled twice. Then, later, when he was in the Base
Room, he heard a loud 'bump' which emanated near the
Chapel. Later that day the heavy shutter in Base Room was heard
to move slightly by Mr. Glanville, Cuthbert, and Kerr-Pearse.

On October 25, at 2 o'clock in the morning, three of the
observers, who were keeping watch on the landing outside Blue
Room, heard 'heavy shuffling footsteps outside Base Room. At
first we did not investigate, being certain they were made by
Cuthbert whom we had left asleep in that room. On descending,
we found him still sound asleep.'[1]

At 3.40 a.m., while they were still in the Base Room, a distinct
thud was heard upstairs. Investigation revealed nothing unusual.

Readers will remember the extraordinary experiences which
Mr. Foyster and Dom, Richard Whitehouse have so often
recorded concerning the spontaneous locking of doors. We were
present[2] at one of these manifestations.

On October 26, while alone in the house (the Glanvilles and
friend had returned home), Kerr-Pearse witnessed a similar
phenomenon. I will let him relate the story:

'Oct. 26, 10.48 p.m. When sitting in Base Room, finishing
supper, I heard a small "click" of which I did not take much
notice, thinking it was caused by a draught shaking the door.
A few seconds later, when going to the pantry to wash up,
I found that I had been locked in the Base Room. Fortunately, the key
was on the inside of the door.'

Kerr-Pearse had only just previously entered the Base Room
from the pantry with his supper things. Whatever it was that
locked the door must have been in the room while he was having
his supper.

Next day (October 27) while he was in the Base Room, he
heard a 'shuffling noise' that appeared to come from the w.c.
upstairs. It lasted about three seconds. When he mounted to the
upper floor he could find nothing to account for the noise.

A few hours later, when he was resting in the Base Room, he
'heard from the kitchen a crash as though several saucepans
had fallen to the ground. On investigation found nothing.'

On October 28, I paid one of my rare visits to the Rectory to
see how Kerr-Pearse was getting on. I was accompanied by
three friends. I stayed a few hours, and during our first inspection
of the house we found a large pencil mark on a wall of the Base

---

[1] Confirms Glanville's account, page 201.   [2] See page 70.

Room. It was a new one. Then we all (at about 11 p.m.) heard footsteps in the Blue Room above us. I rushed upstairs: no one was there. We left the Rectory soon afterwards. Similar footsteps, from the same direction, had been recorded by Kerr-Pearse, *at the same hour*, on October 25, 26, and 27: 'At times they appeared to be pacing up and down the room alongside the wall dividing it from the passage.'

During this evening Kerr-Pearse had his *coat pulled twice*. The interval between was about 15 seconds. No one was near him, and the pull was quite definite.[1]

On October 30, someone—or something—unscrewed the handle of the cupboard door in the hall. On this same day Mr. Glanville and his son arrived and, when the three of them made their next inspection of the house 'a large pencilled "M"' was discovered on the landing wall opposite w.c. Later, they heard 'a succession of heavy metallic sounds in bathroom, lasting some 20–30 seconds.' They were then standing *outside* the house, in the drive, immediately below the bathroom window. Mr. Henning arrived later and when the whole party was outside the kitchen, they all heard a distinct 'thump' in the hall. Two minutes later a second 'thump' was heard. Next morning, at 10.35, three distinct thuds came from the Blue Room while the party was in the Base Room. These were followed by two more thuds about ten seconds later. This was the last phenomenon that Kerr-Pearse heard in Borley Rectory, as he left for London —on his way to Geneva—the same day.

In sending me the account of his last week at Borley, Kerr-Pearse says in a covering letter: 'This is quite the most interesting report.' With which I agree. If the phenomena witnessed by him and his friends were the only manifestations ever recorded at Borley, the Rectory would still be an outstanding example of a really haunted house.

COLONEL WESTLAND'S DISCOVERY

Among the many good observers who answered my call for help in solving the mystery of Borley Rectory, some were particularly useful and skilful. Lieut.-Col. F. C. Westland was one of them. He is not only a clever draftsman—he is attached to the Royal Army Ordnance Corps—but he is also a very clever photographer and supplied us with perfect photographs of all the wall writings that he found.

Being such a shrewd observer, he very soon discovered the 'Marianne' messages in the various parts of the house. These,

[1] Compare similar experience recorded by Mr. F. A. Mansbridge, page 233.

of course, 'appeared' during Mr. Foyster's occupation of the Rectory and are dealt with in Chapter XXIV.

Colonel and Mrs. Westland paid their first visit to Borley on Friday, June 25, 1937, and stayed in the Rectory until the following morning. He sent me his minute-by-minute log, with all incidents recorded, weather conditions, etc. As I have not previously reproduced verbatim any observer's routine log, I will print a short section of Colonel Westland's report, in order that the reader can assess with what care the investigation of the Rectory was carried out. Here is the first page of Colonel Westland's log, begun on his arrival at the house. It is dated June 25, 1937:

'6.15 p.m. Arrived and briefly inspected house outside and inside. Found all objects on their chalk marks. Weather fair, but overcast. Warm. No wind.

'6.40. Unloaded car.

'6.50. Went to Long Melford for supplies.

'7.35. Returned and unpacked.

'8.0. Made a round of inside of house. Taped door on attic. All objects in place. Shut all windows and doors with one or two exceptions, locking those [interior doors] that had keys. Oiled lock of cellar door and locked it.

'8.45. Had supper.

'9.22. Visited Blue Room.

'9.50. Went to summer-house.

'10.45. Left summer-house, having seen nothing. Made a round of exterior of house. Weather fine. Sky clearer, some stars showing. Moon was clear of mist on horizon.

'11.5. Returned inside house and made coffee.

'11.50–12.15 a.m. Made a round of inside of house, pausing for ten minutes in the Blue Room in darkness. All objects unmoved, but discovered a small, blue lacquered box containing pins in the store-room [i.e., large cupboard] nearest the hall or passage to garden door. We had not noticed the box on our previous rounds at 8 o'clock, but it is possible that we overlooked it. A chalk ring was drawn round it.'

And so it goes on—a good example of our observers' records. In a covering letter to his report, Colonel Westland said that the blue box that he found at, midnight was three inches in diameter and contained pins. It was a flat box. It was found on the lower shelf of the stack in the cupboard. At eight o'clock when he and Mrs. Westland thoroughly examined the cupboards, they used torches to look into all corners, although it was not yet dark.

I made inquiries concerning the blue box, but could not trace the ownership. Mr. Glanville was doing duty at the Rectory a few days previously and it did not belong to him. The blue box was just one of the many curious objects that appeared in the Rectory in a curious way.

Colonel Westland and his wife next visited the Rectory on Monday, July 7, 1937, and remained there until the following Friday evening.

Here are extracts from his log :

'The phenomena which occurred during our stay were: On our 4 a.m. round of the house on Tuesday, July 6, we found the door of the dressing-room (*i.e.*, the small room next the Blue Room) [Room No. 5] unlocked and ajar. We certainly thought we had shut and locked it on our 2 a.m. round, but may have omitted to do so.

'Whilst taking measurements of the rooms between 6 and 7 a.m. on Wednesday [July 7] I found a blue serge lady's jacket hanging behind the door of the S.E. bedroom [Room No. 7] which we had not noticed before. The door opens to the left against the wall and the jacket would not be seen unless one shut the door after entering the room.

'On our 12 a.m. round on Thursday, July 8, we noticed a cross in red chalk on the outside of the door of the room over the kitchen. This again may have been overlooked on previous rounds.

'On our 4.40 a.m. round on Friday, July 9, we found that the Eucryl tin on the slate shelf of the larder had moved half an inch. On the same round we found signs of writing on the wall of the kitchen passage. It looked as if an attempt had been made to rub it out. It was illegible.

'At 9.20 p.m., July 9, I found a piece of wood 3 inches by 1 inch by 1 inch on the stairs in the kitchen passage. Mrs. Westland had noticed it at 6 p.m., but thought it was due to my having been photographing in the passage and that it was connected with my work. This was not the case, and I do not remember having noticed it though I was using these stairs a good deal.

'On Saturday morning . . . we found that the round blue box in the store room [large cupboard] *had moved half an inch*. We had left the door open the evening before.'

Whether the 'strange coat' was there before Colonel Westland saw it, I cannot say. But he is such a very careful observer that it seems incredible that he could have missed it on his patrols. The same applies to the piece of wood.

During his stay, Colonel Westland made plans of every room in the house, and took many photographs, some of which are reproduced in this volume. He took with him on this visit his Aberdeen terrier, which behaved quite normally—unlike Captain Gregson's two dogs, both of which disappeared.

Concerning the movement of the blue box in the cupboard, it is interesting to note that Mr. Drinkwater, in his report,[1] also records the fact that on December 13 following, the box *moved one inch* off its chalked ring while he and his friends were on guard in the house. In fact, it moved twice.

When Colonel and Mrs. Westland visited the 'Psychic Fête' at Borley Rectory on June 21, 1939, four months after the fire that gutted the Rectory, they were amazed to find that the 'blue box' that so strangely appeared at midnight, June 25, 1937, *was still in its chalked ring in the cupboard* where they originally found it! They took it away with them as a souvenir.

DR. BELLAMY'S EXPERIMENT

Among our official observers were Dr. H. F. Bellamy, engaged in medical research, and his son, Mr. F. C. Bellamy. Accompanied by a friend, Mr. Hugh E. Fee-Smith, they visited Borley Rectory on the night of October 16–17, 1937.

Included amongst the 'gadgets' and bits of apparatus was a simple electric bell contact-breaker. It consisted of the contacts, bell, and an electric battery, the whole kept steady by a pile of books. If a book was disturbed or displaced, the circuit was closed by two pieces of metal coming together. This indicator had been made by Mr. S. H. Glanville and installed by him on the marble mantelpiece of the dining-room.

At 12.20 a.m. on October 17, Dr. Bellamy and his friends were quietly watching in the Blue Room. They were sitting on the floor with their backs to the wall, and the moon was streaming in at the window. They sat there until 12.50 a.m. when (to quote their united signed report):

'Electric bell in circuit with contact-breaker under pile of books on marble mantelpiece in living-room, to right of main hall, started ringing and continued to ring for the space of about a minute, when it ceased abruptly. This apparatus had been tested for delicacy of adjustment earlier in the evening and the books replaced. Now, on our arrival in the room, *the books were displaced, no book occupying its original position,* and the bottom one was right off the contact breaker. The window of the room was found to be sealed. . . . Nothing else in the room was disturbed. In view of the displacement of the books we are quite unable to account for this phenomenon.'

[1] Pages 234–5.

In sending the report, Mr. Francis Bellamy said in a covering letter:

'The ringing was a very startling experience, occurring as it did during our vigil in the Blue Room. Knowing something about the vagaries of electrical contacts, I should not have attached much importance to the incident had the books not been so greatly displaced and the apparatus moved out of the chalk marks. The fact that it ceased so suddenly also added to our bewilderment. We have omitted to mention in the report that we tested it before we left at 6 a.m. and we found that everything was in working order.'

The house, after sealing and fastening of all windows and external doors, was patrolled at 4.50 p.m., 9 p.m., 10.30 p.m., 2.30 a.m., and 4.40 a.m.

Other phenomena experienced that night was 'a faint knocking, from somewhere above Base Room.' Duration about ten seconds. Two strange pencil marks were also discovered on their fourth tour of inspection at 2.30 a.m. One of these was on the wall just outside the Chapel, the other over the mantelpiece in Room 7. They ringed and dated them.

Dr. Bellamy—and his party—comments on the quietness of the house. He says: 'One feature which impressed itself on all our minds was the extraordinary quietness of the house. There never seemed to be a board creaking nor any sign of mice or rats. In fact, the silence was almost uncanny.'

Dr. Bellamy and his party visited the Rectory in the following spring, and in the report, dated May 26, 1938, sent me by Mr. Francis C. Bellamy, it is stated:

'About 1 a.m. we found and marked a pencil line in the room [No. 7] next to the Blue Room. We also had a peculiar experience which oddly enough made very little effect on us at the time. When we first went round the house at about 7 p.m., we were standing outside the two large cupboards, off the hall in the short corridor which leads to the side door of garden, when the friend we took down had a distinct feeling that someone had ruffled his hair lightly. Again, about 1 o'clock we chose the same place to stand in the dark, and Fee-Smith had the sensation of someone touching his face. Was it not through this garden door that the nun sometimes was seen to enter? Other than this, we got much less "feeling" in the house than on our previous visit.'

THE B.B.C. INVESTIGATES

The British Broadcasting Corporation is nothing if not enterprising, and the Department of Outside Broadcasts is always the first to investigate the possibilities of radiating anything of a topical nature, if interesting enough to the general public. It will be remembered that I broadcast from the 'haunted house' at Meopham on March 10, 1936, when the ghost-hunting technique employed was very successfully relayed. Mr. S. J. de Lotbinière was in charge of the transmission.

Mr. de Lotbinière was also interested in Borley Rectory and wished to visit the place. Of course I agreed. I particularly wanted him to visit the house by himself, or with friends, but he insisted upon my accompanying him and Mr. H. Douglas-Home, who was also interested.

We arrived at Borley on the afternoon of July 21, 1937, at 4 o'clock and found that our other official observers, Mr. J. M. Bailey and Mr. C. V. Wintour,[1] two undergraduates, who were staying for some days, were still in possession. They left an hour later, and slept out.

After a cursory tour of the house, Bailey and Wintour showed us some new wall marks that had appeared during the previous night.

I will now quote de Lotbinière's report verbatim, reserving any comments until later:

'6.0 p.m. Went into Sudbury for a meal, leaving all doors bolted on the inside, except the front door, which was locked and had a piece of transparent paper stuck across the crack.

'7.30 p.m. Returned to Borley and found everything intact.

'8.15 p.m. Made a thorough examination of the house. Found a certain number of small wall marks and ringed them with chalk. Found that the clapper of the bell communicating with the Blue Room had been tied up with a piece of silk material.

'9.15 p.m. The Rev. A. C. and Mrs. Henning arrived and came in through the garden door into the Base Room. In the course of a cursory tour of the house, we found a long new pencil mark on the wall next to the pantry.

'9.30 p.m. Watched the garden from the summer-house. A full moon came up. It was quite warm and there was very little wind. No clouds.

'10.30 p.m. Returned to house and did some "challenging" from the Base Room with light very low. No result.

'11.0 p.m. Tour of house. Found a substantial new pencil mark in each of the following rooms: The Chapel, Room 8, and Room 3. We found other small, but apparently new pencil marks in Room 7, the Blue Room and the room next door [Room 5]. During this tour the five of us were together, but it was not possible to watch everyone's movements.

'11.50 p.m. The Hennings left.

[1] See their report, pages 222–4.

'12.40–1.05 a.m. Sat in the Blue Room in the dark. Both doors were open. By now there was a considerable wind, but there were no clouds. Heard prolonged rustling downstairs. Not accounted for. Sounded like mice amongst paper.

'1.10 a.m. Tour of house. Carton on chimney-piece in room [No. 4] next to Chapel had been moved eighteen inches. Marked new position with dotted line and replaced. Must have been *lifted* as intervening dust unmarked. Found a number of small pencil marks in room [No. 3] next bathroom.

'1.46 a.m. Returned to Base Room for food and talked.

'3.15–3.50 a.m. Listened in Blue Room. Heard one "click" from stairs as we were settling down. "Challenged" a few minutes later and heard another sharp click before the sentence was even finished! By now it was a good deal cooler and this might have been contraction. But apart from this the house was very silent.

'4.45 a.m. Went for a walk.

'5.15 a.m. Made another tour of house. Nothing to report.

'5.45 a.m. Left for London.

'Throughout the visit we did our best not to separate, but I cannot say for certain that the "manifestations" could not have been done by one or other of us. I am certain that no one could have got into the house in the course of our visit. This report is written on July 24, 1937, from notes made at the time of the visit.

[*Typed signature*] 'S. J. DE LOTBINIÈRE.'

Mr. de Lotbinière's report, which should be read in conjunction with the report of Bailey and Wintour, is accurate and agrees with the notes I made during the visit. My only comments are that the 'rustling noise' came from the Base Room immediately below us and lasted for from 7 to 10 minutes. It was quite loud and we discussed in whispers how the sounds might be caused. I do not think they were caused by mice. No one suggested mice. I reiterate that I have never seen signs of mice in the Rectory. On the table in the Base Room were the remains of a box of chocolates, with the loose paper wrappings lying in the box. I mentioned during the occurrence of the sounds that the 'ghost' was a long time choosing one. It sounded exactly as if someone was turning over the box and contents.

Though Mr. de Lotbinière does not emphasize the incident (except by means of an exclamation mark), the 'click' in the passage was very striking. But it was more than a 'click'—it was a sharp 'crack.' And I think it came from the passage outside the Blue Room, in which we were standing. And, as Mr. de Lotbinière observes, the 'crack' which instantly answered our challenge, was startling in the extreme. In fact, it made me

'jump'! I think it was Mr. de Lotbinière who said 'If they want
to impress us, let them do something *now*.' Before he had finished
speaking, the 'crack' was heard. Mr. de Lotbinière, in his
report, suggests 'contraction,' but that was impossible. It was
a sharp, hard knock—twice. And, as I have previously observed,
there was never a suspicion of crepitation in the house. It was the
most soundless place I have been in, and this is confirmed by
every observer.

In his concluding remarks Mr. de Lotbinière says that 'I cannot say for certain that the "manifestations" could not have been
done by one or other of us.' This argument could not possibly
apply to the 'rustling noise' or the 'cracks,' as we were all
together in the Blue Room while the alleged phenomena occurred
in the Base Room and passage (or stairs) respectively.

On December 14, 1937, Mr. de Lotbinière, Mr. John Snagge
and Mr. Home again visited the Rectory, but 'things seemed so
quiet and uneventful that we decided to return to London.'

On January 8, 1938, Mr. W. S. Hammond, a member of the
staff of the B.B.C., visited the Rectory. He was accompanied
by Mr. C. S. Taylor, Mr. G. J. Bell, and Mr. J. Thurley. After
a thorough inspection of the house, and the sealing of all doors,
etc., they began their hourly patrols of the building.

I will now quote their report:

'10 p.m. Another unproductive tour of the house. . . . Before
starting this tour and while standing in passage opposite the Base
Room, we heard a door being closed. But on investigation nothing
could be found to account for it.

'12 p.m. Examined every room and stayed for a while in the
Blue Room in silence and complete darkness. Nothing occurred.
At 12.25 a.m., when coming down the main staircase there was
the sound of a door being gently closed, but careful investigation
failed to trace the origin.

'2 a.m. Inspected grounds and outside of house. Nothing to
report. We then inspected every room carefully and found
everything in its place with the exception of a piece of zinc on
the floor in Room 10. This we had previously placed in the
centre of a chalk mark and it was now partly outside. A rather
unpleasant odour was noticed in Room 5, which somewhat
suggested the lavatory. The same kind of smell was afterwards
noticed in the Blue Room—*i.e.*, when we returned after com-
pleting the tour.

'3.15 a.m. Tour of house, but nothing to report except the
sound of a door closing again, which was apparently outside and
might have been caused by the wind which had risen slightly.'

[The report is signed by all four observers.]

Another party from the B.B.C. visited Borley Rectory on Friday, February 18, 1938. They were Mr. C. Gordon Glover and Mr. Lloyd Williams (a Director of the B.B.C. Educational Department), and their respective wives.

They arrived at 4.30 p.m., and closely examined the Rectory. Then they all adjourned to the garden and took up their position in the famous summer-house in order to watch the Nun's Walk. I will now cite Mr. Glover's report (dated February 26, 1938) verbatim:

'5.45 p.m. My wife and I watched the open part of the walk while Mr. and Mrs. Lloyd Williams kept their eyes fixed on the line of trees at the Rectory end. At about 6.10 Mrs. Lloyd Williams suddenly tensed. She said nothing for some ten seconds, at the end of which time she declared that she had distinctly seen "a round, dark object." This might, she said, have been a short, stooping figure. It appeared to move from the tree closest to the Rectory to the central fir-tree at which spot it vanished. Mrs. Lloyd Williams told us that she had not seen it actually *progress*, but it had somehow covered the distance between the two trees. The light was bad, it being deep twilight. The other three of us walked across the lawn and walked in front of the trees to test whether or no we were visible from her position in the summer-house. We were, she declared, just visible, though we were clothed in light-coloured coats. So much for the "Nun." One witness only whose faith that she saw *something* is not to be shaken. We have since, as you know, ascertained that this "Nun," when seen, has always been observed at this particular spot.

'I find that I omitted one point in connection with our first inspection of the house between 4.30 and 5 o'clock. This was that while standing outside the Chapel, my wife declares that she heard a door downstairs quietly close. It was a dead still afternoon, and all doors and windows were shut.'[1]

Mr. Glover continues:

'Towards eleven o'clock we made another tour of the house. We observed and chalk-marked a pencil mark by the Butler's Pantry. This, to the best of our knowledge, had not been there on our previous tour. While in the scullery Mrs. Lloyd Williams said she heard in the passage outside "Six quick, young footsteps." No one of the rest of the party heard these. It is our opinion that these steps were imagined. When upstairs during this same tour of inspection, my wife and I were standing in the doorway of the Chapel, when both of us heard coming from downstairs a dull, heavy thud followed by a short shuffle. The

[1] Compare similar experiences by Mr. Hammond and his friends, page 218, and other observers.

other two of the party were at the back of the Chapel and heard nothing.'

Mr. Glover and his party spent the next hour and a half in the Base Room and heard nothing, though the door was left open. Then they went upstairs again. Mr. Glover continues:

'At 12.30 a.m. we all went upstairs again, closing the door of the Base Room behind us, and stationed ourselves in the Blue Room. We remained here in darkness until 1 a.m. During this period we are all agreed on the following occurrences: This was (a) two heavy thuds coming from downstairs and one of a lighter character. A kind of vague shuffling was also heard, giving an impression of "general activity of some kind going on"; and (b) a staccato and isolated "crack."[1] I described this as being like the crack of a whip, while the others likened it to an electric light switch—of which there are none—being snapped on. It is unlikely that this was made by the fire in the Base Room, since the Blue Room is some distance away and the door of the former was closed. We returned to the Base Room, and made a final tour of the house at about 2.15 a.m., during which nothing of any kind occurred.'

That concluded the Glover report and the party returned home.

The next B.B.C. observer to visit the Rectory was Mr. M. Savage, an electrical engineer, of the Television Service, Alexandra Palace. He was accompanied by a friend, Mr. Bridgewater. The date was Saturday, March 12, 1938. During this week-end the Glanvilles and Mr. Cuthbert were also 'observing' at the house.[2] Mr. Savage and the party inspected the house and garden at intervals, and neither saw nor heard anything with the exception of:

(1) 'We made a second tour of the house and on visiting the Chapel at about 10.20 p.m. we discovered on the floor some curious gluey material, which we are all practically certain, as we should almost have been bound to have walked over it on our previous tour, was not there before. It was not in such a position where it could have fallen from the ceiling without leaving a mark and it certainly did not appear to be due to any small stray animals. As a matter of interest, Mr. Glanville photographed this.'[3]

(2) 'The only other occurrence which I can report was that at 1.43 a.m one extremely heavy knock occurred while we were

[1] Compare the 'cracks' that we heard (de Lotbinière report), *ante*, page 217.
[2] See their report, page 202.
[3] From Mr. Savage's letter. The discovery has already been mentioned in this monograph, page 202.

all sitting in the Base Room. This knock appeared to emanate from the top of the bookcase towards the left-hand end, and appeared to be too heavy to be accounted for by normal house movements caused by changes in temperature, but on the other hand I should not like to say that this was not so.'

Mr. Savage again visited Borley Rectory on May 7, 1938, just before my tenancy expired. He was accompanied by a friend, Mr. Bowden. I cannot do better than quote Mr. Savage's own words, a policy of first-hand written testimony that I have adopted throughout this monograph, where possible. · This is what Mr. Savage says in his report, dated May 10, 1938:

'We arrived at about 4.30 p.m., obtained the keys from Mr. Arbon, and proceeded straight away to do a very thorough inspection of every room in the house. Everything appeared to be in order; all seals were intact on windows and doors. During the inspection, we noticed that a number of new marks had been noted by observers on the night of Thursday, May 5, but over and above these marks, we found a fair number of fresh pencil marks on the walls in various places. As we could not be sure of the origin of these, we merely ringed them and noted the date in the usual manner.'

During their stay in the Rectory, Mr. Savage installed a number of 'electrical traps' for the 'entities,' and 'the alarm in the kitchen was inadvertently tested by us on each of these tours and was found in perfect order!' A further alarm was fitted over the 'cold spot' on the landing outside the Blue Room. Mr. Savage continues:

'At about 9.0 p.m. another very thorough search was made. *As usual, the Blue Room was subjected to a microscopic examination,*[1] but nothing further was found. Once more, just before 11 o'clock, we commenced a search through the house. Upon arriving in the Blue Room at almost exactly 11 p.m., we noticed, above the right-hand side of the fireplace, a small vertical pencil mark about three-sixteenths of an inch long. It was obviously new, and we are as definite as one can be that it was not there on any of our previous inspections. We had hardly ringed this mark, when we were surprised to see a second rather smaller mark about four inches below it. This we also ringed. We then transferred our attention along the top of the mantelpiece to the left-hand side, but found nothing. We returned to the right-hand side within about one or two minutes, and yet a further mark had appeared an inch or two to the left of the first two marks. Once more we examined the left-hand side of the mantelpiece, and this time found a pencil mark similar to the others, at approximately

[1] My italics. H.P.

the same height from the floor. The examination over the area round the mantelpiece was continued backwards and forwards for a further five minutes or so, but no further marks appeared. I do not think we could have both missed these marks, either on our earlier inspections of the house or on our first examination during this particular inspection, and it therefore seems almost certain that they must have been produced while we were actually within a yard of the mantelpiece. Nothing further was observed in the Blue Room throughout the night.

'During this tour of the house, in Room 5 a number of scratched markings were observed about five feet above the ground to the left of the window. These were obviously new and unringed, and we had not noticed them during our earlier inspections. I have endeavoured to sketch these markings at the bottom of this report. In the corridor, within the rectangular "ringing" of the "Marianne-please-help-get" message, two new pencil marks were observed, one either end of the writing, and a third one below it just outside the ringing. In Room 3, behind the door, a number of very distinct markings were observed covering an area of about two feet by just over one foot wide. Again, I have tried to illustrate these roughly in the freehand drawing given below. Throughout the whole night the house was absolutely silent.'

The two sets of drawings that Mr. Savage enclosed were (1) a series of markings comparable with an attempt to draw the 'Prince of Wales's feathers'; and (2) a long series of marks like the letter 'B.' They were very curious.

And so ended the investigation by the various members of the British Broadcasting Corporation. Their reports are interesting and valuable.

ACADEMIC INQUIRIES

Among the many persons who answered my *Times* advertisement for observers were a number of undergraduates from Oxford and Cambridge universities. Some of their letters were in a facetious vein, and were immediately consigned to the waste-paper basket. But we had replies from a few young students who were obviously deeply interested in psychical research, and who took the matter seriously. These were duly appointed official observers. I will now deal with their respective reports, which are not in strict chronological order.

The first of the undergraduates to visit the house were Mr. J. M. Bailey and Mr. C. V. Wintour. They arrived at 9 p.m. on July 18, 1937. After a thorough inspection of house, during which they 'found a deeply scrawled "M" at the end of ground floor passage,'[1] they visited the garden and returned to the

[1] I am quoting from their detailed log.

house. At 9.40 p.m., the Rev. A. C. Henning and Mr. Mark Kerr-Pearse (who had been dining with him) arrived at the Rectory. The party decided to hold a little séance: 'We tried some table rapping in the dining-room without any result. Subsequently we went upstairs and knocked on the floor of the Blue Room. We were answered by one small explosive sound, not very loud. (Note. I am convinced this was not a natural sound; we never heard another noise like it.)'

The Rev. Mr. Henning and Kerr-Pearse left at 10.26 p.m. The house was again inspected and they went to bed at 11.30 p.m. At 9 a.m. the next morning (July 19) they again inspected house. Then they went to Sudbury, locking all doors. They returned at 12.5 p.m. 'and discovered deep scratch or incision on the ground floor passage wall near the pencilled "Ma" discovered by Kerr-Pearse. The scratch, which was not there before, was clearly artificial. The mark was in the form of an arrow-shaft and its head.'

At 6 p.m. they 'discovered one bow-shaped pencil mark in downstairs passage near the end, and one small pencil mark in the chapel bringing total to eight.' Nothing occurred during the evening and, before retiring to rest, they stretched black threads across all the doorways and passages. Wintour slept in the Base Room, and Bailey in the Blue Room. They heard nothing.

They inspected house at 8 a.m. next morning (July 20) and found nothing new. Their threads had not been disturbed. But at 10 a.m. they discovered the letter 'C' opposite the stairs leading to the attics.

At 11 a.m. they found a pencilled 'G' by the door of Room 8, and a line behind it. At 11.15 a.m. they discovered several small marks in Room 11. Then they returned to Room 8 'and we discovered (at 11.23) that three circles had been added behind the door. We are both certain that these were not there at 11.15.' Therefore, they *must* have appeared while they were in Room 11, examining the other marks. Other small marks appeared during the day.

As the reader knows, Mr. de Lotbinière and I visited the Rectory next day, July 21 (at 4 p.m.). Mr. Bailey and his friend slept out that night. When they returned at 11 a.m. the next morning, July 22, they of course saw the pencillings that had 'appeared' during our visit, and confirmed that they were new.

Nothing of note occurred during this day until the evening. At 10 o'clock they inspected the house, as usual, and when they reached Room 3 . . . but I will quote from the report:

' 10 p.m. Inspect house on return from Long Melford. Nothing new except a mark like the beginning of an "M" appears in Room 3, above the kitchen, while we were in the room. Wintour had looked at the wall there on entering the room and noted nothing fresh, but flashing his torch on to the wall again a minute or two later noticed this not very large mark. Both Bailey and Wintour thought they saw it grow in front of their eyes, but are now inclined to think it was an optical illusion. We left it for ten minutes, but nothing more was added.'

Wintour slept in the Blue Room that night, and heard nothing. Bailey slept in the summer-house and he, too, was undisturbed. During the day of July 23, the usual inspections were carried out, but no new pencillings were recorded, and no other phenomena were noted. On the evening of this day, Bailey slept in the Blue Room, and neither saw nor heard anything unusual. They left for home at 10.15 a.m. on July 24.

On the night of February 16–17, 1938, a party of four under-graduates from the University of Oxford visited Borley Rectory. They were Mr. S. G. Welles, Rhodes Scholar of University College; Mr. R. Hawkin, Mr. Samuel J. Milberg, and Mr. M. P. Knox. They were all from University College. Mr. Welles subsequently sent me a long and detailed report of the night's events; the others sent me very short comments, as Mr. Welles had taken so much trouble in writing up his log. I will take Mr. Welles's account first, extracting from it any passages that should be quoted verbatim.

After having settled themselves in the Base Room, they made the usual inspection: 'We scanned every room and its contents with minute attention, ringing bells, seeing whether objects were within their chalked marks, etc.' They tied threads across a few doors and passages. After mentioning that at 8 o'clock the four of them saw 'a small puddle of brownish water' on the passage floor, which no one had noticed previously (though they had traversed it repeatedly), Mr. Welles went up to the Blue Room while his friends were preparing supper in the Base Room.

He tells us that he was in the Blue Room exactly 25 minutes by his watch, from 8 to 8.25 p.m. He was alone in the darkness, and saw a remarkable luminous phenomenon, which I will let him describe himself:

'I had taken for my position the corner of the room between the fireplace and the window, from which I was able to see the entire room (as my eyes grew accustomed to the darkness) as well as the four exits from it—two doors, fireplace, and window. Standing there and looking at the corner diagonally opposite (between 8.15 and 8.20 p.m. I should judge, not being able to read my watch though my eyes had by then clearly distinguished the outlines of the room), I became aware of a luminous patch of light on the ceiling, about six inches from the moulding that ran round the top of the walls and opposite the centre of the window. This luminous patch, a roughly rounded rectangle of perhaps a foot by five inches, moved slowly about half-way towards my corner from its original position (I was standing five feet from a point opposite the centre of the window, so that it shifted some two or three feet), poised there a moment, moved as slowly back, disappeared for an instant, again appeared just where it had first done so, and moved forward and back exactly as it had done before, and then disappeared a second and last time at the spot where it had both appeared and disappeared. This whole proceeding took not more than a minute.

'I may say at once that though I myself spent at least two hours more in solitary darkness in the Blue Room during the night, and each of my friends a shorter period, none of us again saw anything remotely resembling this phenomenon. And it was the only occurrence of our stay for which we were unable to conceive a more or less logical explanation. It was definitely not one of those patches or lines of white, one's eyeballs, straining into darkness, so often see. I saw many of these during that and my other stays in the darkened Blue Room, and they in no way resembled it. The light had none of the dim haziness, general all-pervading sense over the vision for the moment, or swift movement of these: it was clearly outlined and made its motions in leisurely yet precise fashion, and impinged itself on my perception not directly through my forward-seeing vision, but gradually, through a feeling that something was shining down on me. I had ample time to turn my eyes upwards and follow its movements; was near enough the window to be able to lean forward noiselessly from where I stood, and perceived no outside agency that could have been responsible for the light, though headlights of passing cars and other outside disturbances had been clearly visible.

'We later conducted extensive experiments, I being in the unlighted room while various sorts of lights (torches of varying power, candles, matches, glowing cigarette ends, etc.—I am a non-smoker myself and of course lit no lights of any kind during my periods of watch) were shone in at me, from under the window, the foot of the garden, the hall, and the room adjacent. None of these even remotely suggested what I felt I had seen. What they tended to establish in my mind was:

'(1) That any light whatsoever coming in through the window lit up a far greater area than that one luminous patch so close (six inches, as I have said) to the window and yet only visible on the ceiling.

Q

'(2) That all lights entering through the window cast patches
of light (representing its panes) separated by narrow dark bars
(the sashes and frames).

'(3) That even the smallest pinprick of illumination cast high-
lights and shadows in all parts of the room, whereas during my
memorable moment the whole room had been in a neutral darkness save for this one patch.

'(4) All the lights we made cast into strong relief the metal
curtain-hanger projecting from the corner of the window between
me and the spot where the luminous patch had appeared, and
about opposite the point where it stopped its advance each time
and began to move back, whereas during the time of that
illumination I never noticed it, which seems possibly to indicate
that this patch, unlike any ordinary light shining in darkness,
cast no shadow of objects near it or contrasted itself with those
objects.

'As I spent most of my remaining time during that and my
following visits to the Blue Room in thinking over this appearance
from every angle that I could, and have written this account
within twelve hours, I sincerely believe it to be as full and
accurate as I can make it.

'After supper, Milberg and I at 9.15 began another round of
the house. . . . In the scullery we found on the floor a piece of
lath, 42 inches by 1 inch. We were both convinced we had not
seen it on our previous visit, and owing to its size and the fact
that one end of it was within 4¾ inches of a slightly crumpled
cigarette card we perfectly well remembered having seen, we
were rather startled. When Knox and Hawkin came in, we took
them to it and Hawkin, who had been with Milberg and me on
our previous round, also remembered the card well and the lath
not at all. It had no chalk marks round it when first noticed,
which was in itself unusual, since every object of any size scattered
about the house did. We chalked it at once, Milberg doing so
while I held my light for him, and it had not moved when we
brought back Knox and Hawkin to see it; nor did it move during
the rest of the night.

'On our next visit, at 10.20 p.m., when Hawkin and I were
making the rounds, we were still more startled to find a piece
of dried grass, 9 inches long, lying parallel to this lath—so close
as almost to be touching it—this at the opposite end from that
near the cigarette card. Again, none of us could remember
having seen this before, though as Hawkin and Knox had come
straight from the long dry grasses of the summer-house path to
see the lath, it is quite possible that one of them tracked it in on
the sole of his shoe and left it there while examining the lath,
none of us happening to notice it until this next visit, though as
the blade was lying its full length parallel to and almost touching
the lath and no one set foot on the lath once Milberg had chalked

it in its position, it would seem difficult to have tracked unconsciously to that particular position.

'I have discussed this and our other experiences thoroughly with Joseph W. Burden, who spent four nights at the Rectory just two months before we visited it. He clearly remembers a lath of those dimensions being in the scullery. In his time it was stretched diagonally across the lead sink of the pump there and he chalked it into that position. He also remembers the slightly crumpled cigarette card, the position of which was just under the outside edge of this sink, about two feet from the wall. None of us remember seeing the lath on the sink during our first visit, any more than we remember seeing it in the position on the floor where we observed it on our second visit.'

Mr. Welles neither heard nor saw anything further that night that calls for comment. He slept on the floor of the Base Room for an hour or so, visiting the Blue Room at half-hour intervals.

Between 11.40 p.m. and 12.20 a.m. the four investigators, Welles, Knox, Milberg, and Hawkin, separated and took up their positions respectively in the following rooms; No. 9, the Chapel, Blue Room, and Base Room. Mr. Welles, who says he is slightly deaf, heard nothing during this vigil in complete darkness. But his three companions heard footsteps which appeared to come from the kitchen. Welles continues: 'The three of them likewise heard a series of faint noises at regular short intervals when we were all having tea in the Base Room about 12.30 a.m. I, who am slightly deaf, heard none of these.'

Mr. Samuel J. Milberg confirms Welles's story of the footsteps —or some similar sound—in the following signed report:

'From 11.45 p.m. to 12.20 a.m. I was in the Blue Room alone. Nothing happened till 12.20, when I heard a noise, coming from downstairs or the courtyard (I could not locate it). It was the kind of noise produced when somebody is throwing things against the floor carelessly. I thought at first that the noise was due to the observer [Hawkin] who remained in the Base Room, but when I went downstairs he declared he had made no noise. About 12.30 a.m., we were all having some tea, when three of us heard a faint noise, repeated at intervals of a few seconds for some moments. After it disappeared, nothing else worthy of note happened during the remainder of the night.'

Mr. Hawkin read Mr. Welles's report, and sent me the following confirmation from University College:

'I confirm the report of Mr. Welles with whom I was most of the night, making particular mention of (a) We clearly heard footsteps at 12.17, when I was alone in the Base Room, and the others in distant parts of the house. The footsteps appeared to come from the kitchen, along the passage to the front hall, and towards the drawing-room. I imagined at the time that it was one of the other investigators and, therefore, did not leave the Base Room; and (b) the peculiar thumping noise at 12.30 a.m. (approx.), which could not be traced to any apparent cause.'

(*Signed*) 'ROBT. HAWKIN.'

After 'making careful inspections of the house and grounds by daylight,' the party left Borley at 10.30 a.m. on Thursday, February 17, 1938.

Between December 15 and 19, 1937, Mr. J. Burden and Mr. T. Stainton, both of Christ Church, Oxford, visited Borley. After a very thorough inspection of the house and grounds upon their arrival, and sealing of doors, etc., they set a trap of black thread across the passage between Rooms 9 and 10. At 4.50 a.m., on December 16, Burden spent five minutes in the Chapel, in the dark: 'Chapel seemed to have evil atmosphere, but this probably imagination,' he noted.

At 4.15 p.m. on December 16, Mr. Burden sat in the summerhouse, watching the Nun's Walk until 5 o'clock. His report says:

'Saw and heard nothing except wind and slight rain which had then started to fall. . . . At 6.10, while sitting in Base Room, heard sound of whining or hooting coming from direction of courtyard (faint). Went to door of Base Room and listened in silence without showing light. Noise had stopped (may easily have been wind), but sound of shuffling footsteps heard coming from direction of scullery. We stood listening and at approximately 6.25 heard sound of swishing garments as though someone were walking in upstairs hall. (May have also been wind, but by that time wind had momentarily died down to a slight rustling in trees.)

'8.30 p.m. Burden's watch. House inspected. Wind and rain coming in gusts at intervals. 9.00. Lit two candles in front of Chapel window and hung little silver cross in between them. After twenty minutes of silent watching in dark half-way up main staircase, returned to Base Room at 9.40. . . . 1.30 a.m. [December 17]. Continual wailing sound heard (higher and more continuous note than previous wailing). May have been the wind, but that again had died down. The sound seemed to be coming from the Blue Room, but seemed to penetrate everywhere as it could be heard equally clearly in Base Room, hall, or kitchen passage. At 1.42 wailing stops.

'Stainton's watch. 10 p.m. Brought one of Arbon's cats into house to test reaction. She was extremely nervous and disliked our lantern and torches. Also seemed to be frightened by moonlight on floor and watched it suspiciously. Quieted her with condensed milk and tried, with difficulty, to lead her around house. Was disinclined to enter all the eastern rooms containing moonlight, but was finally tempted to enter them with offers of milk and was then no longer nervous. When confronted with coat "apport" she merely rubbed her back against it. Was alarmed by crackling fire downstairs. Seemed particularly interested by Room 7, but was not frightened when led inside. 11.15 cat put out.'

At 12.10 a.m. (December 18) Burden says: 'Noise heard (too loud to be mistaken) of something being dragged along floor. Two seconds duration, at two seconds intervals. Stainton was standing opposite door of Room 8 and thinks he heard sounds down lower north passage, but is not certain that that was correct location.'

The report continues:

'Burden's watch. 4 a.m. House revealed several new (?) pencil marks along passage and rooms, ground-floor front. 4.5 a.m. Found thread between Rooms 9 and 10 broken. (Assumed this done by cat, but Stainton claims cat did not pass it as he watched her during her tour.)'

Stainton left for home early on the morning of December 19, Burden remaining in the house by himself. At 6.10 on the evening of this day, Burden says:

'6.10 p.m. Heard talking and footsteps coming from direction of main hall, while sitting in Base Room. Stood in hall and listened but could not trace them and thought they must come from Arbon and wife (although could not see them from any windows. . . .) 8.35. Inspection of house with particular attention to ground floor where two new pencil marks were found. (North passage.) 10.15 to 10.35. Last night inspection. Very cold. Heavy frost again and iced windows. Full moon and few clouds. No wind. Heard slight short rattling sound in dairy near north window, but this probably window-bars.[1] Uncanny sense of being watched in Room 2. Retired 10.35 and slept until 8.30 a.m. [December 19].'

Mr. Burden made a final inspection of house and found nothing disturbed and no new pencil marks. He left for home at 10.35 a.m.

In order to see the traditional 'nun' on the night of her traditional appearance, a number of observers visited Borley Rectory on July 28, 1937. Among them were the Rev. A. C.

---

[1] I think this is impossible. The bars were very thick and were screwed solidly to window frame. Also, there was no wind. H.P.

Henning, and Mr. A. C. Elliot Smith, a master at Harrow School. The visit of this party coincided with a period when Mr. Kerr-Pearse was in 'residence' at the Rectory. They waited in the summer-house until 10.40, hoping to see the 'nun,' and were disappointed at not doing so.

In an interesting letter, dated July 29, 1937, Mr. Elliot Smith says:

'I arrived about four in the afternoon, and almost immediately went round the whole house with Kerr-Pearse. I expect you will have thought of all I am going to say long ago, but in case coming fresh to it, any new idea may have come to me, I will tabulate my impressions:

'(1) Though some [pencil] marks (I have no particular one in mind) may be fakes or purely normal pencil marks, I find it difficult to believe the whole lot are. Apart from the testimony of a variety of people and the difficulty of always escaping observation, because a faker would surely endeavour to be more sensational and not content himself with mere jabs.

'(2) The majority seem either 4 feet or 2 feet 6 inches from the ground or just over a mantelpiece.

'(3) Have you ever shown the specimens to a handwriting expert? I find it difficult to believe that the usual "Marianne," the single "Marianne" and "Edwin" are all by the same hand.

'(4) Accepting as an hypothesis a discarnate spirit or psychic factor, where does it get the material lead? Can it sharpen a pencil?

'(5) I had no feeling of atmosphere.

Mr. Elliot Smith left for London the next morning, after a not very exciting time. But as I have before observed in this monograph, July 28, the traditional 'day,' has always been uneventful according to my own experience. The questions raised by Mr. Elliot Smith concerning the pencil marks are dealt with in Chapter XXIV.

Dr. C. E. M. Joad, head of the Department of Philosophy and Psychology, Birkbeck College, University of London, also visited Borley Rectory. Like many other observers, he did not see the 'nun,' but was considerably intrigued with the various pencillings. He, with the others, carefully searched the house and garden, noting especially the pencil marks and dates on the distempered walls. In an article[1] on psychical research, Dr. Joad gives us his experiences:

'On the evening on which I visited the house one observer [Kerr-Pearse] had been staying there for some little time, sleeping

[1] 'Adventures in Psychical Research,' in *Harper's Magazine*, June and July, 1938, pp. 35–41, 202–210.

on a camp-bed, and cooking his meals on an oil stove in one of the empty rooms [the Base Room]. We were alone in the house, and after carefully examining the garden, we had assured ourselves that there was nobody there. We came in, made a tour of all the pencil marks visible on the white-washed walls, and carefully noted their date and position. It was my first visit and I was considerably intrigued by the mysterious marks. At seven o'clock we retired to the room with the camp-bed and the oil stove, securely locking all the doors and windows before we did so, cooked some sausages and made some tea. We were together in this room for the whole of the ensuing hour, and I am positive that neither of us left it. I am also positive that if anybody had entered the house, we should have heard him or her moving about. . . . About eight o'clock we went out again, and on the wall in the passage immediately outside the room in which we had been eating there was another pencil squiggle. I feel reasonably certain that that squiggle had not been there before; it was, indeed, inconceivable that we should have missed it. I am also reasonably certain that it was not made by the other observer, who was in my company during the whole of the period within which the mark must have been made. I am sure that I did not make it myself and, as I have already said, I do not see how anybody could have entered the house without being heard.

'On the other hand, the hypothesis that *Poltergeister* materialize lead pencils and fingers to use them seems to me to be totally incredible; and the question of "why" seems to be hardly less difficult to answer than the question of "how." As so frequently occurs when one is investigating so-called abnormal phenomena, one finds it equally impossible to withhold credence from the facts or to credit any possible explanation of the facts. Either the facts did not occur or, if they did, the universe must in some important respects be totally other than what one is accustomed to suppose. In this particular case my inclination is to doubt the facts; and yet, having reflected long and carefully upon that squiggle, I did not and do not see how it could have been made by normal means.'

MANY OBSERVERS—MANY THRILLS

Among our official observers at Borley Rectory were Flight-Lieut. R. Carter Jonas, and Flight-Lieut. Caunter. They are friends. Together, they visited the Rectory on the night of June 29–30, 1937. During the usual inspection of the house and garden, they found (3.15 p.m.) the circular blue box that, as the reader knows, was discovered by Colonel Westland a day or so before.[1] It was in its chalked circle. But at 7 p.m., on another

[1] See page 212.

round of inspection, they found a nail file that had *not* been noticed by either of the officers. In his report, Jonas says:

'Nothing of interest noticed except a nail-file in the pantry [cupboard], which I do not remember seeing before. Otherwise, no objects had been moved.'

Caunter confirms this incident in a separate report. He says:

'Everything was as we had last seen it, except that in a cupboard or small store room on the ground floor in which we had previously noted a small circular blue box standing in a chalked circle, we now noticed on one of the right-hand shelves a small steel nail file. About a quarter of the nail file was overhanging the edge of the shelf.'

I never discovered the ownership of the file. It seems inconceivable that two very alert young men, when actually looking for objects, should both have missed the file on their first inspection.

They neither saw nor heard anything unusual during their stay, though they were up all night with the exception of two hours' rest in the Base Room.

Both officers comment upon the absolute stillness of the place, though there was quite a wind during the whole duration of their visit. Caunter says: 'During the entire stay the house has been very quiet. We both remarked that it was the quietest house we had ever stayed in. We did not hear the usual creaks and noises usually heard in all houses during the night.' Jonas confirms this. He says: 'I have seldom stayed in a house at night, which had less of the usual noises—such as wood cracking, etc.'

Flight-Lieut. Jonas and his friend again visited the Rectory for two nights on March 16 and 17, 1938. In his report, Jonas said that 'absolutely nothing' occurred. No fresh 'messages' or pencil marks, and no movements of objects. He reiterates the soundlessness of the place. He says: 'The house and grounds at night were as still as a vault.'

Caunter and Jonas paid one more visit to Borley Rectory in November 1938, just after the place had been sold to Captain Gregson, though before he had taken possession. Their visit was, therefore 'unofficial,' as far as we were concerned, as I had relinquished the house the previous May. They stayed one night only, as they were just off to Egypt.

In a letter to me, dated December 12, 1938, and forwarded from Ismailia, Egypt, Flight-Lieut. Jonas says: 'All seemed to be much the same as before, except in one place upstairs there was an *overpowering smell of incense*, which we had not noticed on previous visits.'

Among the many intelligent people who 'observed' for us was Mr. F. A. Mansbridge, an official of the Bank of England, and his wife. They visited the Rectory on Sunday, September 5, 1937, and remained until Tuesday, September 7. Mr. Kerr-Pearse was also on duty during this period, but as there was nothing personal to record during his visit, he sent in no report. What *did* happen concerned Mr. Mansbridge—and his wife—and the following is an extract from his log:

'Sept. 5. Arrived at the Rectory at 7.30 p.m. Met Mr. Kerr-Pearse who kindly showed me round the house. No new marks had appeared. . . . The only unusual thing that happened was that as we (Kerr-Pearse, my wife and myself) stood talking on the first-floor landing [by the "cold spot"], *my wife felt the end of the belt of her coat lifted and dropped again.* The material is too heavy to be lifted by any ordinary draught, and the movement was so definite as to make her look down at it. I might also mention that when we returned to our car, about half an hour later, we found the door open, though we were quite sure we had shut it. It was standing in the drive, out of sight from the road.

'My wife stayed at the "Bull," Sudbury, and when I returned later to the Rectory (11.15 p.m.), Kerr-Pearse and I made another tour of the house, including loft [attics] and cellars. On going outside, before finally turning in at 2.35 a.m. [Sept. 6], I felt a tap on the shoulder as I stood on the lawn. The tap was as heavy as the falling of a large rain drop, though above (I looked up immediately) the night was clear and extremely starry. I was clear of any trees. It might have been a *very heavy* moth or drifting seed pod, or something dropped by a bird–though no mark was to be found on the coat. The weather was very cool and still. No noises were heard during the night, though we slept with the door of the Base Room wide open.'

Mr. and Mrs. Mansbridge left the Rectory on the early morning of September 7.

There was a curious sequel to their visit. Mr. Mansbridge took a number of photographs in the Rectory, but did not develop them for some time afterwards. On January 9, 1938, he sent me a letter containing some prints (and the negative) of the Blue Room. In the recess to the right of the mantelpiece, in the centre of the wall, and about 18 inches from the floor, can be distinctly seen a 'face' on the distemper. Unfortunately, 'faces' can often be seen on surfaces, uneven or broken, such as walls, backgrounds of trees, etc. In the same way, the pattern on a carpet, or the glowing embers in a fire, often produce a 'face' of some sort. I am afraid that Mr. Mansbridge's 'spirit photo' was due primarily to normal irregularities on the Blue Room wall, plus a certain subconscious elaboration of details in the mind of the person looking at the picture. This visual illusion is *not* apparent when one looks at the wall itself.

On the night of November 13–14, 1937, Mr. A. P. Drinkwater, a member of the executive of Messrs. Longmans, Green & Co., Ltd., visited Borley Rectory with three friends. They arrived at 2 p.m. on November 13, and proceeded to make a thorough inspection of the house and grounds. They examined all seals and fastenings, and re-sealed those windows and doors where necessary. The weather 'was clear and cold, temperature about 32° Fahrenheit, and no wind.'

Mr. Drinkwater arranged the following method of watching, as stated in his report:

'Decided to conduct watch in pairs (following instructions in Blue Book), such as waiting in Room 6 (Blue Room) for 10–15 minutes. All seals, objects and walls to be examined. Patrol of house to be followed by patrol of grounds by same watchers. All remainder to stay in or near Blue Room during patrols: this with the object of avoiding confusion. Inspection timed to take 45–50 minutes. One inspection per hour.'

They began their watch at 4.10 p.m. Two members of the party remained in the house, and two stationed themselves near the Nun's Walk.

I will now quote the report:

'4.15 p.m. Two distinct, percussive knocks heard by watchers stationed in Base Room of house. Sounded as if from almost immediately above. [*i.e.* Blue Room.] Investigation showed nothing had moved.'

During the 6 p.m. inspection they found that 'the round tin in small pantry [*i.e.* cupboard] *had moved one inch to the left.*' They marked the new position with another chalked ring.

At 7 p.m. three of the party went to Long Melford to dinner, leaving one on guard in the Rectory. He had nothing to report upon their return.

The four of them inspected the house from top to bottom (taking an hour over each patrol) at 8.30, 10, 11, 12 midnight and at 1 a.m. Nothing of note recorded.

At 1.41 a.m. 'a heavy thump nearly overhead of Base Room [*i.e.* from the Blue Room], like one heavy step. Heard by all members of party on duty. Believed to be the last of several steps which woke them up. [That is, those who were not on duty, but were resting in Base Room.]'

The report continues:

'4.0 a.m. Various light pencil marks discovered in various parts of the house. All these, as far as we know, had appeared after we had taken over the house. The marks we found on dining-room right-hand wall; near window of Blue Room and left-hand side of door; in Room 7 on either side of window; and on pillar between Blue Room and Room 7. All marks ringed as far as possible, but chalk had failed. *Tin in cupboard referred to in 6 p.m. inspection, again moved.*

'5.20 a.m. Inspection. Three more scratches on wall of Room 3 noticed and dated. Inspection ended approximately at 6 a.m.

'8 a.m. House re-examined. No seals found broken. Pencil mark found in Servants' Hall [*i.e.* Sewing-Room] and dated. Marks also found just *outside* the chalk ring enclosing message about "Light-Mass-Prayers" in long passage upstairs. Note: Nearly all the marks we found were of a very tentative nature and seldom consisted of more than one stroke. However, judging from the care with which previous observers marked similar ones, they would seem to be of importance.'

At 9 a.m. the whole party went out for a meal, and returned at 10.30 a.m. for a final look round. Nothing had altered since their 6 a.m. inspection. An hour later they returned to London.

Mr. Drinkwater and his friends had a most interesting evening, and it should be noted that the box in the cupboard, first discovered by Colonel Westland, *moved twice* during the night. Mr. Drinkwater remarks that 'the house was remarkably quiet for an empty house of some age.'

I think the only other of our *official* observers whose experiences I have to relate in this Appendix, were Dr. and Mrs. Joseph, who visited the Rectory on July 30, 1937, when Mr. Kerr-Pearse was on duty. In a letter which Mrs. Joseph sent me on August 1, 1937, she says: 'The house struck me as repellent, but not exactly sinister.' They heard only two sounds which could not be accounted for. One was 'as of a twig snapping'; the other, at 2 a.m., sounded 'as if some small winged insect—a beetle, perhaps—had struck a pane of glass.' Mrs. Joseph speaks of the house as being 'absolutely silent.'

During my tenancy of the Rectory, the Rev. A. C. Henning sent me the following letter, dated November 15, 1937:

'Dear Mr. Price,

'I thought you might be interested to know that a light has
been appearing in the Rectory, and so far we cannot account
for it. It was seen (a *bright* light) by Mr. and Mrs. Payne and
they say it was from the window on the wing looking south
[*i.e.* Room 11]. It looks out towards the fields and is at the
corner close to the garage covered way.

'The light was also seen by our man Herbert Mayes on the
same night at a different window, the large one on the stairs.
This can only be seen at one point on the road opposite the
Tithe Barn at Borley Place.

'I have seen the Arbons and they say the place was all locked
up on Monday night and no one there. . . . Our maid also saw
the light on Thursday night, but is rather vague about its position.

'Yours sincerely,
(*Signed*) 'A. C. HENNING.'

It was, of course, the strange light in the Rectory window that
originally took me to Borley in June 1929. The reader will
remember that it was seen by Mr. V. C. Wall and others on
June 10, 1929.

I have consulted my diary and find that none of our observers
was at Borley on November 8, 1937, and Mr. Arbon's testimony
confirms this fact. Also, there was no one connected with us at
the Rectory on November 11, when Mr. Henning's maid saw the
light. Of the two sets of keys, one was always kept by Mr. Arbon
(except when he handed them to an observer), and the other set
was deposited in London.

When I was at Liston Rectory in March 1939, after my
second visit to Miss Ethel Bull and Mr. Edward Cooper, respectively, I took the opportunity of interviewing Herbert Mayes,
who is gardener-chauffeur to the Rev. A. C. Henning. I first
questioned him about the light he saw in the window of Borley
Rectory on the night of November 8, 1937, and he was quite
definite about it. It was a bright light—bright enough to attract
his attention. He wondered whether any of our observers were
there. But Mr. Henning knew that I had sent no one, and
Mr. Arbon also knew that the place was locked up as he had the
keys, and happened to be at home on this night, working about
the place.

Herbert Mayes was, for a time, employed by the Foysters
during their occupation of the Rectory, and heard a number of
extraordinary sounds and noises for which no normal explanation
could be found. Once, he told me, when he was in the house
by himself, he heard footsteps on the landing. This phenomenon
occurred twice in forty-five minutes. He was in the hall. Investi-

gation proved that no one was there. On another occasion, he was in the hall when he again heard footsteps on the landing at the top of the hall stairs. Suddenly, a terrific crash came from the top of the stairs. Mayes said: 'It was just as if someone with a tray full of crockery had dropped it and smashed the lot.' But no one was there. The reader will remember that Edward Cooper heard[1] a similar crash as if all the china in the cottage kitchen had fallen to the floor, and Mr. Kerr-Pearse records a similar experience.

Another 'thrill' experienced outside the Rectory fell to the lot of a parson. On October 27, 1938, Mr. S. H. Glanville received a letter from Miss Ethel Bull, from her Sudbury home. In it she says:

'The Rectory has been sold. . . . I am very curious to know what will happen when he takes up residence there.[2] He [Captain Gregson] knows all about it, but says he does not mind. Wait a bit, and see! A clergyman friend of ours who was staying in the neighbourhood a few weeks ago, walked up to the Rectory one evening and prowled round outside. He heard an awful noise coming from the house as though a lot of furniture was being thrown about. Nobody was in the house. He felt a bit scared and took himself off.'

Little did Miss Bull dream that within a few weeks the place would be a mass of smouldering ruins.

For the superstitious, I will record that shortly before I leased the Rectory, a parish meeting was held there. It was one of the rare occasions when Mr. Henning used the Rectory. During the meeting, a picture suddenly dropped from its nail on the wall and was smashed.

[1] See Page 54.
[2] Captain Gregson took up residence at the Rectory early in December 1938.

APPENDIX D

ANALYSIS OF PHENOMENA

THE following is a list of the principal phenomena, or alleged phenomena, and the names of those who observed them.

The 'Nun' figure in its different forms:

Miss Ethel Bull	The Misses Bull's cousin
Miss Freda Bull	Mrs. Lloyd Williams
Miss Mabel Bull	Mr. Edward Cooper
Miss Elsie Bull	Mrs. Edward Cooper
Rev. Harry Bull	Mr. Fred Cartwright
Rev. Henry Bull	Miss Mary Pearson
The Misses Bull's cook	Mr. V .C. Wall

'Harry Bull' Phantasm:

Mrs. L. A. Foyster

Headless Man or Men:

Miss Mary Pearson   Rev. Harry Bull

Tall, Dark Man:

Miss Ethel Bull

'An Old Man':

Miss Ethel Bull	Mr. Edward Cooper
Rev. Harry Bull ('old Amos')	Mrs. Edward Cooper

Figure in Grey and Man wearing Bowler Hat:

A police-constable   Some villagers

Girl in White (or Blue):

Three Misses Bull	Mr. C. G. Browne
Miss Rosemary M. Williams	

Shadowy Forms:

Miss Adelaide Foyster   Captain W. H. Gregson

A Black Hand:

Mr. James Ballantyne

Vision of 'Horses':

Miss Mary Pearson   Mr. Edward Cooper

A Strange Insect:

Mrs. Margaret E. Wilson

Appearance of Coach:
Miss Mary Pearson   Mr. Edward Cooper
Rev. Harry Bull

AUDIBLE PHENOMENA

A Woman's Voice:
Rev. G. E. Smith   Mrs. L. A. Foyster
Rev. L. A. Foyster

Whisperings:
     Rev. G. E. Smith

Sound of Horses Galloping:
Rev. Harry Bull   Mr. Herbert Mayes

Dog Padding round Room:
Mr. Edward Cooper   Mrs. Edward Cooper

Sound of Rolling Coach:
     Rev. Harry Bull

Church Music:
     Mr. Hardy, Junr.

'Scratchings':
     Miss Mary Pearson

Bell-ringing:
Misses Bull   Rev. L. A. Foyster
Mrs. Henry Richards   Mrs. L. A. Foyster
Mrs. A. Peel Goldney   Sir George Whitehouse
Miss May Walker   Lady Whitehouse
Rev. G. E. Smith   Dom Richard Whitehouse,
Mr. Harry Price   [O.S.B.
     Katie (the Foysters' maid)

Footsteps, and Similar Sounds:
Rev. G. E. Smith   Mr. Mark Kerr-Pearse
The Misses Bull   Rev. A. C. Henning
Mrs. E. Byford   Mrs. A. C. Henning
Rev. L. A. Foyster   Mr. Herbert Mayes
Mrs. L. A. Foyster   Dom Richard Whitehouse,
Mr. Edward Cooper   [O.S.B.
Mrs. Edward Cooper   Katie (the Foysters' maid)
Mrs. Lloyd Williams   Mr. M. P. Knox
Captain W. H. Gregson   Mr. R. Hawkin
Mr. S. H. Glanville   Mr. Samuel J. Milberg
Mr. Roger H. Glanville   Mr. J. Burden
     Mr. T. Stainton

Raps, Taps, or Knockings:
The Misses Bull   Mr. S. H. Glanville
Rev. G. E. Smith   Mr. Roger H. Glanville

Mrs. G. E. Smith   Mr. Mark Kerr-Pearse
Mr. V. C. Wall   Dr. H. F. Bellamy
Mr. Harry Price   Mr. F. C. Bellamy
Mr. Ellic Howe   Mr. Hugh E. Fee-Smith

Displaced or Projected Objects: Phenomena of true Poltergeist Character:
Rev. G. E. Smith   Mr. G. J. Bell
Mrs. G. E. Smith   Mr. J. Thurley
Mr. V. C. Wall   Flight-Lieut. A. Carter Jonas:
The Misses Bull   Flight-Lieut. Caunter
Mr. Harry Price   Mr. A. P. Drinkwater (and
Mr. Mark Kerr-Pearse   Mr. S. J. de Lotbinière [party)
Dr. H. F. Bellamy   Misses Bull's clerical friend
Mr. F. C. Bellamy   Rev. L. A. Foyster
Mr. Hugh E. Fee-Smith   Mrs. L. A. Foyster
Captain W. H. Gregson   Mrs. Henry Richards
Mr. W. S. Hammond   Mrs. A. Peel Goldney
Mr. C. S. Taylor   Miss May Walker   [O.S.B.
Mrs. F. C. Westland   Dom Richard Whitehouse,
Lieut.-Col. F. C. Westland   Katie (the Foysters' maid)

'Clicks' or 'Cracks':
Mr. S. J. de Lotbinière   Mr. S. H. Glanville
Mr. Henry Douglas-Home   Mrs. C. Gordon Glover
Mr. Harry Price   Mr. Lloyd Williams
Mr. C. Gordon Glover   Mrs. Lloyd Williams

Sound of Door Closing:
Mr. Ellic Howe   Mr. M. Kerr-Pearse [wicket
Mr. Harry Price   Mr. G. J. Bell   closing]
Mr. W. S. Hammond   Mr. J. Thurley
Mr. C. S. Taylor   Mrs. C. Gordon Glover

Knocks, Bumps, Thuds, Jumping or Stamping:
Mr. S. H. Glanville   Mr. J. M. Bailey
Mr. Roger H. Glanville   Mr. C. V. Wintour
Rev. A. C. Henning   Mr. A. P. Drinkwater
Mr. C. Gordon Glover   (and party)
Mrs. C. Gordon Glover   Rev. L. A. Foyster
Squadron-Leader Horniman Mrs. L. A. Foyster
Mr. Lloyd Williams   Dom Richard Whitehouse,
Mrs. Lloyd Williams   O.S.B.
Mr. M. Savage   Mr. Mark Kerr-Pearse
Mr. Bridgewater   Katie (the Foysters' maid)

'Dragging' Noise:
Mr. J. Burden   Mr. T. Stainton

Door-locking Phenomena:

Rev. L. A. Foyster	Mrs. A. Peel Goldney
Mrs. L. A. Foyster	Miss May Walker
Dom Richard Whitehouse, O.S.B.	Mr. Mark Kerr-Pearse
	Mr. Harry Price
Mrs. Henry Richards	

'Wailing' Sounds:

Mr. J. Burden	Mr. T. Stainton

Rustling or 'Scrabbling' Noises:

Mr. S. H. Glanville	Mr. S. J. de Lotbinière
Mr. Roger H. Glanville	Mr. Henry Douglas-Home
Mr. Mark Kerr-Pearse	Mr. Harry Price
Mr. Rupert Haig	

'Metallic' Sounds:

Mr. Mark Kerr-Pearse and the Glanvilles

Sound of 'Rushing Water':

Miss Ethel Bull (and sisters)

'Crashing,' as of Falling Crockery:

The Misses Bull	Mr. Herbert Mayes
Mr. Edward Cooper	Mr. Mark Kerr-Pearse
Mrs. Edward Cooper	

Breaking of Windows:

Rev. L. A. Foyster	Mrs. L. A. Foyster

Sounds of 'Person entering Door'

The Misses Bull	Mrs. Henry Bull

Footsteps heard in Road:

Mr. Walter Bull

Various Noises in the Rectory:

Mr. Walter Bull	Mr. M. P. Knox
Rev. L. A. Foyster	Mr. R. Hawkin
Mrs. L. A. Foyster	Mr. Samuel J. Milberg
Mr. Herbert Mayes	

Sound of Moving Furniture:

Rev. G. E. Smith	Mrs. L. A. Foyster
Mrs. G. E. Smith	Miss Bull's clerical friend
Rev. L. A. Foyster	

VISIBLE PHENOMENA

Wall and Paper-writings:

Rev. L. A. Foyster	Mr. F. C. Bellamy
Mrs. L. A. Foyster	Mr. Hugh E. Fee-Smith
Dom Richard Whitehouse, [O.S.B.	Mr. S. J. de Lotbinière
Dr. C. E. M. Joad	Mr. M. Savage
Mr. S. H. Glanville	Mr. Bowden

R

Mr. Roger H. Glanville
Mr. Mark Kerr-Pearse
Rev. A. C. Henning
Mrs. A. C. Henning
Dr. H. F. Bellamy

Mr. J. M. Bailey
Mr. C. V. Wintour
Mr. J. Burden
Mr. A. P. Drinkwater
(and party)

The Light in the Window:
Rev. G. E. Smith
Mrs. G. E. Smith
(and choir boys)
Mr. Basil Payne
Mrs. Basil Payne

Mr. V. C. Wall
Mr. Herbert Mayes
The Hennings' maid
Many unnamed villagers

Keys Falling from Locks:
Rev. G. E. Smith
Mrs. G. E. Smith

Mr. Harry Price

The Swinging Blind:
Mr. S. H. Glanville
Mr. Roger H. Glanville

Capt. H. G. Harrison
Dr. H. F. Bellamy

Fire Phenomena:
Rev. L. A. Foyster
Mrs. L. A. Foyster
Sir George Whitehouse

Lady Whitehouse
Dom Richard Whitehouse,
O.S.B.

Wine into Ink, etc.:
Rev. L. A. Foyster
Mrs. L. A. Foyster
Mrs. Henry Richards

Mrs. A. Peel Goldney
Miss May Walker
Mr. Harry Price

Personal Injuries:
Mrs. L. A. Foyster

Adelaide Foyster

Appearances, Disappearances, and Reappearances:
Rev. L. A. Foyster
Mrs. L. A. Foyster
Lieut.-Col. F. C. Westland
Mrs. F. C. Westland
Mr. Mark Kerr-Pearse
Mr. Samuel J. Milberg
Mr. R. Hawkin

Mr. M. P. Knox
Mr. S. G. Welles
Flight-Lieut. R. Carter Jonas
Flight-Lieut. Caunter
Mr. Geoffrey Motion
Mr. Harry Price

'Smoking' Phenomenon:
Mr. Hardy, Senior

Luminous Phenomenon:
Mr. S. G. Welles

'Matter-through-Matter':
Captain W. H. Gregson [toad incident]
Alan Gregson   do.
Anthony Gregson   do.

MISCELLANEOUS PHENOMENA

Odours—Pleasant and Unpleasant:

Rev. L. A. Foyster	Flight-Lieut. Caunter
Mrs. L. A. Foyster	Mr. W. S. Hammond
Dom Richard Whitehouse,	Mr. C. S. Taylor
O.S.B.	Mr. G. J. Bell
Flight-Lieut. R. Carter Jonas	Mr. J. Thurley

Sensation of 'Coldness':

Squadron-Leader Horni-	Mr. R. H. Glanville
man's friend	Mr. Mark Kerr-Pearse
Miss Reid	Mr. Alan Cuthbert
Mr. Rupert Haig	

Tactual Phenomena ('Touchings'):

Mr. F. A. Mansfield	Mr. Hugh E. Fee-Smith
Mrs. F. A. Mansfield	Mr. Bellamy's friend
Mr. Mark Kerr-Pearse	

Sensation of a 'Presence':

Rev. L. A. Foyster	Mr. Mark Kerr-Pearse
Mrs. L. A. Foyster	Mr. Roger H. Glanville
Mrs. Margaret E. Wilson	Mr. J. Burden
Dom Richard Whitehouse,	Captain Gregson's visitor
O.S.B..	

Unidentified Footprints in the Snow:

Captain W. H. Gregson	Anthony Gregson
Alan Gregson	

Gluey Substance:

Mr. R. H. Glanville	Mr. M. Savage
Mr. Alan Cuthbert	Mr. Bridgewater

Face-Slapping in Bed:

Miss Bull

Reaction by Animals:

Rev. Harry Bull [recorded by]
Captain W. H. Gregson [recorded by]
Alan Gregson [recorded by]
Anthony Gregson [recorded by]
Mr. Joseph Burden [recorded by]

A Camera Phenomenon:

Mr. W. Davey

Phenomenon in Church Vaults:

Miss Ethel Bull [recorded by]

A Fulfilled Prediction:

Miss Helen Glanville [Planchette prediction of Rectory fire]

LIST OF OFFICIAL OBSERVERS AND OTHERS, REFERRED TO IN THIS MONOGRAPH, WHO WITNESSED PHENOMENA OR ALLEGED PHENOMENA

Bailey, Mr. J. M.
Ballantyne, Mr. James
Bell, Mr. G. J.
Bellamy, Mr. F. C.
Bellamy, Dr. H. F.
Bellamy's friend, Mr. F. C.
Bridgewater, Mr.
Browne, Mr. C. G.
Bull, Miss Elsie
Bull, Miss Ethel
Bull, Miss Freda
Bull, Miss Mabel
Bull, Rev. H. D. E. [Henry]
Bull, Rev. H. F. [Harry]
Bull, Mrs. H. D. E.
Bull, Mr. Walter
Bull's clerical friend, Miss
Bull's cousin, The Misses
Bull's cook, The Misses
Burden, Mr. Joseph W.
Byford, Mrs. E.
Cartwright, Mr. Fred
Caunter, Flight-Lieut.
Cooper, Mr. Edward
Cooper, Mrs. Edward
Cuthbert, Mr. Alan
Davey, Mr. W.
Douglas-Home, Mr. Henry
Drinkwater, Mr. A. P. [and party of 3 friends]
Fee-Smith, Mr. Hugh E.
Foyster, Miss Adelaide
Foyster, Rev. L. A.

Foyster, Mrs. L. A.
Glanville, Miss Helen
Glanville, Mr. Roger H.
Glanville, Mr. Sidney H.
Glover, Mr. C. Gordon
Glover, Mrs. C. Gordon
Goldney, Mrs. A. Peel
Gregson, Mr. Alan
Gregson, Mr. Anthony
Gregson, Captain W. H.
Gregson's visitor, Captain
Haig, Mr. Rupert
Hammond, Mr. W. S.
Hardy, Junior, Mr.
Hardy, Senior, Mr.
Harrison, Captain H. G.
Hawkin, Mr. R.
Henning, Rev. A. C.
Henning, Mrs. A. C.
Henning's maid, Rev. A. C.
Horniman, Squadron-Leader
Horniman's friend, Squadron-Leader
Howe, Mr. Ellic
Joad, Dr. C. E. M.
Jonas, Flight-Lieut. A. Carter
Katie [Rev. L. H. Foyster's maid]
Kaye, Miss Lucie
Kerr-Pearse, Mr. Mark
Knox, Mr. M. P.
Lotbinière, Mr. S. J. de
Mansfield, Mr. F. A.

Mansfield, Mrs. F. A.
Mayes, Mr. Herbert
Milberg, Mr. Samuel J.
Motion, Mr. G. H.
Payne, Mr. Basil
Payne, Mrs. Basil
Pearson, Miss Mary
Police-constable, A.
Price, Mr. Harry
Richards, Mrs. Henry
Savage, Mr. M.
Smith, Rev. G. Eric
Smith, Mrs. G. Eric
Stainton, Mr. T.
Taylor, Mr. C. S.
Thurley, Mr. J.

Villagers of Borley
Walker, Miss May
Wall, Mr. V. C.
Welles, Mr. S. G.
Westland, Lieut.-Colonel F. C.
Westland, Mrs. F. C.
Whitehouse, Sir George
Whitehouse, Lady
Whitehouse, O.S.B., Dom
    Richard
Williams, Mr. Lloyd
Williams, Mrs. Lloyd
Williams, Miss Rosemary M.
Wilson, Mrs. Margaret E.
Wintour, Mr. C. V.

APPENDIX F

CHRONOLOGICAL RECORD OF PRINCIPAL EVENTS,
1362–1939

1362. Edward III gave Manor of Borley to Benedictine monks.
1375. Simon of Sudbury appointed Archbishop of Canterbury.
1381 (June 14), Simon of Sudbury murdered on Tower Hill.
c. 1500–1800. Borley Manor in possession of Waldegrave family.
1833 (Nov. 23). Rev. H. D. E. Bull born.
1862–1892. Rev. H. D. E. Bull Rector of Borley.
1862 (Jan. 24). Rev. H. F. Bull born.
1863. Rev. H. D. E. Bull built Borley Rectory.
1875–6. New wing added to Borley Rectory.
1886. Mrs. E. Byford left Rectory on account of 'ghostly foot-
    steps.'
1892 (May 2). Death of Rev. H. D. E. Bull.
1892–1927. Rev. H. F. Bull Rector of Borley.
1900 (July 28). The Misses Bull saw 'nun' in daylight on
    Rectory lawn.
1900 (Nov.). Miss E. Bull and a cook saw 'nun' in garden.
1916 (April). Mr. and Mrs. Edward Cooper took up residence
    in Rectory cottage.

1916–19. The Coopers disturbed by 'padding dog' phenomenon in cottage; saw 'nun' many times; and Mr. Cooper saw coach and horses 'with glittering harness' sweep across Rectory grounds.

1919. Mr. and Mrs. Cooper saw 'black shape' in their bedroom.

1920 (March). The Coopers left cottage.

1922. Rev. Harry Bull informed Mr. J. Harley about his 'communications with spirits.'

1927 (June 9). Death of Rev. H. F. Bull.

1927 (Autumn). Fred Cartwright four times saw 'nun' standing at gate of Borley Rectory.

1928 (Oct. 2). Rev. G. Eric Smith inducted to living of Borley.

1929.

June 10. Borley hauntings first mentioned in Press. Mr. V. C. Wall saw 'mysterious light' in Rectory window.

June 11. Harry Price invited to investigate.

June 12. Harry Price paid first visit to Borley Rectory. Mr. Wall saw 'nun.' Various objects hurled at Wall and Price, who was told story of the Rev. G. E. Smith's experiences. Price interviewed Miss Mary Pearson, who stated she saw coach and horses, etc.

June 12–13. Early morning séance in Blue Room, when Harry Bull alleged to manifest himself. Soap jumped to floor.

June 13. Price interviewed the Misses Bull and Mr. and Mrs. Cooper. Heard their respective experiences.

June 27. Price and party visited the Rectory. A Roman Catholic medallion and other articles 'appeared.'

July 5. All Rectory bells rung simultaneously.

July 10. Small table in Blue Room hurled across room.

July 14. Rev. G. E. Smith and wife left Rectory.

August 7. Window in Rectory thrown up from within though house was empty and doors locked.

1930.

February 22. Half of one of the fireplaces in Rectory deposited on main staircase, though place empty and locked.

February 22. Rectory was put up for sale.

March 4. Main staircase found covered with lumps of stone and villagers saw 'lights' in the Rectory, though place locked and unoccupied.

March 18. Stones and glass scattered about the Rectory, and 'horrible sounds' heard in the house at full moon.

March 24. 'Light' still seen in Rectory window.

April 20. Rev. G. E. Smith preached his farewell sermon at Borley.

October 16. The Rev. L. A. Foyster and his wife took up residence at Borley Rectory. A voice heard calling 'Marianne,' and Mrs. Foyster saw phantasm of 'Harry Bull' in grey dressing-gown.

October. Mrs. Foyster lost her bracelet mysteriously and a lavender bag 'appeared.'

1931.

February 25. Crockery, having previously unaccountably disappeared, spontaneously reappeared.

February 26. Mrs. Foyster given a black eye.

February 27. A cotton-reel and hammer thrown at the Foysters as they lay in bed.

March 7. Mr. Foyster exorcises the Borley spirits—is pelted with stones.

March 8. Both doors of Blue Room spontaneously locked.

March 10. Cabin trunk, china box and wedding ring, origin unknown, spontaneously 'appeared.' Ring disappeared next morning.

March 11. Rectory again exorcised by two priests. Stones thrown.

March 13. Mrs. Foyster hit on head with piece of metal.

March 23. Flat-iron thrown at Mrs. Foyster.

March 24. Mrs. Foyster saw 'Harry Bull' again.

May. Bells rung; pepper dropped on Foysters in bed; house 'exorcised' with creosote; papers with 'Marianne' written on them appeared about the house.

May 4. All bells rung; room on fire, which Lady Whitehouse helped to put out. The Foysters left the Rectory for a few days' peace.

June 8. Dom Richard Whitehouse, O.S.B., investigated. Found things scattered all over the house. Mrs. Foyster thrown out of bed three times. Objects precipitated. Lady Whitehouse's parasol 'moved' across the room.

June 8–16. Mrs. Foyster and Dom Whitehouse made a Novena near Chapel for guidance. They became aware of a 'presence' and a message 'appeared' on a wall.

June 12. A bed found overturned in the Rectory, though the Foysters were staying with Lady Whitehouse, and the house was locked.

August. Foysters held a séance.

September. More doors 'miraculously' locked: they were opened with help of relic of Curé d'Ars. Study attacked, and writing desk thrown on its face.

September 29. The Misses Bull called on Harry Price and told him that manifestations at Borley Rectory were more frequent, and more violent.

October. Rev. Foyster awakened by bedroom water-jug dropped on his head.

October 13. Visit of Harry Price and party to Rectory. Wine turned into ink, doors were locked, bottles were thrown, etc.

October–November. Adelaide Foyster injured by a 'nasty thing.'

November 13. Mrs. Foyster, Dom Richard Whitehouse, and Katie the maid, were seated in kitchen with doors and windows closed, when bottle after bottle 'materialized' and crashed to floor. Bells rang of their own volition.

1932.

January. More door-locking: opened by help of relic. Spontaneous return of key on Chapel altar.

January 23-4. Great manifestations previous to holding séance. Bottles flying, bells rang. Different 'atmosphere' noticed after séance.

1933.

June. Strange noises heard in the house.

1935.

Manifestations began again, and more things disappeared. Foysters heard many 'bangs' in the Rectory.

October. The Foysters moved out of the Rectory.

1936 (March 13). Rev. A. C. Henning inducted to the combined livings of Liston and Borley.

1937.

May 19. Harry Price visited Borley Rectory and decided to rent it for a year. His tenancy began on this day.

May 25. Price inserted advertisement in *The Times* and invited persons to join a rota of investigators.

June 1–2. A 'strange coat' appeared in the Rectory.

June 2. Price visited Rectory with Ellic Howe and both heard 'thumps' and a door being closed.

June 20. S. H. Glanville visited Rectory and heard 'cracks,' 'thumps,' and new pencil markings were found.

June 25. Col. Westland found a blue box in Rectory cupboard.

June 26. Kerr-Pearse at Rectory and heard raps, 'thump,' etc.

July 7. Col. Westland present when 'strange coat' 'appeared' again.

July 13. Kerr-Pearse at Rectory and more pencil-marks appeared. Wicket gate mysteriously opened.

July 16. More pencil marks discovered by Kerr-Pearse. Rev. A. C. Henning and Kerr-Pearse held a séance and 'extraordinary noises were heard coming from the kitchen.'

July 18. Kerr-Pearse found lump of touch-wood and more pencil marks.

July 22. Mr. de Lotbinière and friends heard 'rustlings' in Base Room, and a 'sign' was given when entities were 'challenged.'

July 28. Dr. C. E. M. Joad witnessed new pencil marks.

August 5. Kerr-Pearse found petrified frog.

August 14. Glanville found cats' cemetery disturbed.

August 23. Miss Reid felt 'icy cold' outside Blue Room.

August 28. Glanville's friends heard 'light tripping footsteps' on main stairs of Rectory.

September 5. Mrs. Mansfield had her belt lifted by an invisible presence.

September 20. Squadron-Leader Horniman's friend 'came over desperately cold' outside Blue Room.

September 21. Kerr-Pearse discovered that 50-pound bag of coal had moved 18 inches of its own volition. Rupert Haig became 'icy cold' in Base Room.

October 17. Dr. Bellamy and party heard electric bell phenomenon.

October 23–25. Glanville and friends held séances in the Rectory and tried Planchette writing.

October 26. Kerr-Pearse locked in Base Room while he was having his supper, the key being on *inside* of door.

October 27. Kerr-Pearse heard 'shuffling noise' coming from w.c., and later a 'crash' from kitchen. Footsteps were heard.

October 28. Kerr-Pearse had his coat pulled twice.

October 31. The Glanville family tried more Planchette writing and the name—'Mary Lairre'— of the 'nun' was given. She was 'strangled in 1667.'

November 8. Herbert Mayes saw light in upstairs window of Rectory, when place was shut and unoccupied.

November 13–14. A. P. Drinkwater and friends found new pencil marks and heard 'thumps.'

November 15. Report of 'strange light' in Rectory window.

1938.

February 16. S. G. Welles saw luminous phenomenon on Blue Room ceiling.

February 18. Mrs. Lloyd Williams saw 'nun' on Nun's Walk,

and Mr. C. G. Glover and party heard thuds, shuffles and cracks.

March 12.   Mr. Savage, Glanville and others found gluey substance on Chapel floor: could not be accounted for.

March 27.   'Sunex Amures' threatened to burn down the Rectory (*vide* Planchette 'message').

May 7.   Savage and friend recorded new pencil marks which 'appeared' while they actually watched the walls.

May 9.   Price 'moved out' from Borley Rectory and Motion and he found 'golden apport.'

May 19.   Price's tenancy of Rectory ended.

August 12.   Mrs. Margaret E. Wilson saw and painted 'strange insect' in Rectory garden.

October.   Visiting clergyman heard 'furniture being thrown about' at Rectory.

November 1.   Price broadcast story of Borley Rectory and, through it, became acquainted with its new owner, Captain Gregson.

November.   Caunter and Jonas visited Rectory and experienced 'overpowering smell of incense.'

November 9.   Marion psychometrized Rectory 'apport.'

December.   Captain Gregson took possession of Borley Rectory, which he renamed Borley Priory, and experienced many strange phenomena.

1939.

February 27.   Borley Rectory destroyed by fire at midnight, and strange figures were seen walking in the flames.

March 16.   Herbert Mayes heard 'horses,' invisible to him, stampeding in lane outside Rectory.

March 26.   Miss Rosemary M. Williams and C. Graham Browne saw 'woman in white' (or blue) at burnt-out Blue Room window.

March 28–30.   Price revisited Borley, examined ruins of Rectory, and interviewed a number of witnesses.

March 30.   Herbert Mayes related to Price story of footsteps at the Rectory, and 'crashing crockery' phenomenon.

April 10.   Mr. Davey saw camera 'phenomenon.'

April 15.   Captain Gregson broadcast in 'In Town To-night,' and related his strange experiences.

June 21.   'Psychic fête' amongst the ruins of Borley Rectory and Harry Price's last official visit.

INDEX

The titles of books, articles, periodicals, manuscripts, lectures and society publications are printed in italics. Appendices A, B, D, E, and F have *not* been indexed.

Walton-on-Thames, Surrey, 190
Wedding-ring 'apport,' 142–3
Well, a curious, 20, 21
Welles, S. G., 126, 224–8
Wesley, John, 182
Westland, Lieut.-Col. and Mrs. F.
 C., vi, 123, 128, 148, 211–14,
 231, 235
'White Horse Inn,' Sudbury, Suf-
 folk, 56
Whitehouse, O.S.B., Dom Richard,
 v, 12, 71 n. 1, 80, 82, 82 n. 1, 85,
 87 n. 1, 88–101, 147, 170, 187,
 191, 210
Whitehouse, Sir George and Lady,
 v, 80, 80 n. 1, 2, 85–9, 170

Whitton Church Lane, Ipswich,
 Suffolk, 179
William the Conqueror (of Eng-
 land), 11
Williams, Captain, 176
Williams, Miss Rosemary M., 176–8
Williams, Mr. and Mrs. Lloyd, 124,
 125, 219–20
Wilson, Mrs. Margaret E., 132–6
Window Tax, 17
Wintour, C. V., 126, 151, 216,
 222–4

Zugun, Eleonore, 101 n. 1

THE MOST
HAUNTED HOUSE
IN
ENGLAND

TEN YEARS' INVESTIGATION
OF BORLEY RECTORY

•

Harry Price

" The book has furnished possibly the most fully documented account of an example of this class (Poltergeist) of localised supranormal happenings in existence. A conscientious and well-written record." *Manchester Guardian (Oct.* 4, 1940).

" A lively record." *Star (Sept.* 23, 1940).

" Conscientiously learned and exciting. . . . It would be stupid, as well as unscientific, to be sceptical."
Philip Page (Daily Mail, Sept. 26, 1940).

" A wonderful antidote to a night of Blitzkrieg."
Daily Telegraph (Oct. 2, 1940).

" The most excitingly rich case in psychic annals in this country."
Glasgow Herald (Oct. 5, 1940).

" Mr. Price has collated his facts carefully and marshalled a hundred witnesses to prove a phenomenon stranger than fiction."
Cavalcade (Sept. 28, 1940).

" The chronicle will rank high in the bibliography of occult science . . . the case will stand as a classic in the annals of psychic lore." *Nottingham Journal (Oct.* 11, 1940).

" Of unique value to the student of psychical matters. It may also be commended to the general reader as a well-told ghost story ; one that happens to be true."
Campbell Nairne (John o'London's, Oct. 4, 1940).

" The result is a very readable mixture of science and spicy taletelling." *News Review (Oct.* 3, 1940).

" This record of ten years' investigation of Borley Rectory is a model of what such a record should be."
Notes and Queries (Oct. 5, 1940).

" Perhaps the most completely documented case ever published. A most interesting story. Mr. Price writes well."
Two Worlds (Oct. 11, 1940).

" A most intriguing and baffling story. It seems safe to say that there will not be a more teasing book published this year."
Howard A. Gray (Observer, Oct. 13, 1940).

" Mr. Price's story abounds in interest and excitement."
Reynolds (Oct. 13, 1940).

" Mr. Price has written one of the best ghost stories ever told."
Star (Oct. 21, 1940)

" Admirable, and a fascinating book."
Dr. C. E. M. Joad (Star, Oct. 21, 1940).

" This history . . . is just about the most convincing account of a *Poltergeist* I have ever read. One of the most extraordinary stories imaginable." *Richard King (The Tatler, Oct.* 23, 1940).

" Thank God for Mr. Price, who seeks ghosts so successfully, pursues them so indefatigably, and writes about them so excitingly. The book could not have been better done."

Dr. C. E. M. Joad (Spectator, Oct. 18, 1940).

" Mr. Price is a sensible observer and tells an astonishing story."

V. S. Pritchett (Bystander, Oct. 23, 1940).

" A real creepy book."

Newsagent-Booksellers' Review (Oct. 5, 1940).

" A thrilling and fully documented account."

Liverpool Daily Post (Oct. 5, 1940).

" Mr. Price's record is one of absorbing interest for all lovers of ghost stories as well as for those interested in the deeper aspect of the subject." *Sunday Mercury (Oct. 13, 1940).*

" A collection of most extraordinary psychic episodes . . . all carefully and soberly documented by Mr. Price and others."

H. E. Bates (Books of the Month, Oct., 1940).

" It will be found absorbing." *Current Literature (Oct., 1940).*

" Psychical research owes Mr. Price one more debt for his monograph." *A. T. G. Edwards (Western Mail, Oct. 22, 1940).*

" This fully documented account of Borley Rectory is likely to remain among the most remarkable contributions ever made to the study of the paranormal." *Church Times (Oct. 25, 1940).*

" The book is entertaining and exciting and really overwhelming in its mass." *Country Life (Oct. 26, 1940).*

" The book should be read by every intelligent man and woman."

Border Standard (Oct. 25, 1940).

" One must congratulate Mr. Price on having so admirably stated its case. This volume could scarcely have been improved as a record of open-minded investigation."

H. F. Prevost Battersby (Light, Oct. 31, 1940).

" A tribute is due to Mr. Price for the entirely unbiassed way in which he has chronicled the happenings."

Northern Whig (Oct. 26, 1940).

" Mr. Price has won an unique place as an investigator of paranormal phenomena . . . a fascinating book."

Daily Telegraph (Nov. 11, 1940).

" Mr. Price gives an astonishing report of the phenomena witnessed by his official observers." *Magic Circular (Nov., 1940).*

" Of especial value to those interested in psychical research."

Yorkshire Post (Nov. 5, 1940).

" It is certainly a wonderful story." *Listener (Nov.* 7, 1940).

" The most amazing ghost story of our time."
Sunday Graphic (Nov. 10, 1940)

" The most remarkable unvarnished ghost story ever written."
Prediction (Dec., 1940).

" Few will dismiss this extraordinary narrative as negligible."
Illustrated London News (Nov. 9, 1940).

" This is a book to please the logical thinker."
Psychic Times (Nov., 1940).

" A valuable addition to works on psychical research."
West Herts Observer (Nov. 8, 1940).

" Coldly scientific and very interesting."
Irish Times (Nov. 11, 1940).

" Very interesting." *Bristol Observer (Nov.* 9, 1940).

" It is a record to shake the most sceptical."
Book Window (Christmas, 1940).

" This thrilling book . . . is a remarkable contribution to the study of haunted houses."
Aidan Elrington, O.P. (Catholic Herald, Nov. 22, 1940).

" A noteworthy book." *Times Literary Supplement (Dec.* 7, 1940).

"Any reader who is not hide-bound against the possibility of such happenings must accept much of the evidence. A spine-chilling story." *Universe (Dec.* 6, 1940).

" A most interesting tale . . . it possesses a strange fascination for the reader. The story of Borley is quite unique."
Prescriber (Dec. 1940).

" We do not advise people to read it late at night."
Scottish Guardian (Oct. 25, 1940).

" A remarkable book. Abundant material for thought and argument. *Hampshire Telegraph (Oct* 18, 1940).

" A book as enthralling as any thriller."
Huddersfield Examiner (Dec. 7, 1940).

"A masterly survey and analysis of the happenings at Borley Rectory." *Light (Dec.* 19, 1940).

With many Plans, Facsimiles and Photographs

10s. 6d. net

(Postage 7d. inland ; 6d. extra abroad)

LONGMANS, GREEN & CO. LTD.
39 Paternoster Row, London, E.C.4

Library of Congress Cataloging-in-Publication Data

Price, Harry, 1881-1948.
The most haunted house in England : ten years' investigation of
Borley Rectory / by Harry Price.
p. cm. — (Collector's library of the unknown)
Reprint. Originally published: London ; New York : Longmans,
Green, 1940.
ISBN 0-8094-8058-1. — ISBN 0-8094-8059-X (lib. bdg.)
1. Haunted houses—England—Borley. 2. Ghosts—England—Borley.
BF1472.E53P75 1989   133.1'29426715—dc20   89-27207 CIP